POPULAR CULTURE

The R&L Series in Mass Communication

This exciting new series of "compact core" textbooks provides clear, concise overviews for key mass communication courses. These accessible and engaging texts feature illustrations, pedagogical tools, and practical guidelines to show students how to apply concepts outside the classroom.

Future topics in the series may include media and politics, law, ethics, international communication, online communication, mass communication theory, research methods, economics, gender and media, comparative media systems, new communications technology, history, media effects, policy and regulation, management, advertising, public relations, film, visual communication, and media literacy.

Editorial Board

Titles in the Series

Media and Society: A Critical Perspective, second edition
Arthur Asa Berger

Popular Culture: Introductory Perspectives
Marcel Danesi

POPULAR CULTURE

Introductory Perspectives

MARCEL DANESI

ROWMAN & LITTLEFIELD PUBLISHERS, INC.
Lanham • Boulder • New York • Toronto • Plymouth, UK

ROWMAN & LITTLEFIELD PUBLISHERS, INC.

Published in the United States of America
by Rowman & Littlefield Publishers, Inc.
A wholly owned subsidary of The Rowman & Littlefield Publishing Group, Inc.
4501 Forbes Boulevard, Suite 200, Lanham, Maryland 20706
www.rowmanlittlefield.com

Estover Road, Plymouth PL6 7PY, United Kingdom
Copyright © 2008 by Rowman & Littlefield Publishers, Inc.

British Library Cataloguing in Publication Information Available

Library of Congress Cataloging-in-Publication Data

Danesi, Marcel, 1946-
    Popular culture : introductory perspectives / Marcel Danesi.
        p.   cm.— (R & L series in mass communication)
    Includes bibliographical references and index.
    ISBN-13: 978-0-7425-5546-4 (cloth : alk. paper)
    ISBN-10: 0-7425-5546-1 (cloth : alk. paper)
    ISBN-13: 978-0-7425-5547-1 (pbk. : alk. paper)
    ISBN-10: 0-7425-5547-X (pbk. : alk. paper)
    1. Popular culture.   I. Title.
HM621.D36   2008
306—dc22

                                             2007012301

Printed in the United States of America

∞ ™ The paper used in this publication meets the minimum requirements of American
National Standard for Information Sciences—Permanence of Paper for Printed Library
Materials, ANSI/NISO Z39.48-1992.

CONTENTS

PREFACE

History records that popular forms of entertainment have always existed. In his *Historia*, Herodotus (circa 485–425 BCE) wrote about amusing performances and songs that he encountered as he traveled the ancient world that seemed rather odd to him but that were highly popular. Fortunately, he thought, such phenomena were the exception, not the rule. Today's popular entertainment culture, or "pop culture" as it is commonly called, is instead the rule, not the exception. It is everywhere—on television, in movie theaters, in sport stadiums, in shopping malls, and so on. Is pop culture on the verge of taking over the hearts and minds of everyone living today? How did it come about? What is it? Why do we hate to love it and love to hate it? What has happened to "high art"? Is "high art" hidden away in the record libraries of a few aficionados or staged for an exclusive group of people in the few remaining opera houses and symphony halls?

These are the kinds of questions that have implicitly guided the writing of this book. In a world that is being managed more and more by those who hold the levers of media power, it is little wonder that the study of the relation between the media and pop culture has been flourishing, with numerous volumes being published every year on all facets of pop culture, from coffee drinking in malls to the appeal of video games. Many of these seek to give theoretical interpretations of the ideological, political, social, or economic conditions that have led to the spread of pop culture as the "default" form of culture. However, very few works have attempted to explore the "psychic structures," as they may be called, that make pop culture so profoundly appealing, even to those who claim to hate it. The purpose of this book is to look at the reasons why we simultaneously love and hate pop culture. Needless to say, the reasons are my own, based on my own perspectives of the pop culture phenomenon. So this book is bound to leave gaps, to occasionally venture into the subjective, and to be somewhat selective. Nevertheless, I have tried to cast the net as widely as possible, so as to offer the reader as complete a menu of ideas and analyses as is possible within two covers.

I have tailored this book for the general reader, and especially for students taking beginning courses in pop culture studies or in related fields such as semiotics, psychology, mythology, education, literary studies, sociology, cultural anthropology, communication studies, and media analysis. In most chapters, I have used a historical framework to contain my perspectives. To facilitate the book's reading, I have avoided making constant references to the technical literature. The works that have informed the various commentaries, descriptions, and analyses that I offer in this book are listed at the back. I have also used a simple writing style and have made absolutely no assumptions about any prior technical knowledge on the part of the reader. A convenient glossary of technical terms is also included at the back.

The first two chapters introduce key theoretical and historical facts and ideas. Chapters 3 through 7 then discuss the various "media stages" on which pop culture has been (and is being) performed—print, radio, recordings, cinema, television, the Internet, and so on. The synergy between pop culture and the mass media is the subtext that drives the discussion in these chapters. Chapter 8 looks at the integration of advertising with pop culture. Chapter 9 considers the role of language in pop culture. The last chapter pulls together the various thematic threads woven in the previous chapters, offering an overall assessment of the pop culture phenomenon.

I should mention from the very outset that I love pop culture, no matter how crass it can sometimes be. It is liberating to know that entertainment can be as much a part of everyday life as anything else, including religious rituals and serious art (whatever that is). One does not preclude the other. On the other hand, I also feel that there must be a balance between entertainment and serious artistic engagement, between distraction and philosophical reflection. It is that balance that will be the target of my concluding remarks.

ACKNOWLEDGMENTS

I thank Alden Perkins, production editor, and Rebekka Istrail, copyeditor, for their contributions in transforming my manuscript into a book.

1

WHAT IS POP CULTURE?

> The bosses of our mass media, press, radio, film, and television suc-
> ceed in their aim of taking our minds off disaster.
>
> Ernst Fischer (1899–1972)

In 1923, a landmark event occurred, changing American society radically. The event was a Broadway musical, *Running Wild*, which helped turn a sexually suggestive dance called the Charleston into a craze for the young (and the young at heart) throughout the nation. It was evidence that the American psyche had started to yearn for a new, carefree public form of sexuality. This yearning found its expressive vehicle in the form of a dance that symbolized the birth of an exciting popular form of culture. Of course, there was a reaction against the craze from society's elders and moral guardians. This admonishment is captured cleverly in the 2002 movie *Chicago* (based on the 1975 Broadway musical). A social censure of the Charleston and its attendant lifestyle and fashions—considered to be vulgar and crude—was the main consequence of the adverse reaction.

But the condemnation could not stop the dance's spread, as *Running Wild* had predicted. Burlesque and vaudeville theaters, speakeasies (night clubs), and dance halls cropped up in the 1920s to satisfy Americans' desire to freely express themselves sexually. As a consequence, the 1920s came to be called the Roaring Twenties. The decade marked, in fact, the crystallization of *pop culture*, as we now call it. By the 1930s, pop culture was spreading to all corners of American society and to other parts of the world as well. It could not be curtailed, despite the severity of the legislative measures taken, from Prohibition to movie censorship. It was then, and is now, unstoppable as a form of expressive culture, challenging moral stodginess and aesthetic pretentiousness, while entertaining masses with its earthiness. Pop culture

1

has been the primary driving force behind social evolution since the Roaring Twenties, simultaneously triggering an unprecedented society-wide debate about art, sex, and true culture that is still ongoing.

The purpose of this opening chapter is to trace the origins and evolutionary tendencies of pop culture, discussing its basic features, its close relation to media technologies, and how it can be approached. Along with the next one, this chapter is designed to set the stage for discussing the expressive manifestations of pop culture in subsequent chapters.

DEFINING POP CULTURE

What is *pop culture*? The term is not as easy to define as it might seem at first blush. Let's start with a working definition of *culture*. Most anthropologists would agree that what we call *culture* is a system that includes beliefs, rituals, performances, art forms, lifestyle patterns, symbols, language, clothing, music, dance, and any other mode of human expressive, intellectual, and communicative behavior that is associated with a community during a particular time period. Culture is sometimes subdivided into such categories as *high* and *low*, on the basis of preferences within the system that are associated with differences in social class, education, and other variables within the community. *Pop culture* alludes, essentially, to a form of culture that makes little, if any, such categorical distinctions. The term surfaced in the United States in the 1950s when this noncategorical culture had become a widespread social reality. Pop culture's rise in that era was due, in large part, to post-war affluence and a subsequent baby boom, which gave people, regardless of class or educational background, considerable buying power, thus propelling them into the unprecedented position of shaping trends in fashion, music, and lifestyle through such power. By the end of the decade a full-blown pop culture, promoted by an increasingly affluent population, had materialized. Since then, it has played a pivotal role in the overall evolution of American society (and every other modern society). This is why historians now tend to characterize the periods since the 1950s with terms such as *the hippie era, the disco era, the punk era, the hip-hop era*, and so on—all of which refer to major musical trends within pop culture—rather than, say, *the Truman era, the Roosevelt era*, and the like—which are the kind of labels historians once used to designate historically significant periods.

Culture

The term *culture* requires further commentary. Above all else, it is a phenomenon that reveals that the human species is creative, evolving not only on biology's terms but also on its own terms—through the symbols, arts, technologies, and other artifacts humans make. Culture can be defined essentially as the *memorate* (memory template) of the artifacts that a particular group of people have made in their history and continue to make in order to evolve. As such, culture produces within group members an emotional (rather than rational) connection to the memorate itself, which is used as a template for evaluating life and people. The American anthropologist Franz Boas (1858–1942) claimed that culture is the primary template through which worldview is formed. This theory has come to be known as *cultural relativism*. Several of Boas's students at Columbia University in the 1920s and 1930s—Edward Sapir (1884–1939), Margaret Mead (1901–1978), and Ruth Benedict (1887–1948)—entrenched relativism into the mindset of anthropology generally. Sapir devoted his career to determining the extent to which the language of a culture shaped the thought patterns of its users. Mead sought to unravel how child-rearing practices influenced the behavior and temperament of the maturing individual. Benedict was fascinated by the fact that every culture developed its own particular canons of morality and lifestyle that largely determined the choices individuals made throughout their life cycles. From the moment of birth, Benedict asserted, the culture into which individuals are born shapes their behavior and worldview per-manently. By the time children can talk, they have become creatures of their culture—its habits are their habits, its beliefs are their beliefs, its challenges are their challenges.

The Polish-born British anthropologist Bronislaw Malinowski (1884–1942) contended that cultures originated to provide methods for solving basic physical and moral problems. He claimed that cultures across the world, no matter how divergent they might at first seem, encoded universal concepts of ethics and expressed basic needs, allowing people everywhere to solve life problems in remarkably similar ways. The British anthropologist Alfred Radcliffe-Brown (1881–1955) noted that in a specific cultural con-text even a physical response like weeping was encoded culturally to serve specific purposes. Among the Andaman Islanders in the east Bay of Bengal, for example, he found that weeping was not primarily an expression of joy or sorrow, but rather a response to social situations characterizing such meaningful events as peace-making, marriage, and the reunion of long-separated intimates. In weeping together, the people renewed their ties of solidarity.

Pop Culture

In the history of human cultures, pop culture stands out as atypical. It is culture by the people and for the people. In contrast to historical culture, it rejects both the supremacy of tradition and many of the socially based cultural practices of the past, as well as the pretensions of intellectualist tendencies within contemporary traditional culture. Pop culture has always been highly appealing for this very reason, bestowing on common people the assurance that culture is for everyone, not just for an elite class of designated artists or authority figures. It is thus populist, popular, and public. But, since popularity is unpredictable and highly ephemeral, pop culture is beset by a constant turnover of artifacts, expressive and material. Popular forms of culture quickly grow quaint. As American composer Stephen Sondheim has aptly put it, "How many people feel strongly about Gilbert and Sullivan today compared to those who felt strongly in 1890?" (cited in the *International Herald Tribune* Paris, 20 June 1989). At the same time, pop culture's predictability can give the impression that it is uncreative. The French semiotician Roland Barthes (1915–1980) saw pop culture, in fact, as a "bastard form of mass culture" beset by "humiliated repetition" and thus by "new books, new programs, new films, news items, but always the same meaning" (Barthes 1975: 24).

The term *pop culture* was likely fashioned after the *pop art* (popular art) movement that crystallized in the late 1950s, principally in the United States and Great Britain. Many of the works of pop artists were satirical or playful in intent, devaluing what the artists considered to be unnecessarily difficult and private (subjective) aspects of traditional art forms. Pop art instead validated the everyday experiences of common people. Pop artists represented scenes and objects from mass culture, sometimes with actual consumer products incorporated into their works. The movement began as a reaction against expressionism, an obscure and abstract art style of the 1940s and 1950s. Pop artists sought to depict everyday life, using brand-name commercial products, fast-food items, comic-strip frames, celebrities, and the like as their materials and their subjects. They put on *happenings*, improvised spectacles or performances for anyone, not just art gallery patrons. Perhaps the best known exponent of pop art was the American artist Andy Warhol

(1928–1987), whose paintings and silk-screen prints emblematize the whole pop art movement, as did his famous (some would say infamous) portrait of a Campbell's soup can, painted in 1964.

Pop art caught on widely because it engaged the masses, not just art critics. But was it art, as the critics asked and continue to debate? The terms *high* and *low* have been used constantly in this debate. *High* implies a level of art considered to have a superior value, socially and aesthetically; *low* implies a level considered to have an inferior value. The word *low* is often applied to pop culture generally, along with negative descriptive terms such as *kitschy, slapstick, campy, escapist, exploitative, obscene, raunchy, vulgar,* and the like. Many of these descriptors are applicable to a portion of pop art and pop culture generally—perhaps a large portion. However, pop culture has also produced works such as the Beatles album *Sgt. Pepper's Lonely Hearts Club Band* (1976) and Milos Forman's Hollywood version of Peter Shaffer's *Amadeus* (1984), which hardly merit any of these epithets. Indeed, pop culture has been instrumental in blurring, if not obliterating, the distinction between high and low culture. Already in the Romantic movement of the nineteenth century, artists saw *low culture* or *folk culture* as the only true form of culture, especially since they associated *high culture* with the artificial demands made of artists by the Church and the aristocracy. Pop culture emerged shortly thereafter and effaced any residue of distinctions between levels of culture.

Levels of Culture

The categories of *high, mid,* and *low culture* merit further discussion, since the sense that certain forms of culture are higher than others has not disappeared from modern society, despite the efforts of the Romantics and the advent and spread of pop culture. Paradoxically, the idea of levels of culture exists within pop culture itself. Most people today share an understanding of an implicit *culture hierarchy* (which is judged in an intuitive sense rather than in a formal or critical way). People evaluate movies, novels, music, and so on instinctively in terms of this hierarchy, as illustrated in table 1.1.

The encompassing of all three levels of culture, and the constant crisscrossing that is evident among the levels, are defining tendencies within pop culture. Many works are even designed purposefully to crisscross the levels. For example, any episode of *The Simpsons*, the longest running prime-time cartoon sitcom, might contain references to writers and philosophers locat-

Table 1.1.   Levels of Culture

Level	Examples Perceived to Occur at Each Level
High	Shakespeare, James Joyce, Emily Dickinson, Bach, Mozart, opera, symphonies, art galleries, *Time* magazine, Chanel perfumes, *Frontline*
Mid	newspapers, National Public Radio, Harry Potter, Oprah, CNN, PBS, public museums, jazz, Bob Dylan
Low	tabloids, Jerry Springer, *American Idol*, Howard Stern, infomercials, Budweiser, 50 Cent

able at the highest level of the hierarchy, as well as references to trendy rap groups and blockbuster movies. This admixture of styles and forms is often called *bricolage* or simply *collage*. It is a generic feature that sets pop culture apart from virtually all previous forms of culture.

Therefore, pop culture is not a "bastard culture" as Barthes cynically portrayed it, but rather an eclectic culture. As mentioned, a movie such as *Amadeus* is appealing to masses of people as pure entertainment and at the same time is acclaimed by critics as a cinematic masterpiece. It has a story line that people can follow and understand easily, a soundtrack that moves audiences poignantly, and a visual power that grabs their attention and maintains it throughout the narrative. On the other hand, within the same cultural paradigm, dance fads, magazines, fashion shows, and wrestling matches seem to have little more than a pure recreational function. Pop culture makes little or no distinction between art and recreation, distraction and engagement. Although most of its products are designed to have a short shelf life, some gain permanency as so-called great works of art. Such is the paradox and power of pop culture.

Youth Culture

In the vast literature on pop culture that has accrued over the last half-century, the term *youth culture* surfaces constantly and is often used as a synonym for pop culture. The main reason is that the makers of popular trends have tended to be young people. Already in the 1920s, it was young people who were at the forefront of trends such as the Charleston and jazz music. Although the older generations initially considered these innovations immoral or vulgar, the new forms eventually caught on more broadly for a simple reason—they held great emotional appeal and entertainment value. In that era, therefore, a basic pattern was established—trends in youth culture that held intrinsic appeal eventually made their way into the adult (or more generic) form of pop culture and culture generally.

One of the reasons for this transference of youth-based trends into more generic forms is rather straightforward. Young people become old, but in so doing they do not discard the trends of their youth as they age. Rather, they hang on to them in adulthood. Thus trends once considered to be tied to fleeting youthful fancy eventually become elements of cultural nostalgia. So the main difference between pop culture and youth culture can be seen in the tendency of the former to carry over certain trends that were once considered to be exclusively part of youthful experiences and to spread them more broadly. There is thus a constant dynamic between youth culture and more general forms of pop culture in modern society.

ORIGINS AND SPREAD

Tracing the origins and spread of contemporary pop culture is not an easy thing, since diverse forms of folk culture have existed since time immemorial—that is to say, common folk have always produced music, stories, and other forms of expression that they used for their own recreation and engagement. So, in a way, pop culture has always existed. Modern-day pop culture differs from older varieties in that it is spread widely through the mass media. Pop culture would not have become so widespread without the partnership that it has always had with the mass media. Incidentally, the focus here, and of this book, is American pop culture. There are two reasons for this focus. First, American pop culture is the type with which I am most familiar, and whose categories I have noticed in other pop cultures (European, Asian, and so forth). Second, American pop culture is the model that tends to be exported elsewhere. I will return to this topic in the final chapter.

The most appropriate way to trace the origin, institutionalization, and spread of pop culture is to identify those media events that can be tagged as critical in promoting and spreading its products into the mainstream. The starting point is the early nineteenth century.

The 1820s–1940s

The publication of popular magazines and cheap newspapers, starting in the 1820s, coupled with the publication in the 1860s of dime novels—

A Pop Culture Timeline

1821: The *Saturday Evening Post* is launched, becoming one of the first magazines to appeal directly to masses of people.

1833: The *New York Sun* is published as the first penny press newspaper, costing only one cent.

1836: *Godey's Lady's Book* is launched as the first modern women's magazine.

1860s: The *New York Morning* reaches a circulation of 80,000, highlighting the fact that newspapers had become an integral part of mass culture. The dime novel becomes popular in the same decade.

1887: Emile Berliner develops the gramophone, which can play cheap, mass-produced records.

1888: Guglielmo Marconi invents the first radio transmitter.

1889: Hannibal Goodwin develops film technology.

1894: Thomas Edison opens up the first nickelodeon parlors with coin-operated projectors.

1895: William Randolph Hearst enters newspaper publishing and adopts sensationalistic techniques, promoting so-called yellow journalism. The Lumière brothers show the first short films in Paris.

1896: Thomas Edison invents the Vitascope, which is capable of large-screen projection.

1900: Muckraking (seeking out and publicizing the misdemeanors of prominent people) becomes highly popular in magazine publishing.

1903: Edwin S. Porter's *The Great Train Robbery*, an early western, gains popularity, indicating that the era of movie-going is just around the corner.

1906–1910: Lee De Forest invents the vacuum tube, improving radio reception, and Reginald Fessenden makes the first radio broadcast, from the Metropolitan Opera House in New York City.

1910s: Silent films become popular, and the first movie celebrities emerge.

1916: David Sarnoff, the commercial manager of American Marconi, writes a famous memo, now known as the Radio Box Memo, in which he proposes to make radio a "household utility." Frank Conrad founds KDKA in Pittsburgh, the first radio station, in 1916. The station's broadcast of the 1920 presidential election results on November 2, 1920, is generally considered to constitute the beginning of professional broadcasting.

1920s: The Big Five studios (Paramount, MGM, Warner Brothers, Twentieth Century Fox, RKO) and the Little Three studios (Columbia, Universal, United Artists) are established in the late 1920s.

1922: *Reader's Digest* is launched. The first uses of radio for commercial purposes begin with the airing of the first commercials, by AT&T on station WEAF. This causes an uproar, as people challenge the use of the public airwaves for commercial messages.

1926: The first radio broadcasting network, NBC, is created by RCA.

1927: Soundtrack technology turns silent films into talkies. The first talkie is *The Jazz Singer* (1927), starring Al Jolson. Philo T. Farnsworth transmits the first television picture.

1933: FM radio is developed.

1936: The first television service debuts in Britain.

1939: Robert de Graaf introduces Pocket Books. NBC starts regular television broadcasts from New York City.

1947: Radio starts to lose audiences to television. Magnetic audiotape is developed by 3M. Wynonie Harris records "Good Rockin' Tonight," probably the first rock-and-roll song.

1948: 33 1/3 records are introduced by Columbia Records and 45 rpm records are introduced by RCA Victor. The DJ radio era takes off. Milton Berle and Ed Sullivan go on air with the first television variety shows, ushering in the golden age of television. The first community antenna television channels (CATV) are established.

1949: *Red Hot 'n Blue* becomes one of the first radio rock-and-roll shows.

1950s: Television becomes a dominant medium as previous radio genres and personalities making the move over to television.

1954: *Sports Illustrated* begins publication.

1955: *The Village Voice* is launched as the first underground newspaper in Greenwich Village. Top 40 radio becomes popular, indicating that radio is becoming more and more a marketing arm of the recording industry. Rock-and-roll defines youth culture in the mid-1950s.

1960s: Rock music is linked with social protest, spearheading the counterculture movement.

1962: The first communications satellite, the first digital phone networks, and the first pagers are introduced.

1967: Rock-and-roll gets its own magazine with the launch of *Rolling Stone*. The Beatles release *Sgt. Pepper's Lonely Hearts Club Band*, the first true concept album.

1968: *60 Minutes* starts broadcasting, showcasing the power of television to influence public opinion. The National Commission on

(continues)

the Causes of Violence concludes that television violence encourages violent behavior.

1971: Borders opens its first store in Ann Arbor. Chain bookstores and superstores start springing up across America shortly thereafter.

1972: The first video game, Pong, is introduced.

1974: *People* magazine starts publication.

1976: VCRs are introduced, creating a new rental and purchase industry for movies. *Star Wars* initiates a new era of big-budget blockbusters.

1978: Cellular phone service begins. Nicholas Negroponte of MIT introduces the term *convergence* to describe the intersection of media.

1979–1980: Rap emerges out of hip-hop clubs in New York City.

1980: Ohio's *Columbus Dispatch* is the first newspaper to go online. CNN premieres as a twenty-four-hour cable news network, owned originally by Ted Turner, which revolutionizes newscasting and television formats generally.

1981: Music Television (MTV) is born, becoming a new arm of the recording industry.

1982: *USA Today* is launched, the first paper modeled after television. Compact discs are introduced. Rock fragments into many genres. Rap rises to the top of the pop music industry.

1987: WFAN is launched as the first all-sports radio station.

1989: Tim Berners-Lee develops concepts and techniques that a few years later lead to the establishment of the World Wide Web. A new company called AOL (America Online) is formed, later becoming the first successful Internet service provider.

1991: The Internet opens to commercial uses. The World Wide Web is launched.

1994: The direct broadcast satellite (DBS) industry debuts.

1995: Amazon.com is established, turning its first profit in 2002. The first megaplex movie theater is built in Dallas, leading to a wave of megaplexes and a new cinema-going culture. *Toy Story* is the first completely computer-generated movie, starting a new trend in movie-making.

1997: DVDs make their debut, offering more storage space than VHS.

1998: The *Dallas Morning News* is the first newspaper to break a major story on its website instead of its front page. Increasing use of the Internet leads to the development of blogs, online chat groups, and the like, which take on many of the functions of rubrics in traditional newspapers.

2000s: Microsoft and Adobe start making online books (e-books) available. E-zines, e-toons, and other magazine genres also start proliferating. Movies integrate with the Internet, where trailers are shown and where even full features can be seen. Specialty channels become the norm in the world of traditional television.

2001: MP3 technology shakes up the music industry as Internet users share music files on Napster. Instant messaging services appear.

2002: Satellite and web-based radio and television programs emerge. File-sharing becomes highly popular. Rap and hip-hop remain popular but start losing their market domination.

2003: Apple Computer's iTunes music store makes its debut, making it possible to buy music on the Internet. VOD (video on demand) is introduced.

Mid-2000s and continuing: The Internet converges with previous media (radio, television, etc.) to produce online versions of all media forms. It also becomes a source of new forms of communication and pop culture, including websites such as MySpace, Facebook, and YouTube.

inexpensive novels that dealt mainly with adventure, crime, or romance—planted the seeds from which pop culture would eventually sprout. With the launch of *Reader's Digest* in 1922, the leisure activity of reading for pleasure established a synergy between print media and pop culture that has remained solid to this very day. Magazines and newspapers continue both to propel the spread of pop culture through the stories and images they print and to be shaped by trends within that very culture.

Especially critical in the rise and spread of pop culture were movie theaters, which began as nickelodeons in 1894. By 1905, these early theaters, which opened mainly in commercial areas and in immigrant neighborhoods, attracted large audiences because admission was only five cents. Affordability and popularity have always been decisive factors in promulgating pop culture. Nickelodeons laid the foundation for the expansion of the movie industry and a further spread of popular cinematic genres, from adventure serials to comedies and romance. By the 1910s, the first movie celebrities appeared on the scene. Cinema and pop culture had formed an intrinsic bond. In the 1920s, this bond was further cemented by the institution and rise of the Big Five studios (Paramount, MGM, Warner Brothers, Twentieth Century Fox, RKO) and the Little Three studios (Columbia, Universal, United Artists),

The phenomenon that we understand today as pop culture could never have materialized, however, without jazz. In the early 1920s jazz, once strictly background music in the brothels of Kansas City and New Orleans, started to flourish across America as the musical idiom of young and fashionable people. By the end of the decade, spurred by the cheapness and availability of mass-produced records and the emergence of the radio as a promoter of recordings, a true paradigm shift occurred, resulting in the entrenchment of jazz and its derivative, swing, as culturally dominant music styles. People simply loved the music. Swing band leaders like Glenn Miller, who boasted hits such as "Little Brown Jug," "Sunrise Serenade," "Moonlight Serenade," and "In the Mood," became icons of an ever-expanding pop culture, as did jazz singers and musicians.

Miller disbanded his orchestra in 1942 and enlisted in the U.S. Army, where he formed the forty-two-piece, all-star Army Air Force Band, which entertained World War II service personnel with regular radio broadcasts. His influence on the spread of pop music cannot be underestimated. To this day, his recordings sell in the millions.

The 1950s–1960s

In the years subsequent to World War II, music and fashion trends seemed to spring up on a daily basis. As in previous decades, young people led the trends. By then, the entire society had become aware of pop culture and had begun to tacitly accept it. In 1948, *Life* magazine ran a cover story on this phenomenon, underscoring the fact that, for the first time in American history, young people constituted a demographic unto themselves. The article also pointed out that, due in part to the many extra jobs that were created by World War II, the new market category of teenagers had plenty of spending money. It became Madison Avenue's avowed mission, shortly thereafter, to get them to spend it on clothing, movies, and recordings. By the mid-1950s, the average American teenager had more pocket money than any young person has probably ever had in the history of civilization. In 1955, the movies *Rebel Without a Cause*, starring teen idol James Dean, and *Blackboard Jungle*, starring Marlon Brando as a motorcycle gang leader, made it obvious to one and all that the *Life* article was indeed prophetic. Teenagers had not only become a distinct market category but had also established a youth culture of their own. Elvis Presley became the king of this culture, symbolizing its brash attitude with his hip-swinging style. Television further spread the fledgling youth culture as programs such as *Ameri-*

can Bandstand and the *Adventures of Ozzie and Harriet* gained nationwide popularity. The latter program was, revealingly, the first sitcom to deal with the problems of raising teenaged children (two sons).

Rock-and-roll music started spreading across society by the end of the decade, with the advent of cheap 33 1/3 and 45 rpm records (introduced respectively by Columbia Records and RCA Victor). The DJ radio era also took off, further promoting youth trends broadly. Movies were targeted more and more at younger people, as were magazines, such as *Sports Illustrated* (launched in 1954).

By 1960, it had become obvious that the media, technology, business, and young people had formed a new cohesive partnership. Popular fads spread, from the Hula Hoop to dance crazes such as the twist that instantly cut across generations. Sports, shopping, and fashion became intrinsic components of ever-expanding recreational lifestyles. Radio and television personalities became national celebrities, as did rock musicians. The teenager had become a powerful new social persona, a "rebel without a cause," as the previously mentioned movie title mentioned suggested. Most adults expected the causeless rebellion to fade quickly. But in the 1960s, something truly unexpected happened. The next generation of teenagers became "rebels with a cause," questioning the values of the society in which they were reared as never before. Known as *hippies*, they denounced the adult establishment, seeking inspiration from Eastern mystical traditions to fashion a new form of pop culture that spearheaded a clamor for social change. The rock concert became a *happening* (in the tradition of pop art happenings), in which the lyrics of the performers often spurred youths on to social activism. Drugs were consumed openly to induce or heighten the experience of the happening. Sexual activities were also carried out openly, in obvious defiance of adult moralism. The new musical styles were truly ambitious aesthetically. By the end of the decade, rock operas, such as *Tommy* (1969) by the Who, were being considered as serious musical works by traditional music critics. The high-versus-low dichotomy of culture was becoming more and more meaningless.

In the same decade, television became increasingly powerful as a stage for an ever-expanding pop culture. With the launch of documentary news programs, it was becoming obvious that the trend started by *Reader's Digest* of compressing information into digestible bits and pieces was spreading into the realm of television. *Reader's Digest* culture was morphing into a "viewer's digest" culture.

In the same era, the generally lighthearted music (and movies) of a postmilitary Elvis Presley stood in contrast to an emerging form of truly fascinating musical art emblematized by groups such as Procul Harum and the Beatles. The influence of the latter on the counterculture movement of the late 1960s cannot be overstated. Elvis Presley was the figurehead of youth culture in the 1950s. By the mid-1960s he had crossed over into a more "adult-acceptable" form of pop culture. The Beatles, on the other hand, challenged the status quo. By the time they produced the album *Sgt. Pepper's Lonely Hearts Club Band* in 1967, they had raised rock-and-roll to the level of high musical art. They became the icons of the counterculture. The Beatles' long hairstyles and unusual mode of dress (which included boots) became central features of youth fashion in the mid-1960s. The band's satirical style of denouncing adult culture with songs such as "When I'm Sixty-Four" also became a prominent feature of youth culture. Ironically (and tragically), two of the original members, John Lennon and George Harrison, never made it to that golden age.

The 1970s–1990s

The counterculture movement did not last long. By the early 1970s it had virtually disappeared from the social radar screen. The hippies had simply become less inclined to revolt, as they started to have children of their own. New musical trends emerged, as did new youth lifestyles. The trend that worried adults the most was so-called punk culture, which constituted the first true subculture within the more generic youth culture. Alienating themselves visibly from mainstream society, the punks were deliberately violent and confrontational. Members of punk rock bands spat on their audiences, mutilated themselves with knives, damaged props onstage and in the hall, and shouted, burped, urinated, and bellowed at will to a basic pulsating beat, inciting their audiences to do likewise. The fashion trends that punks introduced—chains, dog collars, army boots, and hairstyles that ranged from shaved heads to wild-looking *Mohawk* hairdos dyed every color imaginable—were designed to communicate degradation, mockery, social caricature, and insubordination all at once. The punks were antibourgeois and anticapitalist in ways that, ironically, their hippie parents found shocking and offensive.

However, the punk subculture, like all previous (and subsequent) youth subcultures, would also recede from center stage. It was, simply, a contemporary form mock theater, having the same function as medieval carnivals. For this reason, punk culture has not changed society radically.

In the same decade, youth culture had become highly fragmented. Other music-based lifestyles crystallized alongside the punk lifstyle. One alternative subculture involved makeup and cross-dressing—another carnivalesque mode of behavior. The rock band Kiss, whose performances on stage were designed to shock adults, symbolized this new trend perfectly. Each musician in the band portrayed a comic book character—a glamour boy, an alien from outer space, a kitty cat, and a sex-crazed kabuki monster. Kiss's stage act included fire-eating, smoke bombs, hydraulic lifts, and instrument-smashing. *The Rocky Horror Picture Show* was another manifestation of this new carnivalesque trend. The movie became a cult phenomenon, as hordes of teenagers went to see it week after week, month after month, year after year. It was both a parody of 1950s rock culture and a glorification of the "transgendered" lifestyle portrayed by bands such as Alice Cooper.

Running totally against the punk and *Rocky Horror* forms of youth culture was disco culture, epitomized by the 1978 movie *Saturday Night Fever,* starring John Travolta. The popularity of disco with hordes of teens was evidence of youth culture's fragmentation. Disco culture was a throwback to the days of swing and ballroom dancing. Punk teens rejected it with the expression "Disco sucks!" So too did other teens, who saw disco as too superficial and much too acceptable to the adult world. Disco culture thrived nonetheless, because it was fun and sexy.By the early 1980s, the youth culture trends of the 1970s had receded to the theatrical periphery, although snippets of the punk, cross-dressing, and disco lifestyles remained and are being recycled even today in movie remakes, television nostalgia programs, Internet websites, and the like. The youth culture of the 1980s continued to split into more and more lifestyle factions. Two performers in particular—Michael Jackson and Madonna—emerged to challenge traditional gender attitudes even more than had Kiss and *Rocky Horror Picture Show* actors. Michael Jackson blended male and female sexual characteristics into his stage persona. He also extolled horror and the occult in his video and album *Thriller* (1982), which earned him an unprecedented eight Grammy awards, becoming the best-selling album in youth culture history up to that time. Madonna's songs "Like a Virgin," "Material Girl," and "Dress You Up" satirized the traditional view of females as objects of male voyeurism. She adopted a Marilyn Monroe "sex kitten" peep show pose as one of her performance trademarks, but at the same time she held the reins of the performance simply by looking into the camera, thus taking possession of her own sexuality. As Madonna knew and showed, lookers who are themselves looked at become powerless.

By the end of the 1980s, youth culture continued to fragment, as hard rockers, mods, preps, goths, adherents of grunge, and other teen subculture groups emerged with their own fashions, music, and lifestyles. But one trend rose above them all to capture center stage—rap music and its accompanying hip-hop lifestyle. Already in 1961, the Tokens had recorded a highly popular song, "The Lion Sleeps Tonight," which some critics consider to be a forerunner of rap style since the lyrics were spoken rhythmically rather than set to melody. Jamaican reggae style is also thought to be a predecessor. It was imitated by the Beatles in their 1968 song "Ob-La-Di, Ob-La-Da." Reggae also influenced the songwriting styles of Sting, The Police, Eric Clapton, and Led Zeppelin. The term *rap* was used for the first time in the mid-1970s to describe an eclectic mix of funk, soul, and hard rock played by disc jockeys in the dance halls of Harlem and the South Bronx. The more enthusiastic members of those audiences would improvise singsong rhymes, exhorting other teens to dance and "get into it." These were called *rapping* sessions.

Along with such youth-based trends, the decades of the 1970s to 1990s also saw several other developments that further entrenched pop culture as increasingly the default form of culture. The first Borders store in Ann Arbor led to the popularity of chain bookstores and superstores, which started springing up across America shortly thereafter, making the bookstore a part of popular reading culture and a vehicle for the mass consumption of books. Since then, bookstores have become entertainment centers, including coffee shops and DVD and record sections as part of their ambiance. Television, radio, and other media began converging through digital technologies. By the end of the 1990s, pop culture was moving away from the traditional media stages, and more and more to the new and exciting online venue.

The 2000s

As computer technology improved steadily after World War II, smaller and cheaper computers could be built for many purposes. By the 1970s, it became economically feasible to manufacture personal computers (PCs) for mass consumption. The first PCs were mainly word processors; that is, they simply added computer-based capacities to typewriters, making the writing of printed text significantly easier and more sophisticated. In 1975, the first microcomputer was introduced to the world. It had the power of many of the previous larger computers but could fit onto a desktop. This feat was accomplished using new miniaturization technologies. The first commercial software appeared shortly thereafter in 1978.

At the same time that computers were becoming faster, more powerful, and smaller, networks were being developed to interconnect them. In the 1960s, the Advanced Research Projects Agency (ARPA) of the U.S. Department of Defense, along with researchers working on military projects at research centers and universities across the country, developed a network called Arpanet for sharing data and mainframe computer processing time over specially equipped telephone lines and satellite links. Used at first for military purposes, Arpanet became the first functional major electronic mail network when the National Science Foundation connected university and nonmilitary research sites to it. By 1981, a couple of hundred computers were connected to Arpanet. The military then divided the network into two organizations—Arpanet and a purely military network. During the 1980s, the former was absorbed by NSFNET, a more advanced network developed by the National Science Foundation. It was that system that soon came to be known as the Internet.

One of the main reasons for the slow growth of the Internet was its complexity. To access it, users had to learn an intricate series of programming commands. A major breakthrough occurred in 1991 with the arrival of the World Wide Web, developed by Tim Berners-Lee (b. 1955), a British computer scientist at the European Center for Nuclear Research (CERN). The advent of the World Wide Web simplified use of the Internet considerably. The arrival of browsers in 1993 further eased use, bringing about astronomical growth in traffic on the Internet. In the history of human communications, no other technology has made it possible for so many people to interact with each other, irrespective of the distance between them. Moreover, because of the Internet, it is no longer accurate to talk about "competing" media. Advances in digital technologies and in telecommunications networks have led to a convergence of all communications systems into one overall digital system. This development has led, in turn, to the emergence of new digitally based lifestyles and careers, to the creation of new institutions, and to radical paradigm shifts in all domains of mass communications and culture.

The first telecommunications medium to be digitized was the telephone, with the installation in 1962 of high-speed lines, capable of carrying dozens of conversations simultaneously, in phone networks. Phone equip-

An Internet and World Wide Web Timeline

1822: Charles Babbage develops a computer prototype.

1844: Telegraphy constitutes a data network forerunner.

1866: Transoceanic telegraph service begins.

1876: The telephone is introduced.

1915: The first transcontinental phone call is made.

1939: John Vincent Atanasoff of Iowa State University is credited with designing the first modern computer.

1946: ENIAC, the first general-purpose computer, is developed by J. Presper Eckert and John Mauchly, mainly for military purposes.

1951: Eckert and Mauchly introduce UNIVAC as the first civilian computer.

1962: The first communications satellite, the first digital phone networks, and the first pagers are introduced.

1964: The first local area network (LAN) is initiated to support nuclear weapons research.

1965: A highly usable computer language, BASIC, is developed.

1969: Arpanet, the first communication network, is established by the American defense department.

1971: Microprocessors are developed, leading shortly thereafter to personal computer technology.

1972: The first video game, Pong, is introduced. E-mail is developed on Arpanet.

1975: The first personal computer, Altair, is launched.

1977: The first fiber optic network is created.

1978: Cellular phone service begins.

ment of all kinds is now fully digitized. A new high-speed phone technology, called Digital Subscriber Line (DSL), is being installed across the globe. It has the capacity to transmit audio, video, and computer data over both conventional phone lines and satellite.

Stories of similar or parallel convergence can be told with regard to other technologies. The digitization of print media, for instance, started in 1967. Today, most major newspapers are produced by means of digital technologies and are available in online versions. The special effects created for the movie *Star Wars* in 1977 introduced digital technology into filmmaking. The first computer-generated movie, *Toy Story*, debuted in 1995. Digitally produced movies are now common. In the domain of home video technol-

1980s: Hypertext is developed in the mid-1980s, leading eventually to the creation of the World Wide Web.

1982: The National Science Foundation sponsors a high-speed communications network, leading to the Internet.

1983: Arpanet starts using TCP/IP, essentially launching the Internet.

1984: Apple Macintosh is the first PC with graphics.

1989: Tim Berners-Lee develops concepts that a few years later are converted into the World Wide Web. A new company called AOL (America Online) is formed, later becoming the first successful Internet service provider.

1990: The first Internet search engine, Archie, is developed.

1991: The Internet opens to commercial uses, HTML is developed, and the World Wide Web is finally launched.

1993: The first point-and-click Web browser, Mosaic, is introduced.

1994: The first Internet cafés open. Jeff Bezos launches Amazon .com.

1995: Digital cellular phones are introduced. The first online auction house, eBay, is launched.

1996: Google makes its debut.

2000: Cookies technology allows for information profiles to be created, enabling data-mining practices to burgeon.

2001: Instant messaging services appear.

2002: Broadband technology is developed in South Korea.

Mid-2000s and continuing: The Internet converges with previous media (radio, television, etc.) to produce online versions of all media forms. It also becomes a source of new forms of communication, including websites such as MySpace, Facebook, and YouTube.

ogy, the DVD supplanted the VHS tape in the mid-1990s. The digitally produced compact disc (CD) started replacing vinyl records and audiocassette tapes already in the mid-1980s, shortly after its introduction in 1982. Further compression technologies, known as MP3, are further enhancing the miniaturization process. The Internet itself has also become a source for uploading and downloading music, and for showcasing new forms of music. Cable television went digital in 1998, allowing broadcasters to increase their channel offerings. This technology was introduced primarily to meet competition from the Direct Broadcast Satellite (DBS) industry, which started producing digital multi-channel programming for reception by home satellite dishes in 1995. So-called high-definition television (HDTV), which consists of transmitters and receivers using digital formats, became commercially available in 1998. Digital Audio Broadcasting (DAB) is the corresponding technology in radio broadcasting. Radio stations now use digital technology universally to create their programs.

Until the early 1990s, most information on the Internet consisted mainly of printed text. The introduction of the World Wide Web made it possible to include graphics, animation, video, and sound. Today, the World Wide Web contains all kinds of documents, databases, bulletin boards, and electronic publications, such as newspapers, books, and magazines in all media forms (print, audio-oral, visual). The plethora of information it enfolds, and the rapidity at which that information can be accessed, are leading to the Internet's gradual replacement of such traditional institutions as reference libraries. More to the point of the current discussion, the Internet is providing an important stage for the performance of new music, the showcasing of new movies, and so on. The online venue has made *indie culture*, as it is called, a budding form of pop culture. People can post their own art, writings, music videos, movies, and the like on popular websites or on personal blogs. The Internet is further democratizing an already largely democratic form of culture. Alongside indie producers, media and entertainment enterprises are now using the Internet. Scientists and scholars access the Internet to communicate with colleagues, to conduct research, to distribute lecture notes and course materials to students, and to publish papers and articles. The "Internet galaxy" is expanding at the speed of light. The Internet has also become a highly effective medium of advertising, making it possible for all kinds of businesses and individuals the world over to communicate effectively and inexpensively with the entire globe.

Push technology, also known as webcasting, is starting to overtake previous forms of broadcasting. Push technology programs have no fixed schedules. A producer can offer audio or video presentations to anyone who subscribes to them. The user might wish to download the entire audio or video clip for later playback or play it in real time over the Internet. Real-time play, moreover, is possible through a technology called *streaming*. Radio and television often stream their programs in real time so that people throughout the world may listen or watch over the Internet. Some media outlets have started creating programs specifically for the Internet. Some television news organizations now use the Internet to post additional stories, constantly updating the news. These media outlets offer extended versions of interviews and other features. Popular online news programs include weather reports, global financial information, sports scores, and breaking news.

The Internet is also leading to a redefinition of the roles of the author and the reader of a text. Online novels, for instance, allow for multiple plot twists to be built into a story. They also enable readers to observe the story as it unfolds from the perspective of different characters. Readers may also change the story themselves to suit their interpretive fancies. While the author sets a framework for the narrative, the actual narrative is realized by the reader. The same kind of editing power is now applicable to all kinds of Internet documents, from web-based encyclopedias and dictionaries to online textbooks. Electronic documents can always be updated and thus always kept up to date. The *popular* in pop culture is now taking on more and more of a literal meaning, as readers interact with authors, scholars, artists, and others in determining how they will ultimately be informed, engaged, or entertained.

Online documents can store the equivalent information of myriad paper books. As a consequence, cyber libraries have already sprung up and may eventually replace traditional libraries. Already in 1971, a venture called Project Gutenberg was established by volunteers to digitize, archive, and distribute online the full texts of books in the public domain. The project continues to make these texts as free as possible, in formats that can be used on almost any computer. As of 2006, Project Gutenberg had over nineteen thousand items in its collection, with an average of over fifty new e-books being added each week. Most are in English, but there are also growing numbers in other languages, as similar projects are established in non–English-speaking countries. There are now similar projects posting various materials in the public domain on websites of their own.

The main lesson to be learned from studying the development of pop culture through its association with changes in media technologies is that there is no turning back the clock once an innovation is introduced that makes communication more rapid, cheap, efficient, and broadly accessible. Nevertheless, this does not mean that previous media outlets for pop culture will disappear. As in the past, forms of media will evolve new functions as they converge with new technologies. For example, an audience for traditional paper books not only continues to exist but is actually augmented by online versions of the books, which paradoxically help to promote the paper versions. Moreover, purchasing books in a super bookstore is a diverting and distracting experience in itself—which bookstore chains have come to realize, as evidenced by their joining of forces with coffee chains. The market for paper-based print materials such as novels, trade books, magazines, and newspapers continues to be strong, even though online versions are springing up constantly.

POP CULTURE AND TECHNOLOGY

As the foregoing discussion emphasized, the spread of pop culture has been brought about largely through its partnership with media and communications technologies. The rise of music as a mass art, for instance, was made possible by the advent of recording and radio broadcasting technologies at the start of the twentieth century. Records and radio made music available to large audiences, converting it from an art for the elite to a commodity for one and all. Similarly, the spread and appeal of pop culture throughout the globe today is due to technology—most importantly, satellite technology. Satellite technology has had profound social, political, and cultural repercussions. Satellite television, for example, is often cited as bringing about the disintegration of the former Soviet system in Eastern Europe, as people became attracted to images of consumerist delights by simply tuning into American television programs.

As the late Canadian communications theorist Marshall McLuhan (1911–1980) often claimed, culture, social evolution, and scientific innovation are so intertwined that we hardly ever notice their interconnection. Some inventions become so intertwined with trends in pop culture that they morph into symbolic artifacts within that culture. Two examples include the jukebox and the automobile.

The Jukebox

The invention of jukeboxes in 1906 constitutes a classic case of how technology is linked with trends and patterns in pop culture. Originally found in *juke joints*, places where southern field workers went to dance and interact socially, jukeboxes were adopted by diners and soda shops in the 1920s so that customers could enjoy the pop tunes of the era as they ate or drank. By 1941 there were nearly four hundred thousand jukeboxes in the United States.

The jukebox became a symbolic part of the early rock culture of the 1950s, functioning as a magnet for teenagers after the Seeburg Company produced the first jukeboxes in 1950 to play 45 rpm singles. Jukeboxes

The jukebox was a symbolic part of the early rock culture of the 1950s.
©iStockphoto.com/Barbara Henry

quickly became a fixture in soda shops, bowling alleys, and other teen hang-outs. The 1970s television sitcom *Happy Days* perfectly illustrated this development. After school, the adolescent characters of that program hung out at a diner that featured a jukebox that blurted out the rock tunes of the 1950s, putting them in a good frame of mind to interact socially and romantically. The jukebox was an icon of the golden age of rock. In the 1953 movie *The Wild One*, Marlon Brando delivered his now classic juvenile delinquent's retort to the question "What are you rebelling against?" by drumming his fingers on a jukebox and answering, "Whaddaya got?" A number of other movies and television programs also featured jukeboxes. In its heyday, the jukebox was part of a social experience, defining an era of pop culture for groups of teenagers across the country.

The Automobile

Like the jukebox, the automobile became a symbolic prop in pop culture almost right after its invention. By the Roaring Twenties it had far exceeded its original function of transportation. In the 1920s many low-income families could afford to buy an inexpensive automobile called the Model T, which Henry Ford had developed in 1908. The number of passenger cars in the United States jumped from fewer than 7 million in 1919 to about 23 million in 1929. Traffic started spreading throughout the nation's highways, creating a need for new kinds of businesses, including gas stations and roadside restaurants, all of which became parts of an expanding road-based pop culture.

The media picked up on the automobile's role in this new type of social experience. Nicholas Ray, for example, showcased the symbolic value of the automobile to 1950s teenagers in his 1955 movie *Rebel Without a Cause*, in which a game of "car chicken" is particularly memorable. In that scene, two male suitors are seen vying to win over a female paramour through what becomes, essentially, a form of virility-proving combat. Before the car duel there is a ritualistic rubbing of the earth. Then the camera zooms in on James Dean, one of the two combatants, behind the wheel of his car, showing him with a cigarette dangling confidently from the side of his mouth; the camera then shifts to his competitor in his own car, self-assuredly slicking down his hair. Cars, hairstyle, and cigarettes are, clearly, the primary symbolic props in that memorable depiction of teen sexual and virility rituals. *Rebel Without a Cause* caught on throughout the teen universe. The movie radiated a sense of restlessness and alienation that could be felt more easily than articulated. *Rebel Without a Cause* is now part of general pop culture lore.

The car as a symbolic prop is everywhere in pop culture, from television programs like the now defunct *Knight Rider* to movies such as the series of *The Fast and Furious* of the mid-2000s. The car, of course, also appears in many pivotal scenes in the set of James Bond movies and in many other adventure flicks. The widespread fascination with cars is also manifest in the current hobby of collecting, maintaining, and displaying cars from certain periods in history. There are now even television channels, websites, magazines, radio programs, and the like that cater to lovers of antique or period cars.

Some car models have unique historical value as pop culture symbols. Two classic examples are the 1957 Cadillac Eldorado and the 1964 Ford Mustang. The former became a part of the pop culture lore in the late 1950s. The name Eldorado alludes to a magical city of the New World, often thought to be in the northern part of South America, fabled for its great wealth of gold and precious jewels. The name fit perfectly—in its convertible design, with its large tail fins and its expansive body, the Eldorado epitomized the large cars that were the craze of America's era of expanding wealth. Although its showy features did little for the performance of the vehicle, consumers loved the look and demanded fins of similar size and style for many different car makes until the mid-1960s. The Mustang was associated, from the outset, with youth culture. More than one hundred thousand were sold during the first four months of 1964, when the Mustang was introduced, making it Ford's best early sales success since the Model T. The Mustang's design as a quasi–sports car for the young (and the young at heart) was indisputably a key to its success. Marketed as a low-priced, high-style car, the Mustang appealed instantly to a large segment of people. It imparted a sense of artistry that was previously associated only with luxury cars. Also, it was intended to attract men and women equally. It had elegant, narrow bumpers instead of the large ones common at the time and delicate grillwork that jutted out at the top and slanted back at the bottom, giving the car a forward-thrusting look. The car's visual appeal was increased by the air scoops on its sides which cooled the rear brakes. The Mustang's hefty logo of a galloping horse adorned the grille—as on a Maserati—and itself became an icon of pop culture. The car's name and design matched perfectly: A mustang is a horse that, although small, is powerful—like the car. Also, a mustang is a horse that is wild—as the youths of the era at the threshold of the counterculture movement were perceived to be.

Convergence

The integration of the jukebox and the car with various domains of pop culture, from movies to music, now falls under the rubric of *convergence*—a term introduced into pop culture studies in the mid-1990s by Nicholas Negroponte (b. 1943), an influential author on digital media. Although Negroponte coined the term to describe the digitization process previously discussed, it is now used to refer more generally to the phenomenon of the integration and merging of media, technology, and cultural forms.

The convergence of the computer with all other technologies, for example, is a defining characteristic of mass communications today, and is turning the world into a true digital global village. But although convergence has greatly facilitated many developments, it has also faced setbacks. Overreliance on computers has fostered a mindset in which people see them as intrinsic components of human life. This attitude became apparent on the threshold of the year 2000 when the "millennium bug" was thought to be a harbinger of doom. So reliant had people become on the computer that a simple technological problem—making sure that computers could read the new *00* date as *2000* and not *1900* or some other date—was interpreted in moral and apocalyptic terms. That fear was striking evidence that computers had acquired a meaning that far exceeded their original function as computing machines.

Constant interaction in cyberspace, moreover, is leading surreptitiously and gradually to the entrenchment of a bizarre modern form of Cartesian dualism—the view that the body and the mind are separate entities. Computers allow users to move and react in simulated environments and to manipulate virtual objects rather than real objects. Constant engagement in such environments is conditioning people more and more to perceive the body as separable from the mind. In effect, the modern-day human being is interacting more and more in an artificial space. This trend is featured in the 1999 movie *The Matrix*. As online interaction becomes even more widespread, and less dependent on external devices, it will further entrench the process of disembodiment. So too will the continuing process of creating "cyber places" and "cyber events." Incidentally, the term *cyberspace* was coined by American writer William Gibson (b. 1948) in his 1984 science fiction novel *Neuromancer*, in which he described cyberspace as a place of "unthinkable complexity." The term has given rise to a vocabulary including *cyber cafés* (cafés that sell coffee and computer time), *cyber malls* (online shopping services), and *cyber junkies* (people addicted to being online).

It is wise to keep in mind, however, that the foregoing discussion may be somewhat overdrawn. The media stage has changed drastically, but the script remains essentially the same. Means of cultural expression from independent movies on YouTube to webcasts of various kinds are still based on the same sorts of concepts and styles that have characterized pop culture spectacles since the Roaring Twenties. The online narratives and songs still have to prove themselves as popular in order to catch on. Pop culture is simply continuing to perpetuate itself, as it always has, through the technologically changing media that deliver it to large masses of people. And while pop culture today is bringing about broad social change, that is not a new occurrence. The social fabric of America in the 1960s, for instance, was shaped by hippie culture, which garnered media attention through protest and music. Before the advent of the media, the culture that most readily survived was that which received support from authority figures or traditional institutions, from the Church to the nobility. With the advent of cheap print materials, gramophones, radios, and so on, the conditions for delivering popular forms of culture independently of sponsoring institutions became a reality, ushering in the age of pop culture—an age that is as vibrant today as it was a century ago.

FEATURES OF POP CULTURE

The remaining parts of this book will explore the mass psychology behind pop culture. The movie *Chicago*, mentioned earlier, is particularly useful in this regard because it highlights the main features that give pop culture its particular appeal. Most significantly, *Chicago* underscores how pop culture's basis in spectacle and variety makes it very emotionally appealing. Pop culture is an emotional culture. That is why even after a spectacle or an artifact has become passé, it tends to become part of a society-wide memory and nostalgia.

A perfect example is the spectacle called The Ziegfield Follies, produced in 1907 by the American theatrical producer Florenz Ziegfeld (1867–1932). In its heyday, these performances became popular for extravagant musical follies, beautiful chorus girls, dazzling sets, and catchy tunes. Today, the Follies are hardly seen as "folly" but rather as part of an early chapter in the history of American society itself.

Spectacle

Spectacle is all about entertainment. Musicals, blockbuster movies, the Super Bowl, rock concerts, shopping malls, and bookstores all constitute spectacle. Most historians trace pop culture's origins to a specific kind of theatrical spectacle that featured a wide variety of acts, called *vaudeville*. Vaudeville was the most popular form of entertainment in the United States from the 1880s to the early 1930s and produced many of the celebrities who later gained success in other entertainment media, especially the motion pictures and radio. These crossover celebrities included Jack Benny, George Burns, Eddie Cantor, W. C. Fields, Al Jolson, Ed Wynn, and Sophie Tucker. Some vaudeville theaters featured more than twenty acts in a single bill. But the standard pattern was a dozen acts that ranged enormously— from juggling, animal acts, comedy skits, recitations, songs, and magic shows to burlesque performances by actresses, usually involving various forms of striptease (generally sanitized for broader consumption). Vaudeville was an offshoot of the circus, where the term *spectacle* had a specific meaning—it referred to the segment that opened and closed performances and included many performers, animals, and floats. As the band played and the ringmaster sang, performers dressed in elaborate costumes walked around the circus tent or arena. The spectacle usually ended with a trick called a long mount, in which the elephants stood in a line with their front legs resting on each other's backs.

Through the efforts of powerful producers and theater owners, vaudeville became a highly organized nationwide big business with its own theater chains. In its heyday it was the most popular form of live entertainment for family audiences. The term *variety show* eventually replaced *vaudeville*.

Jazz music was an intrinsic part of vaudeville in the Roaring Twenties. As mentioned above, one cannot overstate the role of jazz in the spread and development of pop culture. Jazz originated around 1900. Its roots lay in the musical traditions of African Americans, including both West African music and black folk music. Most early jazz was played by small marching bands or by solo pianists and included musical references to ragtime, marches, hymns, spirituals, and the blues. In 1917 a group of New Orleans musicians called The Original Dixieland Jazz Band recorded a jazz piece, creating a sensation throughout society. Two other groups soon followed: in 1922 the New Orleans Rhythm Kings and in 1923 the Creole Jazz Band, led by cornetist King Oliver. The most influential musician nurtured in New Orleans was King Oliver's second trumpeter, Louis Armstrong, who showed the power of jazz to move people emotionally and to entertain them at the same time. By the 1930s and early 1940s, jazz developed into swing, and also spawned a new and highly popular style known as bebop. Bebop was based on the principle of improvisation over a chord progression, but its tempos were faster and its phrases longer and more complex.

The term *cool jazz* surfaced in 1948 when tenor saxophonist Stan Getz recorded a slow, romantic solo of Ralph Burns's composition *Early Autumn* with the Woody Herman band. The work profoundly influenced many younger musicians. In 1949 and 1950, a group of young musicians that included trumpeter Miles Davis, alto saxophonist Lee Konitz, baritone saxophonist Gerry Mulligan, and arranger Gil Evans recorded several new compositions in this style. These recordings emphasized a lagging beat, soft instrumental sounds, and unusual orchestrations that included the French horn and the tuba. The recordings, with Davis as leader, were later released as *The Birth of Cool*. This term *cool* has come to characterize the popular lifestyle ever since.

The movie *Chicago* highlighted the importance of jazz in the constitution of pop culture, encapsulated in its opening musical piece titled "All that Jazz." *Chicago* also shows the role of women in pop culture—a new role that led to a redefinition of womanhood in American society at large. The main character, Roxie Hart, becomes an overnight sensation after murdering an unfaithful lover. People react against her at first because she is a burlesque star, associated with jazz and sexuality, which are considered the two evils in society. For courtroom purposes, Roxie and her lawyer devise an acceptable persona for her—the persona of a pregnant and loving mother figure. The sexual persona that she assumes on stage, however, is the one that gives Roxie great appeal.

No one has realized the appeal of the female sexual persona more than Madonna. With songs such as "Like a Virgin" and "Material Girl" Madonna showcased the emotional power of that persona. Her videos were, in effect, about "all that jazz." As will be discussed subsequently, by the end of the 1980s Madonna had helped to bring about a powerful new form of feminism, called *post-feminism.*

Madonna's performances are a throwback to the Roaring Twenties, an era of spectacular economic growth, rising prosperity, and far-reaching social change. In the 1920s, large numbers of Americans wanted simply to enjoy life and to amuse themselves with liquor, short skirts, jazz music, and listening to the radio. The Roaring Twenties was also an era of women's liberation, which was expressed through lifestyle and fashion rather than political protest. Before World War I, women had worn long hair, ankle-length dresses, and long cotton stockings. In the 1920s, they wore short, tight dresses and rolled their silk stockings down to their knees. They cut their hair in a boyish style called the bob and wore flashy cosmetics. They danced cheek-to-cheek with men to blaring jazz music. Like Roxie, they decided to put on a sexual persona in public. The era of pop culture had clearly arrived. The literature, art, and music of the 1920s also reflected the nation's changing values. In his novel *Main Street* (1920), Sinclair Lewis attacked what he considered the dull lives and narrow-minded attitudes of people in a small town. Many American authors, including F. Scott Fitzgerald and Ernest Hemingway, analyzed the attitudes and experiences of the era's so-called Lost Generation. H. L. Mencken, in his witty magazine *The American Mercury,* ridiculed the antics of dimwitted politicians, prohibitionists, and others.

The foregoing discussion is not mean to imply that women have controlled the economy of pop culture. On the contrary, with few exceptions the controllers have been men. Moreover, pop culture has not been immune to sexism (or racism, for that matter). But the fact remains that pop culture—like no previous form of culture—has also allowed women to flaunt their sexual persona publicly and to become artists in their own right. The duality of women's sexual liberation but limited economic power has been constant in the history of pop culture. Members of the female rap group Sequence, for example, wore miniskirts, sequined fabric, high-heeled shoes and prominent makeup to emphasize the female form with its voluptuous curves at the same time that they decried social inequities. The example of Sequence is not unique but rather part of a pattern. In pop culture, differentiating sexuality from sexism has always been a delicate balance.

Collage, Bricolage, and Pastiche

Thee French words—*collage, bricolage,* and *pastiche*—are often used in the relevant literature to describe the character of pop culture spectacles, movements, lifestyles, and products. *Collage* is a term taken from the domain of modern painting, describing a picture or design made by gluing pieces of paper or other materials onto a canvas or another surface. By arranging the materials in a certain way, the artist can create strange or witty effects not possible with traditional painting techniques. Many pop culture spectacles, from early vaudeville to *The Simpsons*, are created by a collage technique. Vaudeville was made up of a collage of acts, ranging from skits to acrobatic acts; *The Simpsons* uses diverse elements from different levels of culture in the same episode, as mentioned, to create effects similar to collage paintings. *Bricolage* is a type of collage that emphasizes disproportion, parody, and irony. The goth lifestyle is an example of bricolage, featuring implicit references to themes of horror, difference, and vampirism in an essentially ironic juxtaposition against the mainstream culture. Finally, *pastiche* refers to an admixture of elements in a work or spectacle intended to imitate or satirize another work or style. In my view it is this term that best describes the character of pop culture, which is essentially a pastiche of spectacles, fashion, fads, and other accouterments that together give pop culture its distinct character.

Nostalgia

The sustaining power behind pop culture is its emotional nature. This feature is likely the reason that people hang on to the trends and fads that they found meaningful in their younger years—that is, they react to them nostalgically in their later years. Whether it is Elvis movies, Disney cartoons, Beatles albums, disco dancing, Barbie dolls, or even punk clothing, people react nostalgically to the pop culture symbols and works of their eras. Boomers react nostalgically to the truly beautiful strains of the Platters, and Gen Xers to those of Donna Summers and Madonna. By clinging to their memories, people have made it possible for pop culture to perpetuate itself.

Memorabilia is a product of this mindset. And it is a profitable one indeed, as sales of Elvis and Beatles records continue to show. Pop culture nostalgia has permanently changed the sociology of the modern world. More and more people maintain and cherish their youthful pop culture experiences well beyond adolescence.

This does not mean, though, that pop culture is incapable of producing truly meritorious and lasting forms of "high" art. Indeed, some of the modern world's most significant artistic products have come out of pop culture (as previously mentioned). The comic book art of Charles Schulz (1922–2000) is a case in point. His comic strip *Peanuts*, which debuted in 1950 under the original title *Li'l Folks*, appealed—and continues to appeal—to mass audiences. Through the strip Schulz dealt with some of the most profound religious and philosophical themes of human history in a way that was unique and aesthetically powerful. The same kind of story can be told in other domains of pop culture, from music to the movies.

STUDYING POP CULTURE

Studying culture is the aim of disciplines such as anthropology and semiotics. Other disciplines, such as linguistics, focus on specific aspects or components of culture, such as language. The findings and insights garnered in these disciplines are, clearly, useful to the study of pop culture. In fact, since its inception in the 1950s, pop culture studies have been characterized by *interdisciplinarity*—the adoption and integration of findings and ideas from various disciplines.

On one hand, the study of pop culture is fundamentally an exercise in unraveling the psychological reasons that such things as sports spectacles, hula hoops, recipes, posters, cars, songs, dances, television programs, clothing fashions, and the like gain popularity. On the other hand, the way that scholars study pop culture is akin to the approach taken by literary critics to the study of literary texts. Like literary critics, pop culture analysts identify

Nostalgia: What Was Popular?

1950s

Music: "The Song from Moulin Rouge" (Percy Faith), "Hound Dog" (Elvis Presley), "Your Cheatin' Heart" (Hank Williams), "Great Balls of Fire" (Jerry Lee Lewis)
Cars: drop-top Corvette, models with fins
Posters: Audrey Hepburn, Marilyn Monroe, Jane Russell, Deborah Kerr, Burt Lancaster, Humphrey Bogart
Movies: *From Here to Eternity*, *House of Wax* in 3-D, *Rebel Without a Cause*, *The Blackboard Jungle*
Publishing: the first issue of *Playboy*
Television: *I Love Lucy*, *The Ed Sullivan Show*
Reading: *The Old Man and the Sea* (Ernest Hemingway), *The Catcher in the Rye* (J. D. Salinger), Agatha Christie's detective novels
Sports: Yankees win the World Series several times

1960s

Music: the Beach Boys, Chubby Checker's "The Twist," limbo dancing, the Beatles, Bob Dylan, counterculture music
Cars: the Corvette Stingray, the Ford Mustang
Posters: James Dean, Elvis, counterculture rock groups
Movies: *Lawrence of Arabia*, *To Kill a Mockingbird*, *Tom Jones*, *The Pink Panther*, *The Great Escape*, Elvis's musical movies
Publishing: Betty Friedan's *The Feminine Mystique*
Television: *Bonanza*, *The Fugitive*

1970s

Music: Pink Floyd, Roberta Flack, punk rock, disco
Cars: small import cars
Posters: Al Pacino, John Travolta, Janis Joplin
Movies: *American Graffiti*, *Last Tango in Paris*
Publishing: *The Joy of Sex* (Alex Comfort)

Television: *M*A*S*H*, *All in the Family*
Gadgets: electronic calculators
Sport: jogging

1980s

Music: *Thriller* (Michael Jackson), "Like a Virgin" (Madonna)
Cars: Hondas, Toyotas
Posters: Farrah Fawcett, Jennifer Beals
Movies: *Star Wars*, *Cujo*, *Raiders of the Lost Ark*
Publishing: Stephen King
Television: *Dallas, Dynasty, Falcon Crest, Knots Landing, Married . . . with Children, The Simpsons*
Sport: frisbees

1990s

Music: Nirvana, Pearl Jam, hip-hop
Posters: Cosmo Kramer (Seinfeld)
Movies: *Philadelphia, Schindler's List, Boyz 'n the Hood*
Publishing: Madonna's *Sex*
Television: *Beverly Hills 90210*
Gadget: Intel Pentium processor

2000s

Music: *Get Rich or Die Tryin'* (50 Cent), *A Rush of Blood to the Head* (Coldplay), *Come Away with Me* (Norah Jones), *Elephant* (The White Stripes), Il Divo, Andrea Boccelli
Cars: Hummer H2
Posters: Doisneau's *Kiss at the Hotel de Ville* (two Parisians in a lip-lock circa 1950s)
Movies: *The Matrix Reloaded, The Matrix Revolutions*
Publishing: Harry Potter
Television: *CSI: Crime Scene Investigation*
Pasttime: surfing the Internet

and dissect the various *genres* that make up their subject and also explore the nature of *audiences* for each genre.

Genres

The books, movies, and television programs that are produced for mass consumption are categorized into various *genres*. The term, as mentioned, originated within literary criticism but was adopted by pop culture analysts in the 1960s.

Genres are identifiable by certain conventions that audiences have come to recognize through regular exposure. On television, a soap opera, for instance, is a serial drama, involving stock characters and romantic entanglements; a talk show, on the other hand, involves an announcer who interviews people, such as authorities in a particular field or common people with specific kinds of problems or issues that they wish to discuss publicly. Since each genre attracts a particular kind of audience, its programs are sponsored ordinarily by specific types of brand manufacturers. Indeed, the term *soap opera* comes from the fact that the genre was originally sponsored by soap companies, since it was designed to appeal to homemakers who stayed at home to do house chores such as washing dishes and clothes.

Audiences

Audience is the term used to refer to the typical readers, spectators, listeners, or viewers attracted to a certain genre. In broadcasting theory, most audiences are divisible into segments defined by specific sociological and lifestyle characteristics. The contemporary specialty radio stations and television channels in particular have seriously taken this aspect of broadcasting into account by providing programming that is aimed at audiences with specific kinds of interests. To describe this type of programming, the term *narrowcasting,* rather than *broadcasting,* is now used.

Many audiences tend to perceive their favorite type of genre as consistent with their own life experiences; others may view the same genre more critically. For example, a nonreligious viewer of a televangelism program will tend to interpret it critically and skeptically, whereas an audience of faithful viewers will perceive it as relevant directly to their personal life experiences.

Pop Culture Study Today

As will be discussed in the next chapter, pop culture study now has its own set of theories and analytical frameworks for studying genres, audiences, and the whole phenomenon itself. These theories and frameworks provide concepts and discourses that can be applied in part or in whole to a study of a particular pop culture trend or product. But the appeal of such study is that it leaves the interpretation of a pop culture text or spectacle flexible and open to variation. This openness to interpretation is the reason that there is not one theory of pop culture, but many. Pop culture analysts today use a blend of concepts and techniques at various stages of analysis and for diverse purposes.

Pop culture courses and entire programs are springing up throughout the academic landscape. The probable reason is that differences between high and low culture have broken down, as discussed throughout this chapter. This change has brought about a veritable explosion of scholarly interest in popular culture. In turn, pop culture studies has now become a source of insight for other disciplines, including media studies, communications, and even the traditional disciplines of anthropology and psychology. The pages that follow will, hopefully, impart a sense of the excitement that such study now offers and, above all else, provide a framework for understanding the world we live in and probably will live in for the foreseeable future.

2

EXPLAINING POP CULTURE

There is no comparing the brutality and cynicism of today's pop culture with that of forty years ago: from *High Noon* to *Robocop* is a long descent.

Charles Krauthammer (b. 1950)

Why is pop culture *popular*? Why do some people hate it or love to hate it? Does television violence lead to real-life violence and other aberrant forms of social behavior? Given its broad diffusion, and often controversial aspects, explaining the nature of pop culture and the reasons for its emergence and spread has become a major focus of psychologists, anthropologists, and other social scientists over the last five decades. Some of the studies have concentrated on the general character of the phenomenon and the role it plays in communal life; others have attempted to understand the core of pop culture and to show why it has emerged in human life. The purpose of the present chapter is to look at the main explanations of pop culture in outline form. In my view, theoretical models and discussions of pop culture are useful only insofar as they allow us to ask appropriate questions about it. None of the rubrics provide a truly satisfactory answer, either by themselves or in combination. As in most theoretical enterprises, it is impossible to capture in language all there is to know or understand about the phenomenon studied.

More than anything else, the available explanations of pop culture provide complementary templates for viewing its aspects in systematic and sometimes insightful ways. These frameworks will thus be referenced as needed in the remaining chapters, which look in detail at the products of pop culture, from music and movies to fads and celebrities.

COMMUNICATIONS MODELS

As mentioned in the previous chapter, the importance that communications technologies have played in the formation, rise, and spread of pop culture cannot be stressed enough. Scholars who made early contributions to the formal study of pop culture focused, understandably, on its relation to such technologies.

The Bull's-Eye Model

The earliest *communications model* of pop culture emerged from the work of the engineer Claude Shannon (1916–2001), who had devised a framework in the late 1940s intended originally to improve the efficiency of telecommunications systems. Known as the *bull's-eye model*, it aimed to identify the main components of such systems and describe in precise mathematical terms how they functioned in the transmission and reception of information. In bare outline form, the communications model consists of a *sender* targeting a *message* at a *receiver.*

Four other components complete the overall outline: channel, noise, redundancy, and feedback. The *channel* is the physical system carrying the transmitted signal. Words, for instance, can be transmitted through the air or through an electronic channel (for example, through the radio). *Noise* is any interfering element (physical or psychological) in the channel that distorts or partially effaces the message. In radio and telephone transmissions, it consists of electronic static; in verbal communication, it can vary from any interfering exterior sound (physical noise) to the speaker's lapses of memory (psychological noise). Communication systems have built-in *redundancy* that allows for messages to be understood even if noise is present. For instance, in human communication the high predictability of certain words in some utterances (*Roses are red, violets are . . .*) and the patterned repetition of ele-

Figure 2.1. The Bull's-Eye Model

ments (*Yes, yes, I'll do it; yes, I will*) are redundant features of conversation that greatly increase the likelihood that a verbal message will be received successfully. Finally, *feedback* refers to the fact that senders have the capacity to monitor the messages they transmit and modify them to enhance their reception or their audience's understanding. Feedback in human communication includes, for instance, the physical reactions observable in receivers (facial expressions, bodily movements, and so forth) that indicate the effect that a message is having as it is being communicated.

The bull's-eye model provides a minimal nomenclature for describing pop culture as a form of communication between makers or performers (*senders*) and their audiences (*receivers*), with feedback consisting of everything from audience reactions to a joke recited on stage to ratings on the popularity of a television sitcom taken by professional statisticians. Noise is viewed as any element interfering with the effective reception of a performance or text, such as competition from another sitcom, poor timing of a punch line (for example, delivery of the punch line while the audience is still busy laughing at a previous comment, and therefore distracted), and so forth.

The SMCR Model

The bull's-eye model was adopted by pop culture analysts early on because of its simplicity and its flexibility—it provides a simple terminology and general conceptual framework for studying how culture and communications have become interlinked. The main components of this model for pop culture study were elaborated as far back as 1954 by the American communications theorist Wilbur Schramm (1907–1987), who added two other components to the original model—the *encoder*, the component (human or electronic) that converts the message into a form that can be transmitted through an appropriate channel; and the *decoder*, which reverses the encoding process so that the message can be received and understood successfully. The revised framework was called, logically, the *Sender* (or *Source*)-*Message-Channel-Receiver* model, often shortened to the SMCR model. It continues to be used in media and pop culture studies because of its plainness and its applicability to all types of mass communications systems.

The SMCR model can, for instance, be used to portray the components of television broadcasting, whereby *source* = the broadcaster, *message* = words (such as those used in a dialogue in a sitcom or in comments by a newscaster), sounds (such as musical background), and images (such as pictures or video clips), *encoder* = studio personnel and their equipment, *channel* = the actual broadcast transmitter, *noise* = static or visual "snow," *decoder* = the television sets or systems that have the physical capacity to turn the broadcast signal into the words, sounds, and images of the program, *receiver* = the viewers or audience, and *feedback* = the ratings garnered by the broadcast:

A further elaboration of the SMCR model for pop culture study was put forward by George Gerbner (1919–2005) in 1956. Encoding and decoding, according to Gerbner, involve knowledge of the *codes* used in constructing the message, including social ones, such as relations between the sexes in, for example, a sitcom, or the features that make a hero superhuman. The concepts of code, encoding, and decoding are now generally accepted within pop culture studies.

Marshall McLuhan

The scholar most associated with linking mass communications to culture was Marshall McLuhan, who claimed throughout his writings that there existed an intrinsic synergy between communications media and culture. Each major period in history takes its character from the medium used most widely at the time. McLuhan called the period from 1700 to the mid-1900s the "Age of Print" and the "Gutenberg Galaxy"—after the invention of modern print technology by Johannes Gutenberg (c. 1395–1468)—because in those centuries printed books were the chief means through which mass communications took place. The advent of the modern printing press had consequences that were felt throughout the world and changed cultures permanently—print literacy encouraged individualism and the growth of nationalism. The "Electronic Age" displaced the Gutenberg Galaxy by the middle part of the twentieth century. Again, the consequences of this displacement have been monumental. Because electronic modes of transmission increase the speed at which people can communicate and allow messages to reach many more instantly, these new technologies have altered people's interaction. Phones, radios, computers, and instant messaging devices have influenced the lives of everyone, even those who do not use them. The Electronic Age may be leading, as McLuhan suspected it would, to the end of individualism and of traditional literacy-inspired notions of nationalism.

Today pop culture embraces all media, from traditional print (maga-

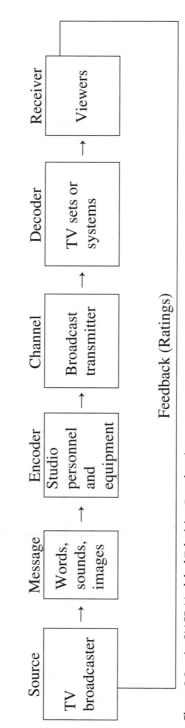

Figure 2.2.   An SMCR Model of Television Broadcasting

Marshall McLuhan (1911–1980)

Marshall McLuhan was a professor at the University of Toronto from the 1950s to the 1970s. His theories on the relation between mass communication systems and culture caused widespread debate. McLuhan claimed, essentially, that changes in communications technology affect our ways of thinking as well as our social institutions. He wrote his ideas in widely read books including *The Mechanical Bride* (1951), *The Gutenberg Galaxy* (1962), *Understanding Media* (1964), *The Medium Is the Massage* (1967), and *War and Peace in the Global Village* (1968).

zines, newspaper) to online forms. As British critic Raymond Williams (1921–1988) argued, pop culture is self-perpetuating because of its ability to adapt to media changes. Williams called the mainstream form of culture in place at any given time *dominant*. But he saw in it *residual* tendencies from previous forms of culture, including nondominant ones, and *emergent* tendencies, which point to the future. It is in tapping into the latter that pop culture begets its power to change and thus perpetuate itself.

CRITICAL THEORIES

Pop culture—especially in its American version—has been the target of many attacks and critiques from all kinds of academic angles since it erupted onto the social scene at the turn of the twentieth century. Such *critical theories*, as they can be called cumulatively, do not attempt to explain pop culture psychologically or socially, but rather politically or ideologically.

Marxist Theory

Among the first to criticize pop culture from this angle were the scholars belonging to the Frankfurt School, which included Theodor W. Adorno (1903–1969), Walter Benjamin (1892–1940), Max Horkheimer (1895–1973), Herbert Marcuse (1898–1979), Erich Fromm (1900–1980), and Leo Lowenthal (1900–1993). In one way or another, these scholars took a highly negative view of pop culture. Some of them saw it as part of a hidden

---

The Frankfurt Institute for Social Research

The Institute was founded at the University of Frankfurt in 1922. It was the world's first Marxist school of social research. Its aim was to understand the way in which human groups create meaning collectively under the influence of modern technology and capitalist modes of production.

"culture industry" controlled by capitalist rulers and made to obey only the logic of marketplace capitalism. Adopting Italian Marxist Antonio Gramsci's concept of *hegemony*, they claimed that the domination of society by the group in power occurs in large part through the control of the levers of mass communications. Gramsci had used the term in reference to his belief that the dominant class in a society used social "instruments" which varied from outright coercion (including incarceration, the use of secret police, and threats) to gentler and more "managerial" tactics (including education, religion, and control of the mass media) in order to gain the consent of common people. The concept of hegemony has found widespread use in current pop culture studies, where it generally refers to the cultural manufacturing of consent by politicians in power rather than to overt forms of coercion.

The Frankfurt School theorists were, overall, highly pessimistic about the possibility of genuine culture under modern capitalism, condemning most forms of popular culture as modes of propaganda designed to indoctrinate the masses and disguise social inequalities. The School's main contention was that typical pop culture fare was crass and functioned primarily to placate ordinary people. Adorno and Horkheimer traced the source of pop culture's supposed vulgarity to the Enlightenment and the materialistic scientism that developed from it. Breaking somewhat from this mold was Marcuse, who saw in African American and hippie forms of pop culture a renaissance of Romantic idealism, and Benjamin, who put forward a "catharsis hypothesis," in which he claimed that the crude aspects of pop culture allowed people to release pent-up energies and, thus, pacified them. The ideas of the Frankfurt School will be revisited in the final chapter of this book.

Even before the Frankfurt School, British social critic Matthew Arnold (1822–1883) saw mass forms of culture as having become tasteless and homogenized as a result of affluence and urbanization. Arnold popularized the "culture versus civilization" argument, seeing crass materialism as a threat to civilized society. Arnold's attack was taken up by F. R. Leavis (1895–1978) in the 1930s and 1940s. Leavis excoriated American pop culture even more pungently, seeing in it evidence of the decline of civilization. But then, one might ask, who decides what is "good" culture and what is "tasteless" culture? In my view, the critiques put forward by Arnold, Leavis, and the Frankfurt School theorists hide within them an elitist subtext—namely, that only intellectuals (the theorists themselves) know what good culture is and thus what is to be done about eliminating bad culture. The masses are assumed to be zombies, unaware of the manipulation to which they are subjected on a daily basis.

Marxist theory, which also falls under the rubric of *culture industry* theory, has left residues. In the 1970s in Britain, for instance, a Centre for Contemporary Cultural Studies was established at the University of Birmingham to investigate how bourgeois interests are served by the spread of pop culture, employing a basically Marxist framework. The scholars at the Centre took (and continue to take) the view that pop culture has debased all forms of culture by turning art into a "commodity" (whatever that means) controlled by profit-making enterprises. Some British and American critics of contemporary pop culture today who are not affiliated with the Centre draw heavily upon the general arguments made by its members. The argument made by these critics ignores a basic question: Why has pop culture brought about more favorable changes to the social status of common folk than any other cultural experiment in history, including (and especially) Marxism? The emotional appeal of pop culture, moreover, cannot be logically dismissed in a cavalier fashion as part of a mere instrument of pacification. As E. P. Thomson (1924–1993) and others have argued, pop culture has provided the means for people to resist those in power, not be controlled by them.

Propaganda Theory

One of the more interesting contemporary offshoots of culture industry theory is *propaganda theory*, associated primarily with the writings of the American linguist Noam Chomsky (b. 1928). The theory posits that those who control the funding and ownership of the media, and especially the government in power, determine how the media select and present news coverage. The media thus become nothing more than a propaganda arm of the government and put forward mainly its point of view. Pop culture spectacles are seen as complicit in this system of "consent manufacturing." Mainstream news outlets select the topics to be printed or broadcast, establish the character of the concerns to be expressed, determine the ways in which issues are to be framed, and filter out any information assessed to be contradictory. Examples used by propaganda theorists to support their view include mainstream American television coverage of recent wars, from the Vietnam War to the War on Terror (in Afghanistan and Iraq), by which it is shown that the government in power has the ability to influence how the media presents its coverage.

Like Marxist scholars, propaganda theorists see pop culture as an industry serving those in power. Although people commonly believe that the press has an obligation to be adversarial to those in power, propaganda theorists argue that the media are actually supportive of authority, for the simple reason that the press is dependent on the powerful for subsistence. The end result is a vast media and pop culture industry—from movies such as *Rambo* to CNN commentators such as Glenn Beck—that caters to those in power by promulgating a view of the world that espouses an elemental form of patriotism and the essential benevolence of power brokers and the institutions that they head. Like the Frankfurt scholars, propaganda theorists do not seem to believe that common people can tell the difference between truth and manipulation. The solution these theorists offer is to ensure that access to the public media is an open and democratic process. Such access is, in fact, becoming a reality because of the Internet, where basically anyone can post an opinion and garner an international audience for it, almost instantaneously. This very fact shows the untenability of propaganda theory. If consent was really manufactured in the populace as the theorists claim, why is there so much dissent against the war in Iraq online expressed by ordinary people? To my mind, individuals' web-based political critiques are evidence of the capacity of the masses to resist indoctrination.

Feminism

Another critical theoretical assessment of pop culture came from the early feminists in the 1970s and 1980s, who saw it as a construct that was subservient to the desires of the male psyche—essentially a male plot to maintain control over women's minds and, especially, bodies. These feminists argued that representations in the movies, on television, and in print were degrading to women and helped to promote violence against women.

Some of the critiques of the early feminists were well-founded, given the effusion of images of women as either "sexual cheerleaders" or "motherly homemakers" in many domains of pop culture. However, already in the 1950s, alongside sitcoms such as *Father Knows Best* that offered skewed, patriarchal views of womanhood, there were also sitcoms such as *The Honeymooners*, which portrayed femininity as combative against the patriarchal mold. Similarly, *I Love Lucy* featured as the main character a strong-willed, independent female who was completely in charge of her situation. Moreover, by viewing the representation of women's bodies in sports spectacles and erotic movies only as a form of objectification and male voyeurism, the early feminists seem to have ignored the fact that this very mode of display had played a critical role in liberating women from seeing themselves as constricted to the roles of housekeeper and mother—consequently allowing women to openly assume a sexual persona that, paradoxically, was more controlling of the male psyche than it was controlled by it. With the entrance of Madonna onto the pop culture stage in the mid-1980s, the tide in feminist theory changed radically, leading to what is now called *post-feminism*, as will be discussed below.

PSYCHOLOGICAL AND SOCIOLOGICAL THEORIES

Does pop culture truly have an effect on people? Does exposure to violent shows on television predispose people to be more violent and to act out violent fantasies? Does exposure to sitcom humor corrupt true human dialogue? These are, clearly, important questions. Thus, it should come as little surprise that the investigation of the purported effects of the mass media and pop culture on people has been of great interest to psychologists and sociologists.

The power of the media to affect people became evident early on, especially after the 1938 radio broadcast of *The War of the Worlds*. The broadcast was an adaptation of H. G. Wells's novel about interplanetary invasion. It was designed as a radio drama simulating the style of a news broadcast. Many listeners believed that the broadcast was real, despite periodic announcements that it was merely a dramatization. Hysteria resulted, with some people in the New Jersey area (where the invasion was reported as occurring) leaving their homes or phoning the local authorities. The event became a topic of media attention and led, a year later, to the first psychological study on the media. This research project was called the Cantril study, after Hadley Cantril, who headed a team of researchers at Princeton University. The researchers wanted to find out why some people believed the fake reports and others did not. After interviewing 135 subjects, the team came to the conclusion that the key was critical thinking—better-educated listeners were more capable of recognizing the broadcast as a fake than less-educated ones.

Psychological Theories

The Cantril study seemed to demonstrate that the media did indeed produce effects on audiences, opening the door to a host of follow-up psychological studies aiming to determine the extent to which the media influenced people. The studies suggested that media content did not just mirror values and behaviors but, rather, shaped them. Classified under the rubric of hypodermic needle theory (HNT) or magic bullet theory, these studies claimed that the media are capable of directly swaying minds with the same kind of power that a hypodermic needle has to modify bodily processes or that a bullet has to injure or kill. Not everyone agreed with the findings. A number of other studies showed, in contrast, that audiences got out of media content views toward which they were already inclined. For example, in an influential 1948 study titled *The People's Choice*, American sociologist Paul Lazarsfeld (1901–1976) and a team of researchers found that the media had virtually no ability to change people's minds about how they would vote in an election. People took out of newspapers or radio broadcasts only the views that matched their preconceptions and ignored the others.

Follow-up research seemed to corroborate Lazarsfeld's findings. The research—which led to what became known as *selective perception theory*—found, for example, that anti-pornography individuals who watched a television debate on the relation of pornography to freedom of expression took away from the debate only the points that were consistent with their particular view—namely, that pornography should be restricted under any and all circumstances. On the other hand, libertarian individuals tended to feel triumphant due to the fact that the debate occurred in the first place (thus legitimizing the topic). In some cases, it was found that perception was mediated by "leaders." Lazarsfeld and Elihu Katz (b. 1926) had argued as far back as the mid-1950s that people tended to come up with interpretations that are consistent with the values of the social class or group to which they belonged. Audiences are, in other words, interpretive communities, which crystallize from real communities such as families, unions, neighborhoods, and churches. Such groups contain members known as "opinion leaders" who influence how the other members interpret content. In contrast to hypodermic needle theory, which viewed the spread of media's messages as a one-step flow reaching a homogeneous audience directly, Lazarsfeld and Katz saw this process as a two-step flow. In the first step, the opinion leader takes in media content and interprets it; in the second step, this leader passes on an interpretation to group members.

However, the power of media to affect people psychologically through the power of images cannot be easily dismissed. The importance of the media's visual component was shown dramatically by another well-known media episode—the Kennedy-Nixon television debate, which turned the 1960 election around in favor of Kennedy. People who heard the debate on radio maintained that Nixon had won it, coming across as the better candidate; those who saw it on television claimed the opposite. Nixon looked disheveled and worried; Kennedy looked confident and came across as a young, idealistic, and vibrant "president of the future." Kennedy went on to win the election and a society-wide debate emerged on the effects of media images on all viewers, not just a niche audience whose opinions are mediated by a leader.

One-Step Flow:

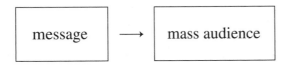

Two-Step Flow:

Figure 2.3.   Two-Step Flow Theory

Sociological Theories

In partnership with George Gerbner (1919–2005), Lazarsfeld argued in another work that the media have a conservative social function—namely, to enforce existing norms. For example, the display of deviancy on television crime programs and in serial killer movies will hardly lead to more crime in society. The reason is that such representation is designed to have the same effect as a medieval morality play—to warn people about the dangers of such deviancy and, thus, to evoke its condemnation, not its justification. This framework of thought has come to be known, logically, as *functionalist theory*. In its wider scope, it is also called *cultivation theory* because it claims that media "cultivate" the status quo. Again, in this view, the over-representation of violence on television is intended to reinforce the respect for law and order, constituting a kind of "divine justice spectacle" in which the "bad guys" will ultimately pay for their sins.

Cultivation theory is an example of a sociological theory—that is, of a theory that takes into account the relation between media, culture, and social values and norms. Perhaps the most widely known of all the sociological theories is the one associated with the work of American sociologist Elihu Katz (mentioned previously). Katz claims that people are not passive consumers of media representations. On the contrary, they are opportunistic users of the media. Employing a framework known, logically, as *uses and gratifications theory*, he suggests that the media do nothing to people. It is the other way around—people use media for their own purposes and gratifications.

A third major sociological theory has been put forward by British cultural theorist Stuart Hall (b. 1932). Hall argues that people do not absorb texts passively but rather *read* them (interpret them) in one of three ways, known as preferred, negotiated, and oppositional readings. The *preferred* reading is the one that the makers of texts have built into them and which they hope that audiences will take from them. The *negotiated* reading is the one that results when audiences partly agree with or respond to the meanings built into texts. An *oppositional* reading is one that is in opposition to what the maker of the text intended. A simple way to understand the difference between the three types is to consider a comedian who has just told a joke onstage. If the audience laughs wholeheartedly, then the joke has produced the preferred reading. If only some of the audience laughs wholeheartedly, while others chuckle or sneer, then the joke has brought about a negotiated reading. Finally, if the audience reacts negatively to the joke, with resentment, then it has produced an oppositional reading.

SEMIOTICS

The concept of *reading* leads directly to the discipline of semiotics. Indeed, Hall's *reading theory* is often considered to be part of a semiotic approach to the study of the media and pop culture.

Semiotics is the science of meaning. In many theories of pop culture today, it plays a central role. Three of its rudimentary notions—opposition, mythology, and representation—are, in fact, used throughout the relevant literature. *Opposition* implies that we do not perceive meaningful differences in absolute ways, but in relational ones. For example, if we were to think of *day*, its opposite, *night*, would invariably pop up in our mind. Indeed, we seem incapable of understanding *night* unless we contrast it to *day*, and vice versa. *Mythology* theory claims that texts, performances, and spectacles are linked to each other through a chain of mythic themes, such as good versus evil and male versus female. *Representation* refers to the fact that any text or

---

Founders of Semiotics

Ferdinand de Saussure (1857–1913): The Swiss philologist Ferdinand de Saussure is considered to be one of the founders of modern-day semiotics. He taught at the École des Hautes Études in Paris from 1881 to 1891 and then became a professor of Sanskrit and of comparative grammar at the University of Geneva. After his death, two of his assistants collated the lecture notes of some of his students and published them in 1916 as a book (*Cours de linguistique générale*) that names Saussure as the author. A comprehensive model of semiotics (or semiology, as Saussure called it) is found in that book.

Charles S. Peirce (1839–1914): The American philosopher and mathematician Charles Peirce is another founder of modern-day semiotics. Peirce is also known for his philosophical system, later called pragmatism, which maintains that the significance of any theory or model lies in the practical effects of its application.

spectacle stands for something that is not immediately obvious in the text. The text defers to that "something else" instead of referring to it directly.

Opposition

The notion of opposition has proven itself to be highly productive in the study of pop culture because it allows us to flesh out the hidden meanings built into characters, plots, performances, and so forth. As a simple example, consider the differences that are associated with the opposition of *white* vs. *black* in Western culture. The color *white* suggests *purity, innocence,* and so on, while its counterpart *black* suggests *impurity, corruption,* and the like. This opposition manifests itself symbolically in all kinds of pop culture texts and spectacles. In the early Hollywood cowboy movies, for example, the heroes wore white hats and the villains black ones. This does not mean, however, that *black* is never associated with the positive pole of the opposition. Since it also suggests *mysteriousness* and *dauntlessness*, it can be embedded in the symbolism of the hero. Therefore the Zorro character of television and movie fame wears black, as did several Hollywood western heroes of the past (such as Lash LaRue).

The French anthropologist Claude Lévi-Strauss (b. 1908) has claimed that such binary oppositions (*night* vs. *day, white* vs. *black*) are built unconsciously into all human texts (myths, fables, and so forth) and social systems (kinship, language, and so forth), which are constructed through their combination, recombination, interweaving, and intermingling. Lévi-Strauss's argument has suggested to some semioticians that the very structure of human thought is oppositional—that is to say, relational and associative, rather than linear and categorical. Whether or not this is true, as an analytical technique in pop culture studies, opposition is highly useful because it provides a template for reading (interpreting) spectacles and texts.

Mythology Theory

One of the more interesting and pertinent semiotic approaches to pop culture was put forward by the French semiotician Roland Barthes (1915–1980) in the mid-1950s. It has come to be called *mythology theory.*

Barthes claimed that pop culture gains a large part of its emotional allure because it is based on the recycling of unconscious mythic meanings, symbols, narratives, and spectacles. To distinguish between the original myths and their pop culture versions, Barthes designated the latter *mytholo-*

gies. In early Hollywood westerns, for instance, the heroes and villains are mythological reconstructions of the ancient mythic heroes and their opponents. The heroes are honest, truthful, physically attractive, strong, and vulnerable; the villains are dishonest, cowardly, physically ugly, weak, and cunning. As in many of the ancient myths, the hero is beaten up at a critical stage, but against all odds he survives to become a champion of justice. Because of the unconscious power of myth, it is no surprise that early Hollywood cowboys such as Roy Rogers, John Wayne, Hopalong Cassidy, and the Lone Ranger became cultural icons, symbolizing virtue, heroism, and righteousness above and beyond the movie scripts. Although early Hollywood also showcased female characters as heroic, usually the women played a supporting role to a male hero. Hollywood has broken away from this male-centered western mythology in recent times, as exemplified in Clint Eastwood's *Unforgiven* (1992). However, the tradition of the maverick male loner fighting for justice surfaces often as a central mythic image even in contemporary cowboy narratives.

The Superman character of comic book and cinematic fame is another perfect example of the recycled mythic hero, possessing all the characteristics of his ancient predecessors but in modern guise—he comes from another world (the planet Krypton) in order to help humanity overcome its weaknesses; he has superhuman powers; but he has a tragic flaw (exposure to the fictitious substance known as kryptonite takes away his power); and so forth. Sports events, too, are designed to emulate mythic dramas by juxtaposing good (the home team) vs. evil (the visiting team). The whole fanfare associated with preparing for the "big event," such as the Super Bowl of American football or the World Cup of soccer, has a ritualistic quality to it similar to the pomp and circumstance that ancient armies engaged in before going out to battle and war. Indeed, the whole spectacle is perceived to represent a battle of mythic proportions. The symbolism of the team's (army's) uniform, the valor and strength of the players (the heroic warriors), and the skill and tactics of the coach (the army general) powerfully effects the fans (the warring nations). As Barthes observed, this unconscious symbolism is the reason that pop culture is powerful and has enduring appeal. Like their ancient ancestors, modern-day people subconsciously need heroes to "make things right" in human affairs, at least in the world of fantasy.

Because it constitutes a mythological system, Barthes argued that pop culture has had a profound impact on modern-day ethics. In the historical development of ethics, three principal standards of conduct have been proposed as the highest good: happiness or pleasure; duty, virtue, or obligation; and perfection, the fullest harmonious development of human potential. In traditional (historical) cultures, these standards were established through religious and philosophical traditions. In pop culture, they are established through mythologies. Ethical issues that are showcased on television, for example, are felt as being more significant and historically meaningful to society today than those that are not. This has led people to stage events for the cameras. The social critic W. T. Anderson (1992) has appropriately called these scenes "pseudoevents" because they are not spontaneous but rather planned for the sole purpose of playing to huge audiences. Most pseudoevents are intended to be self-fulfilling prophecies.

Representation

In 1997 a tragic event occurred that greatly affected people living in Western societies—the death of Princess Diana (1961–1997) at a young age. Her death was felt by many to be analogous to the premature deaths of legendary heroines. It was portrayed as such on British and American television, despite the fact that the majority of people did not know her personally. In other parts of the world, her death was portrayed in much less dramatic ways. In some countries, it was ignored. In effect, her death represented different things to different people and was thus represented in varying manners in the media. *Representation*, shown in this example, is the process of depicting or recounting something in a specific way. The intent of the representer, the historical, cultural, and social contexts in which the representation is made, the purpose for which it is made, and what it is designed to depict all play a role in how it is interpreted and received by audiences.

As another example, consider the representation of fatherhood in television sitcoms. In the 1950s, the father was portrayed as someone who was all-knowing and in charge of his family. The sitcom that best represented this portrait of fatherhood was *Father Knows Best*. In the 1980s and 1990s, however, the same figure was represented in the sitcom *Married . . . with Children* in an opposite manner—as an ignorant figure who had absolutely no control over his family. These different representations of fatherhood on American television reflected changing concepts of fatherhood in society. We tend to understand representations as mirroring real life—an effect achieved through the creation of characters and places that remind us of real people, settings, and situations (including the home, the workplace, relationships, marriage, and children). Sitcoms are emotionally powerful because they are fictional representations of real life.

Among the first to consider the connection between representation and real life were the Greek philosophers Plato (c. 427–c. 347 BCE) and Aristotle (384–322 BCE). Aristotle considered the common modes of representation—verbal, visual, and musical—as the primary means through which human beings came to perceive reality. He identified *mimesis* (imitation or simulation) as the most basic and natural form of representation. Nonetheless, Aristotle also warned that representations create illusory worlds and, thus, can easily lead people astray. Plato believed that representations never really tell the truth but instead "mediate" it, creating nothing but illusions that lead us away from contemplating life as it really is. He argued that representations had to be monitored because they could foster antisocial reactions or encourage the imitation of evil things. Plato's argument has not disappeared from the social radar screen. It undergirds such phenomena as movie ratings and other restrictions on our freedom. These are modern society's "Platonic attempts" to limit or modify representations in order to protect people (especially children).

In semiotics, representation is defined as a process that involves creating a *text* in a specific *context* according to a *code* or set of *codes*. To understand what this means, consider again the case of the fictional hero Superman, who was introduced in 1938 by Action Comics. What or who does Superman represent? The answer is, as we saw above, a recycled hero in the tradition of mythic heroes, such as Prometheus and Achilles. Superman has, of course, been updated and adapted culturally—he is an American hero who stands for "truth, justice, and the American way." Like the ancient heroes, he is indestructible, morally upright, and devoted to saving humanity from itself. And, like many of the mythic heroes, he has a tragic flaw—in his case, exposure to kryptonite, a substance that is found on the planet where he was born, renders him devoid of his awesome powers.

Now, answering the question of why Superman (or any comic book action hero, for that matter) appeals to modern-day audiences requires us to delve into the origin and history of the archetypal heroic figure. There we find the *code* that guides any representation of Superman in comic book or movie form. In myth and legend, a hero is an individual, often of divine ancestry, who is endowed with great courage and strength, celebrated for his bold exploits, and sent by the gods to Earth to play a crucial role in human affairs. Heroes are character archetypes who embody lofty human ideals for all to admire—truth, honesty, justice, fairness, moral strength, and

so on. Modern-day audiences understand the importance of a hero intu-
itively, as did the ancient ones who watched stage performances of *Prometheus Bound, Prometheus Unbound,* and *Prometheus the Fire-Bringer,* by the
playwright Aeschylus (c. 525–456 BCE). Rather than being sent by the
gods to help humanity (something that would hardly be appropriate in a
secular society), Superman instead came to Earth from a planet in another
galaxy; he leads a double life, as hero and as Clark Kent, a mild-mannered
reporter for a daily newspaper; he is adored by Lois Lane, a reporter for the
same newspaper who suspects (from time to time) that Clark Kent may be
Superman; and he wears a distinctive costume. His red cape suggests noble
blood and his blue tights the hope he brings to humanity. Of course, the
combination of red and blue is also indicative of American patriotism—
these are, after all, colors of the American flag. How Superman acts, how he
behaves, how he looks, and what he does all constitute predictable aspects of
an updated hero code, which was used from one issue to the next by the
creators, making Superman extremely popular. Each story in an issue was a
text derived from that code. In any specific Superman text we can expect to
find our hero fighting a villain, flirting at some point with Lois Lane while
in the persona of Clark Kent, facing a crisis that he must resolve with his
extraordinary powers, and so on. Finally, the meaning of the text is condi-
tioned by *context.* The context is the situation—physical, psychological, and
social—in which the text is constructed or to which it refers. If read in its
comic book format, a Superman text will be interpreted as an adventure
story. However, if a satirist such as the American cineaste Woody Allen were
to portray Superman in a movie, then the movie text would hardly be con-
strued as an adventure story, but rather as a satire or parody of the Superman
figure, of its representations in or of the media, or of some other aspect
related to the Superman code.

TRANSGRESSION

The Charleston and jazz music were seen by many adults in the Roaring
Twenties as part of a transgressive lifestyle. Similarly, Elvis Presley's hip-
swinging performances, goth lifestyle, gangsta rap videos, and many other
forms of pop culture are initially viewed as transgressing against mainstream
values. Paradoxically, it is the act of transgression itself that enhances pop
culture's appeal. From the short skirts donned by flappers to Madonna's
open-mouthed kissing of Britney Spears at the 2003 MTV Video Music

Awards and Janet Jackson's subtle breast exposure during the 2004 Super Bowl halftime show, displays that cross the implicit bounds of decent behavior have always been part and parcel of pop culture performances.

Transgressive symbolism is not, of course, exclusively linkable to public sexual displays. It also manifests itself in many other ways. One other outlet for such symbolism is bodily decoration, such as tattooing and body piercing. Tattooing is one of the most ancient forms of creative body stylizing. Cave paintings date it to at least 8000 BCE. Almost every culture has practiced tattooing for various symbolic reasons. The adoption of tattooing by young people as a rebellious fashion trend started again in the Roaring Twenties but began spreading more broadly in the 1960s and 1970s—a phenomenon captured by the Rolling Stones in their popular 1981 album *Tattoo You*. Since then, tattooing and piercing have evolved into society-wide trends, having lost most, if not all, of their transgressive impact. They have become mere cosmetic practices adopted by media icons and common folk alike, crossing the boundaries of age, gender, and social class. There are now television programs, such as *Miami Ink*, devoted to the art of tattooing and the human stories behind it. In reaction to the spread of tattooing, some subcultures have resorted to new and more shocking forms. The tattoos of goths, for example, extol the occult and the macabre; those of punks, the bizarre and the weird.

Transgressive symbolism also manifests itself in popular forms of language. In the 1920s young people spelled *rats* as *rhatz* and shortened *that's too bad* to *stoo bad* to indicate that they possessed (or wanted to possess) their own grammar of English. Similarly, counterculture youths in the 1960s spelled *tough* as *tuff*, *freaks* as *freeks*, and *America* as *Amerika*. Today, the same type of transgressive language is evident in the names assumed by rap artists. Sista Souljah's name, for example, suggests both *soldier* and *soul* while also alluding to Black English Vernacular pronunciation. Such spelling patterns bespeak an attitude that communicates the following message: "I'll do it my way, not the way of the mainstream." Snoop Dogg, to mention one other rap artist, is known not only for his music but also for his use of the suffix *-izzle*, which he employs in phrases such as *fo shizzle*, which is his version of *for sure* and a code for *I concur with you, my African brother*. Phrases such as *BIB* or *boyz in blue* (police) and *government cheese* (welfare) are similarly defiant descriptors of how some young African Americans perceive elements of white America.

Now society-wide trends, tattooing and piercing have lost much of their
original transgressive impact.
©iStockphoto.com/Roberta Osborne

Moral Panic Theory

The features discussed above can be classified under the general rubric of *transgression theory.* This framework posits that trends that gain popularity among young people tend to be those that keep them differentiated from adults, especially if the trends are manifestly transgressive of mainstream norms. For this reason, adults tend to react to new cultural phenomena with "moral panic," sensing that the new features indicate a decline in morality and traditional values. As Stan Cohen (1972) observed his insightful study of mods and rockers, whether it is a panicked reaction to Elvis's swinging hip movements or to the gross antics performed onstage by punk rockers, many people typically react negatively to transgressive behaviors and symbols in youth culture and pop culture generally. However, as these new forms lose their impact, blending silently into the larger cultural mainstream or disappearing altogether, the moral panic evanesces.

Moral panic theory, as it is called, can be enlisted productively to show why certain things have taken place in pop culture history. In 1952, the *I*

Love Lucy program was forbidden to script the word *pregnant* when Lucille Ball (the main character of the sitcom) was truly pregnant; moreover, Lucy and Ricky Ricardo were scripted to sleep in separate beds. Such restrictions were common in early television. On his *Ed Sullivan Show* performance in 1956, Elvis Presley was shot from the waist up, to spare viewers from seeing his gyrating pelvis. But television soon caught up to transgressive culture, coopting it more and more. In 1964, the married couple Darrin and Samantha Stevens were seen sharing a double bed on *Bewitched*. In 1968, *Rowan and Martin's Laugh-in* challenged puritanical mores with its racy skits and double-entendres. In the early 1970s, *All in the Family* addressed taboo subjects such as race, menopause, homosexuality, and premarital sex for the first time on prime-time television. In 1976, the female leads in *Charlie's Angels* went braless for the first time in television history, and one year later the *Roots* miniseries showed bare-breasted women when portraying African life in the eighteenth century. Throughout the 1980s and 1990s Seinfeld and *NYPD Blue* often made reference to previously taboo sexual themes (such as masturbation). In 2000, the winner on CBS's first *Survivor* series walked around naked (although CBS pixilated sensitive areas). Also, as mentioned above, at the 2003 MTV Video Music Awards, Madonna kissed Britney Spears open-mouthed; and a year later, Janet Jackson's breast was exposed by Justin Timberlake during the 2004 Super Bowl halftime show.

All these events caused moral panic initially. However, as Cohen had predicted, the reactions evanesced. Indeed, today some of the things that once evoked moral panic have been incorporated or co-opted by the very people who were most susceptible to moral panic—evangelical groups in the United States, who see youth and pop culture as the ultimate battleground in the culture wars that have surfaced since a radical right-wing government under George W. Bush came into power in 2000. Evangelical Christianity is, in effect, competing with Eminem and 50 Cent for the soul of contemporary youth. Many churches now employ everything from rock or rap bands that sing the praises of Christ to mammoth movie screens that project Bible stories in churches. They also use media products (DVDs and CDs) that promote a "hip religious lifestyle." In contemporary America, pop culture and religion seem to go hand in hand.

Carnival Theory

Why is transgression both so appealing and appalling? Does it reveal something about the human psyche? An insightful theory of pop culture,

Mikhael Bakhtin (1895–1975)

The Russian philosopher and literary theorist Mikhael Bakhtin claimed that pop culture serves the same kinds of social functions as did the medieval carnivals. He also argued that communication in pop culture is not merely an exchange of information but rather an ongoing *polyphonic* dialogue between performers and audiences. Bakhtin's most important works include *The Dialogic Imagination* (1981) and *Rabelais and His World* (1984).

known as *carnival theory*, makes this very claim. Inspired by the work of the Russian social critic Mikhael Bakhtin, the theory asserts that transgression is instinctual. By releasing rebellion in a communal, theatrical way, the ritual of transgression actually validates social norms. In effect, we come to understand the role of social norms in our life through mockery of them. Carnival theory explains why pop culture does not pose (and never has posed) any serious subversive political challenge to the moral and ethical status quo. Pop culture is not truly subversive; it just appears to be. Flappers, punks, goths, gangsta rappers, Alice Cooper, Kiss, Eminem, Marilyn Manson, strippers, porn stars, and all the other usual suspects are, according to this theory, modern-day mockers who take it upon themselves to deride and parody authority figures and sacred symbols, bringing everything down to an earthy, crude level of theatrical performance.

Carnival theory asserts that mockery institutes a vital dialogue between those who feel that expressing the sacred in human life is the only lofty goal to pursue and those who want to emphasize the profane. Through this form of dialogue we come to better understand the meaning of life. Theatrical mockery and the reaction against it constitute an oppositional dialogue, pitting the sacred against the profane in a systematic gridlock. It goes on all the time in human life. It is so instinctive and common that we hardly ever realize consciously what it entails in philosophical and psychological terms. It even manifests itself in conversations and chats and in our internal thoughts. And, of course, it manifests itself in the theatrical and narrative arts, from drama and comedy to rock concerts and social networking websites. As in pop culture, in the tribal and popular festivities associated with traditional carnivals the sacred is made profane and the carnality of all things is proclaimed through the theatricality of spectacles. At the time of a carnival, everything authoritative, rigid, or serious is subverted, loosened, and mocked. It is little wonder, therefore, that pop culture studies are now turning to Bakhtin for insight. Carnival is part of popular and folkloristic traditions that aim to critique traditional mores and idealized social rituals and to highlight the crude, unmediated links between domains of behavior that are normally kept very separate. Carnivalesque genres satirize the lofty words of poets, scholars, and others. They are intended to fly in the face of the official, sacred world—the world of judges, lawyers, politicians, churchmen, and the like.

Bakhtin introduced his concept of the carnivalesque dialogue around 1929. Carnival is a context that emphasizes distinct common voices, which flourish through *polyphonic* expression. For Bakhtin, therefore, carnival is the basic form of human dialogue. People attending a carnival do not merely make up an anonymous crowd. Rather, they feel part of a communal body, sharing a unique sense of time and space. Through costumes and masks, individuals take on a new identity and, as a consequence, renew themselves spiritually. It is through this carnivalesque identity that the *grotesque* within humans can seek expression through overindulgent eating and laughter, and through unbridled sexual acting. In such behaviors, people discover who they really are.

Obviously, not all aspects of pop culture are carnivalesque. Many are, instead, part of the sacred. However, the lifestyles of some subcultures are clearly carnivalesque. As a case in point, consider the goth lifestyle. The goths emerged in the late 1970s as a separate lifestyle clique within the punk subculture, taking their cues initially from Gothic novels, which revolved around mysterious and supernatural events intended to be frightening. The stories were known as *Gothic* because most of them took place in gloomy, medieval castles built in the Gothic style of architecture, which included buildings with secret passageways, dungeons, and towers, all of which provided ideal settings for strange happenings. Most Gothic novels were set in Italy or Spain because those countries seemed remote and mysterious to the English. In the 1800s, elements of the Gothic novel appeared in other forms of fiction that shared its interest in horror and mystery. Novels such as *Frankenstein* (1818) by Mary Shelley and *Wuthering Heights* (1847) by Emily Brontë, and many other historical romances of the time, were cut from the same narrative fabric as Gothic novels. The Gothic novel also influenced such American writers as Nathaniel Hawthorne, Herman Melville, and Edgar Allan Poe. In the 1900s, romantic adventure stories were also known as *Gothic*, but they were of a different narrative nature, placing more emphasis on love than on terror.

Goth youth espoused (and continue to espouse) horror and gloom as their worldview through their fashion and music. Becoming a goth requires a cosmetic makeover consisting of black eyeliner, lipstick, fishnet stockings (worn or cut), black boots, and black hair—all accouterments designed to imprint a gothic look. The goth subculture came to prominence with punk performer Marilyn Manson, after he created widespread moral panic when his music was linked (erroneously) to the Columbine High School massacre. The influence of this subculture has reached deeply into general American pop culture. It can be seen, for instance, in films such as *Edward Scissorhands* and *The Crow*, in Anne Rice's vampire novels, and in bands such as Nine Inch Nails. It can also be seen in the fascination with gothic, supernatural, and horror themes on current and past television programs, in mainstream Hollywood movies, and in cosmetic and clothing trends generally. In effect, goth has become an often subconscious pattern within general pop culture.

Goth clothing fashions are examples of dress styles that are confrontational—that is intended to be antisocial. Such styles showcase transgression. In the 1990s, male hip-hop teens conveyed their confrontational message by wearing baggy pants backward, with ultra-long-sleeved shirts and jackets, unlaced sneakers, and tuques—clothing items that conveyed a message of toughness, since they were stylized in part after the uniforms of prisoners. The jewelry worn by hip-hop artists (neck chains, earrings, and so forth) was similarly intended to be intimidating. Particularly tough-looking was the *gangsta* clothing style, with its heavy jewelry, do-rags, large loose clothing, bandanas, and so on. In most cases, though, the confrontation was theatrical in intent, not real. Rappers such as Tupac Shakur, Eminem, Shaqur Ironman, Dr. Dre, 50 Cent, the Wu-Tang Clan, and The Notorious B.I.G., to name a few, used highly explicit lyrics advocating violence, the use of drugs, sexuality, and the use of weapons. The logo of the Wutang Clan—the killer queen bee—was designed to represent the "killer instinct" of the group. But such performances, lyrics, and images were nothing more than carnivalesque theater. Gangsta artists, punks, goths, and others wear costumes and put on masks (makeup, jewelry, and so on) that are not unlike those worn by the medieval carnival mockers. And like the early carnival participants, members of modern subcultures aim to confuse, intimidate, or parody society. Engagement in the carnivalesque is, ultimately, a condemnation of the emptiness of consumerist society, subcultures' alter ego. Enactment of the carnivalesque intimates that there is nothing left to do but celebrate consumerism's emptiness through ironic postures.

The profane nature of youth culture and pop culture generally is often the theme of movies, novels, and other contemporary works. Consider, for example, Stanley Kubrick's cinematic masterpiece of 1971, *A Clockwork Orange*. The setting for the movie is modern-day Britain. A teenage thug, Alex De Large, engages routinely in criminal and sexual activities in a wanton and reckless fashion. Caught and imprisoned for murder, he volunteers to undergo an experimental shock treatment therapy that is supposed to brainwash him to become nauseated by his previous lifestyle. Mr. Alexander, one of Alex's victims, traps him with the aim of avenging himself. He hopes to drive Alex to commit suicide to the strains of Beethoven's Ninth Symphony. But the actions taken against Alex are condemned by the press as inhumane and, as a consequence, he is released and restored to health. The movie's portrayal of the senseless, aimless violence of which a teenager is capable has a transgressive subtext built into it. Alex is a goalless teen trapped in a weary, decaying environment. His only way out is through intimidation and crime. He is a ticking time bomb ready to explode at any instant. The rage in Alex's eyes is the rage shown by contemporary punks, goths, and rappers. The difference is one between reality and fantasy. Whereas Alex expresses his rage through real crime, punks and goths do so through mockery.

Another main tenet of carnival theory regards the role of occultism in pop culture. Occultism was rampant throughout the ancient world and in the Middle Ages. Even eminent scholars such as thirteenth-century Italian theologian Saint Thomas Aquinas (1225–1274) believed in the powers of occult symbolism. Carvings of animals on roofs and walls, along with sculptures of mysterious animals and female figures, go back tens of thousands of years. According to some estimates, the earliest known visually symbolic artifact might even be 135,000 years old. It is an animal bone with seventy arcs, bands, and chevrons etched in it. Whether for decorative reasons, to record something, or for some mystical rite, the bone was undoubtedly created to symbolize something long before the invention of numbers and alphabets around 1000 BCE. The carvings on the bone appear to show some tribal human's sense of the occult.

By and large, the belief in literal occultism has disappeared from contemporary secular societies, even though it has left some notable residues in practices and artifacts such as daily horoscopes, the widespread wearing of lucky charms and amulets, and the omission of thirteenth floors in high-rise buildings (or more accurately, the intentional misidentification of thirteenth floors as fourteenth floors). The embracing of occultism (or occult symbolism) by groups such as the goths comes as no surprise to carnival theorists. Such behavior, complete with appropriate costume (dark clothes and cosmetics) and sacrilegious activities and rituals (such as devil-worshipping rituals), is essentially part of carnivalesque or the theater of the profane.

In sum, carnival theory asserts that the human psyche holds a basic opposition—the sacred versus the profane—and that both require expression or release. Carnival theory is sustained by the fact that cultures tend to make a distinction between these two categories in their sets of rituals and in the distribution of their institutions. In many religious traditions, for instance, there are periods of fasting (in Catholicism, Lent) preceded by periods of indulgence in all kinds of carnal pleasures (in Catholicism, the carnival period that precedes Lent). The transgressive antics of the latest pop musician, fashion model, movie star, or cult figure are seen as manifestations of an instinct to express the profane in carnivalesque ways. There is, however, a paradox to be noted. In contemporary pop culture, the line demarcating sacred and profane forms of expression is often blurry. Alongside *Dude, Where's My Car?* one finds such movies as *Amadeus* and *Mystic River*. Perhaps it is this ambiguity that gives pop culture its overall power and stability. This theme will be revisited in the final chapter.

Post-Feminism

Perhaps no one has understood the ambiguity of pop culture better than Madonna. A true individualist, the original "material girl" has projected female sexuality front-and-center on the pop culture stage. Madonna's subtext is obvious—no man can ever dictate to her how to pose on that stage. She will do it on her own terms. Men can only watch and behave themselves, as was made evident in her video "Like a Virgin." Madonna has also redefined Western religion in feminine terms, as shown in her video "Like a Prayer." Her artistic trademark was, and continues to be, a blend of sexual (profane) and religious (sacred) modes of expression. The latter are, however, in opposition to the traditional ones, being more in line with pagan or Wiccan (and hence female) modes.

Madonna's embracing of spirituality evokes an ancient mysticism that flies in the face of the moralism predominant in America. Madonna has made it clear that the equilibrium that we all seek between the sacred and the profane is to be found nowhere in the conventional notions present in denominational religions. Madonna expresses her take on the sacred and the profane through spectacle. Her concerts are indeed spectacular, blending peep show images with postures that are evocative of prayer. Using the power of her sexual persona she invites the act of *spectare* (to look) from both male and female audiences. Her intermingling of the sacred and the profane is overpowering.

There is little doubt, in my mind at least, that Madonna turned the tide in feminist theory vis-à-vis pop culture, inspiring the movement known as *post-feminism*. Madonna did this by exposing the latent puritanism and suffocating white middle-class ideology of previous forms of American feminism, which were stuck in an "adolescent whining mode," as Camille Paglia (1992) has argued. Through her performances and music, Madonna taught young women to be fully female and sexual while exercising control over their bodies and their lives.

Like carnival theorists, post-feminists see the display of female sexuality in public places and in media not as exploitation but rather as a transgressive form of dialogue (Phoca and Wright 1999). For this reason, post-feminists view erotic performances, from striptease to pornography, as a crucial part of the ongoing sexual revolution in women's liberation. The post-feminist perspective thus provides a vastly different sense of pop culture's representations of womanhood than do traditional feminist and religious views. For a case in point, consider porn movies. As the most extreme form of sexual explicitness within pop culture, pornography has assailed sexual mores since the 1970s. The early part of that decade marked the premiere of *Deep Throat*, a movie that was perceived not just as a new form of prurient sexual exploitation but also as a serious threat to the political and social order. The reason for *Deep Throat*'s perceived subversiveness was that women appeared to like it as much as men. This equality in reception truly upset those in political and moral power, who saw the movie and the reaction to it as perhaps the greatest threat to their hegemony. The release of *Deep Throat*, and the enjoyment of it, constituted transgression against the patriarchal status quo. It is thus no wonder that a similarly blatant sexual style has been adopted by a number of youth video artists. Pornography continues to be a form of social criticism against political and religious authoritarianism, albeit much less so today since it has become almost mainstream. Pornography continues to be attacked from both the left—as a form of misogyny and social decay—and the right—as a threat to morality and the family. Those who take pornography seriously are its opponents, not its subscribers.

As are other expressive modes of pop culture, pornography is ultimately a form of theater. And when it is relegated to the margin, it is even more effective as spectacle, providing a secretive theatrical context for an engagement in sexual fantasy. As profane theater, pornography is often juxtaposed against the more sacred (acceptable) forms of female sexuality—namely, the romantic forms. But, as Madonna has made clear throughout her career, and as post-feminists have recently argued in their works, the notion that women's fantasy worlds are limited to the type portrayed in romantic novels, movies, and songs is a distortion.

3

PRINT

There are only two or three human stories, and they go on repeating themselves as fiercely as if they had never happened before.

Willa Cather (1873–1947)

One of the most popular activities is to cuddle up with a good book and simply while away the hours reading. Even in the age of the Internet, reading such print materials as novels, "do-it-yourself" books, magazines, comic books, newspapers, and the like is still part of how we get recreation and enjoyment on a daily basis. Recreational print materials and pop culture have always been linked. Starting in the sixteenth century, when the printing press brought into existence the Gutenberg Galaxy, as McLuhan called it (see chapter 2), cheap mass-produced books became not only the primary means for propagating and storing knowledge and ideas, but also props in ensconcing "pleasure reading" into common people's repertory of recreational activities. Books remain popular to this day. The advent of the printing press led not only to widespread print literacy but also to a great growth in the popularity of fiction as a mass form of amusement.

The purpose of this chapter is to look at the role of print in the constitution and evolution of pop culture. Fiction helped to create modern-day pop culture and is still a primary source of entertainment. Its genres became the genres that we enjoy in other media (movies, television, and so on), from the horror story to the ubiquitous adventure and crime story.

BOOKS

As early as 2700 BCE, the Egyptians used material made from stems of the papyrus plant that grows along the Nile River to make pages that they connected to each other. These were the nascent books. Since then, "glued-together pages" have been used for a host of functions and have brought about significant social changes throughout the Gutenberg Galaxy. Shortly after the rise of papyrus books, libraries started sprouting up in the Middle East. One of the largest was built by the Greeks in Alexandria in the third century BCE. By the second century CE public and private libraries had been established in many parts of the world, leading to an increase in the desire to gain literacy and, eventually, to the rise of modern universities in the late eleventh century.

With the rise of literacy came a concomitant need to organize the knowledge contained in books. This led, among other things, to the invention of the *encyclopedia*, a Greek term originally referring to *general knowledge*. The oldest encyclopedia still in existence is the *Natural History* (79 CE) by Roman writer Pliny the Elder (23–79 CE). The modern type of encyclopedia was largely the result of the Enlightenment movement in the eighteenth century, which entrenched the view that knowledge could be arranged logically according to key words, names, or special topics.

Origins and Spread

The Sumerians and Egyptians introduced many of the conventions that are still used today in book production, such as a cover page with a title and the author's name on it. Professional scribes, who either copied a text or set it down from dictation, were responsible for book reproduction. The ancient Greeks, and later the Romans, became aware of books' potential for mass communication, but the books they produced were prohibitively expensive and thus were owned chiefly by temples, rulers, and a few rich individuals.

This pattern continued up until the early Middle Ages, when books were produced chiefly by clerics for other clerics and for rulers. They were written with a quill pen by monks working in the *scriptoria* (Latin for *writing rooms*) of monasteries and either had wooden covers fastened with clasps or were bound in leather. Often they were adorned with gems. Books were artistic objects, commissioned by the very small percentage of the population who could afford them and who knew how to read. Books thus remained mainly the privilege of the clergy and the aristocracy.

In the fifteenth century two developments occurred that broke this pattern. One was the advent of the cheap production of paper; the other was the invention of the printing press. These technological advancements

The Development of Books

2700 BCE: Papyrus made from plant reeds found along the Nile River is used to produce the first books.

350 CE: The *codex* book is produced by the Romans with parchment pages bound together.

600: Illuminated manuscripts featuring decorative designs on each page are created by scribes (primarily monks).

700: Arab traders introduce paper to the West.

1000: Movable clay typesetting is invented in China.

1234: Movable metal typesetting is invented in Korea.

1453: Johannes Gutenberg turns a wine press into a printing machine, leading to the mass production of books.

1455: The Bible is the first mass-produced book published with the new print technology.

1602: The first lending library, the Bodley, is established.

1640: The first book published in the American colonies, *The Bay Psalm Book*, is printed in Boston.

1751: The first encyclopedia is produced by French scholars.

1790: The first U.S. copyright law is passed. Publishing houses start proliferating.

1846: The rotary press is invented in the United States.

1860s: The dime novel becomes a mass culture phenomenon.

1880s: Linotype and offset lithography lower the cost of book production.

1909: The Copyright Act is passed in the United States.

1939: Robert de Graaf introduces Pocket Books.

1960s: Computer-based typesetting begins.

1971: Borders opens its first store, in Ann Arbor, Michigan. Chain bookstores and superstores start springing up across America shortly thereafter.

1980s: Desktop publishing gets under way.

1995: Amazon.com is established. It will turn its first profit in 2002.

1998: The Digital Millennium Copyright Term Extension Act is passed.

2000s: Microsoft and Adobe start making online books (e-books) and other online print materials available.

The book entered popular culture when it could be mass-produced. While electronic and other media continue to challenge the popularity of printed books, books have shown remarkable staying power.

©iStockphoto.com/David H. Lewis

made it possible to inexpensively manufacture books for a mass market. As a consequence, book production flourished. New book genres emerged, as books were being written not only for religious or scientific purposes but also more and more for public edification and for diversion.

By the time of the Industrial Revolution vast numbers of books could be published at a relatively low cost, as printing and paper technologies became highly efficient. The book had become an item of mass consumption. While other media challenged, and continue to challenge, the popularity of paper-produced books in the electronic age, books have shown remarkable staying power. To this day, books remain primary tools for the preservation and dissemination of knowledge, as well as sources for artistic expression and entertainment props.

Narrative

For at least five centuries books have been enjoyed by the masses for leisure. The innumerable works of fiction known as *novels* that have come down to us since the medieval period have been read by millions of people for the pure enjoyment of it. Novels are, basically, stories for the sake of storytelling. They are evidence that *narrative* is a universal expressive form which humans respond to instinctively as pleasurable and meaningful. People all over the world cannot help but think even of their own lives as stories and proceed to tell them as such. An autobiographical story has an inherent "narrative logic" that imparts sense and purpose to the teller's life, not simply mirroring what happened, but exploring and interpreting that life. The "narrative instinct" is as fundamental to human psychic life as breathing is to physical life.

A *narrative* is a text that has been constructed to represent a sequence of events or actions that are felt to be logically connected to each other or causally intertwined in some way. The sequence may be purely fact-based, as in a newspaper report or a psychoanalytic session, or fictional, as in a novel or a fairytale. It is often difficult, if not impossible, to determine the boundary line between fact and fiction. Even in the recounting of life-stories, fiction is often intermingled with fact in order to give the stories more coherence and credibility. The psychologist Paul Ekman (1985) has called the tweaking of autobiographical details the "Othello effect," defining it as lying in order to emphasize reality. As American novelist E. L. Doctorow (b. 1931) has aptly remarked, "There is no longer any such thing as fiction or nonfiction; there's only narrative" (cited by the *New York Times Review*, January 27, 1988).

Making sense of a narrative is not a straightforward process of determining the meanings of the individual words with which it is constructed and adding them together; rather, it involves interpreting the whole narrative at various levels. One level is the *subtext*, as it is called in literary theory. This is the main theme or intent of the narrative, which is not announced explicitly by the characters or narrator. It is implicit or becomes understood by the reader from cues within the main text. Some of these may come in the form of *intertexts,* which are allusions within the narrative text to other texts external to it. For example, the main text of the movie *Blade Runner* unfolds as a science fiction detective story, but its subtext is, arguably, a religious one—the search for a Creator and thus a meaning to life beyond mere physical existence. This interpretation is bolstered by the many intertextual cues to biblical and philosophical themes and symbols in the movie, such as a dove and the eyes.

Narrative can be decomposed into four main constituents—plot, character, setting, and narrator. The *plot* is basically what the narrative is all about; it is interpreted as a series of events connected logically (for example, chronologically or historically) to each other and perceived as mirroring real-life events. *Character* refers to the people or beings who enact the plot. Each character can draw on an archetype standing for a recognizable personality type—the hero, the coward, the lover, the friend, and so on. The *setting* is the location where, and the time when, the plot takes place. The *narrator* is the teller of the story. The narrator is usually a character in the narrative or the author of the text. Each type of narrator provides a different perspective on the story for the reader. The reader can thus feel a part of the narrative, looking at the action as if he or she were in it, or feel aloof from the narrative, looking at the action as if from the outside.

By and large, people think of narrative as fiction (from Latin *fingere*, for *to form, make, put together*). But fiction did not become a popular form of narrative art until the Middle Ages, although there is some evidence that it may have ancient roots. Papyri from the fourth Egyptian dynasty indicate that King Cheops (2590–2567 BCE) delighted in hearing the fictional stories that his sons told him. The Greek statesman and general Aristides (c. 530–468 BCE), moreover, wrote a collection of what we would now call short stories about his hometown, Miletus, to celebrate the Greek victory over the Persians at Salamis. *The Golden Ass* of Apuleius (c. 125–200 CE) was a fictional narration providing social and moral commentary. The tales of the ancient world, however, were hardly perceived as fictional in the modern sense of that word, but rather as dramatic reenactments of historical-mythical events. Fiction became a standard narrative craft only in the Middle Ages, after Giovanni Boccaccio (1313–1375) published *The Decameron* (1351–1353), a collection of one hundred fictional tales set against the gloomy background of the Black Death, as the bubonic plague that swept through Europe in the fourteenth century was called. *The Decameron* is the first real example of fiction in the modern sense. To escape an outbreak of the plague, ten friends decide to take refuge in a country villa outside Florence. There, they entertain one another over a period of ten days with a series of stories told and totally made up for the occasion by each member of the party in turn. Ever since, fictional narration has been a yardstick for exploring the human condition. Why, one might ask? How can a lie (fiction) be perceived as truth-telling? The only plausible answer, as the Argentine writer Jorge Luis Borges (1899–1986) suggested in his *Ficciones* (1944, 1962), is that the mind is inherently structured to understand life as narrative, so we are predisposed to perceive any work of fiction as a probe of reality, not a mere representation of it. Narratives seem to hold up a mirror to the psyche. Sigmund Freud (1856–1939) saw the recounting of conflicts in myths as attempts to come to grips with unconscious psychic life. In the myth of Oedipus—the king who was abandoned at birth and unwittingly killed his father and then married his mother—Freud noticed a narrative mirror for probing hidden sexual desires. Carl Jung (1875–1961) similarly saw narratives as windows into the collective unconscious in the human species—an area of the psyche constituted by primordial images, which he termed *archetypes*, and which are imprinted in narrative forms across the world.

In a famous 1928 study, the Russian critic Vladimir Propp (1895–1970) argued that a relatively small number of innate and, thus, largely unconscious plots, characters, and settings went into the makeup of narratives of all kinds. Propp's theory would explain why stories seem to be so similar the world over and why we tell stories to children instinctively. Stories allow children to make sense of the real world, providing the intelligible formats that give pattern and continuity to their observations of daily life. Stories impart a sense that there is a plot to life, that the characters in it serve some meaningful purpose, and that the setting of life is part of a meaningful cosmos. By age four or five, children are able to manage and negotiate narratives by themselves, especially during play, when they create imaginary narratives designed to entertain onlookers.

Stories are, and always have been, interconnected with ritual, tradition, history, and all other aspects of culture. We listen or read the same stories at specific times of the year—for example, Christmas ushers in tales from *'Twas the Night Before Christmas* to the more contemporary *How the Grinch Stole Christmas*. We are constantly watching movies, enjoying adventure stories, or reading novels for insight and entertainment.

The Novel

There are various media, modes, and devices for delivering narrative. But the one that has been the most influential in cultivating pop culture has been the *novel*. Novels have been popular sources for many cultural practices over the centuries—children were (and still are) named after characters in novels, real places are named or modeled after places described in novels, and so on and so forth. Novels such as Fyodor Dostoyevsky's *Crime and Punishment* (1866) have been used as templates for evaluating human character or the nature of such phenomena as crime. It is amazing indeed to contemplate that a type of text that is essentially a lie has been used throughout its history to get at the truth, about people, life, and the universe.

As mentioned above, proto-fictional narratives were composed in the ancient world, and to these the term *novel* is sometimes applied. But the novel did not emerge as an autonomous narrative genre until the Middle Ages. Many scholars regard the eleventh-century *Tale of Genji*, by the Japanese baroness Murasaki Shikibu (c. 978–1026), as the first true novel, since it depicts the amorous adventures of a fictional Prince Genji and the staid lives of his descendants. The novel paints a charming and apparently accurate picture of Japanese court life in the Heian period. Among its chief delights are the portraits of the women in Prince Genji's life. These women are portrayed as aristocrats, with many talents, especially in the arts of music, drawing, and poetry. As the work nears its conclusion, the tone becomes more mature and somber, colored by Buddhist insight into the fleeting joys of earthly existence.

Etymologists claim that the word *fiction* was first used around 1412 in the sense of "invention of the mind." It is not a far step from this meaning to the sense "imaginative literature," first recorded in 1599, according to the same etymologists. But fictional works predate these events, even though they were not named as such. They became popular with the rise of the long verse tale, the prose romance, and the Old French *fabliau* in the medieval period, culminating, as mentioned above, with Boccaccio's *Decameron*. In Spain during the sixteenth century, the novel gained great social importance with the picaresque novel, in which a hero is portrayed typically as a vagabond who passes through a series of exciting adventures. The most widely known example is a novel by Miguel de Cervantes Saavedra (1547–1616), *Don Quixote de la Mancha* (Part I, 1605, Part II, 1615), which is considered the first great novel of the Western world.

Novels gained enormous popularity in the eighteenth and nineteenth centuries, especially those satirizing contemporary life and morals. During that same era, the novel spawned its own genres, including the Gothic novel, which aimed to horrify readers through depictions of bizarre and supernatural happenings. The first Gothic novel was *The Castle of Otranto* (1764) by Horace Walpole (1717–1797). But perhaps the most well-known example of the genre is *Frankenstein* (1818) by Mary Wollstonecraft Shelley (1797–1851). Another narrative genre of the period was the comedy of manners, which explored the artificial structure of social relations. The novels of Jane Austen (1775–1817) are probably the most important ones in this genre. Throughout the nineteenth century, novelists were as popular and well-known as media personalities are today. The French writer Marcel Proust (1871–1922), the German author Thomas Mann (1875–1955), and the English authors Virginia Woolf (1882–1941) and James Joyce (1882–1941) were veritable icons of the reading public. To this day, novelists are held in high esteem and can become celebrities, whether or not their novels are converted into movies. Writers such as Dan Brown, Judy Collins, and John Grisham are as part of contemporary celebrity culture as are pop musicians, movie stars, and television personalities.

Evaluations of the role the novel has played in human evolution have varied. Twentieth-century Marxist critics (discussed in chapter 2) saw fictional books as meaningful only when they showcased the imbalances that these critics thought existed in capitalist societies. Freudian critics, on the other hand, believed that the value of narrative lay in the insights it provided into the psyche. The conflicts, fantasies, and daydreams of fictional characters, they claimed, are those of ordinary people, and thus can be read as a means to come to grips with one's own real-life psyche. The French philosopher and writer Jean-Paul Sartre (1905–1980) saw narrative art as providing an "escape hatch" from inner psychic turmoil. Perhaps the most radical view of narrative ever to have been formulated comes from the pen of the late French philosopher Jacques Derrida (1930–2004), who contended that the traditional way of interpreting literary fiction as a mirror of life is misleading, as is the view that the author of a work of fiction is the source of its meaning. Derrida has challenged both these beliefs and the idea that a narrative text has an unchanging, unified meaning. The author's intentions in writing, Derrida claimed, cannot be unconditionally accepted. There are an infinite number of legitimate interpretations of a text that are beyond what the author intends.

Pulp Fiction

From its appearance on the stage of human history in the early 1300s, the novel has always constituted a form of popular entertainment (for those who had literacy skills). It is, arguably, the first true fad and, thus, an early congener of pop culture. The novel is a "portable narrative entertainment device" that anyone can enjoy at any time. Novels have been used to fulfill all kinds of interests, from the prurient to the highly intellectual. Moreover, as Bakhtin often pointed out in his writings (see chapter 2), novels are subversive. Novels' potential for subversion, however, is indirect. Because they portray social conditions and characters as fictitious, authors cannot be held legally responsible for libel or political treason. However, readers can easily relate these texts to real conditions and to real people. Novels can thus motivate people to revolt and take action.

By the era of the Roaring Twenties novels were being produced in bulk for mass consumption and entertainment, in response to the rise in popularity of *pulp fiction*—stories published in inexpensive fiction magazines in serial form. The first true pulp is considered to be Frank Munsey's *Argosy Magazine* of 1896. The term *pulp* derives from the fact that the magazines and derivative novels were produced with cheap paper made from wood pulp. In contrast, other contemporary magazines which used higher quality paper were known as *glossies* or *slicks*. The pulps were successors of the *dime novels* of the nineteenth century. Their plots revolved around the themes of crime, adventure, and sex, and they were written in a sensationalistic and lurid way. Fictional pulp detectives and crime fighters such as Doc Savage, the Shadow, and the Phantom Detective became household names. Titles of early pulp magazines included *Dime Detective*, *Planet Stories*, *Startling Stories*, *Flying Aces*, *Amazing Stories*, *Black Mask*, *Spicy Detective*, *Horror Stories*, *Unknown and Weird Tales*, *Marvel Tales*, *Oriental Stories*, and *Thrilling Wonder Stories*. The popularity of these magazines and their spin-off novels was, in no small part, bolstered by their cover designs, which imitated the sensationalistic poster art used by circuses and vaudeville theaters to attract audiences, including scantily dressed "damsels in distress" or virile heroes involved in fisticuffs with villains. The pulps became the basis for the early movie serials, such as those made by Republic Pictures in the 1930s and 1940s. Both the pulps and the serials were designed to keep audiences in suspense as an episode ended with the hero or heroine caught in a dangerous situation. The audience would eagerly come back the week after, or wait for the next issue of the magazine, to find out how the cliffhanger situation would be resolved.

With rising paper costs and competition from other media, the pulps started losing market dominance by the late 1950s. The bankruptcy in 1957 of the American News Company, the main distributor of pulp magazines, marked the end of the pulp era. The pulp cliffhanger formula is still evident in the James Bond movies, the *Raiders of the Lost Ark* films, and other motion pictures. But, more importantly, pulp genres including the detective and mystery story, science fiction, the western, the sword and sorcery story, the horror tale, the romance tale, and many others are now staples of pop culture fare in all media, from movies to comic books. Some of the fictional characters created by the pulp industry have become an enduring part of pop culture lore: Buck Rogers, Fu Manchu, Hopalong Cassidy, Perry Mason, Nick Carter, Secret Agent X, Tarzan, the Shadow, and Zorro, to mention but a few. And, paradoxically, pulp fiction engaged some of the greatest writers of the twentieth century, including Isaac Asimov, Ray Bradbury, Edgar Rice Burroughs, Arthur C. Clarke, Philip K. Dick, Zane Grey, Robert A. Heinlein, Frank Herbert, and Upton Sinclair. Current popular fiction writers such as Stephen King and Anne Rice work in the same tradition as the pulp fiction writers. Although the original pulps have disappeared, the fun of reading pulp genres obviously has not.

Moreover, the close link between pulp fiction genres and the movie industry, established already in the 1930s, has not been broken but, rather, has become even more solid. *The Godfather* (1969), *Love Story* (1970), *The Exorcist* (1971), *Jaws* (1974), and *The Da Vinci Code* (2003) are perfect examples of this link, since all started out as popular novels written in the pulp style and later became popular movies. The venues, plots, and characters of these newer stories may at first appear unlike those in the original pulp genre, but they are not. These are essentially updated pulp fiction stories.

NEWSPAPERS

On most street corners of a big city one finds newspaper racks or dispensing boxes. Newspapers are also delivered to homes on a daily basis. Some, like the Sunday version of the *New York Times*, are so large that it is unlikely that anyone can read them throughout in a reasonable period of time, before the news content in them becomes irrelevant. Indeed, it is unlikely that people will read a newspaper from cover to cover, like they read a novel or some magazines.

Why do we like our newspapers so much, even if we do not actually read them from cover to cover? As anything else in pop culture, this has both a short and a long answer. The short answer is that they are fun to read—we like them because they provide pleasure in the same way that the pulp magazines did, only in this case the crime and prurience are real. The long answer is that they are props in the overall pop culture collage of materials and spectacles, serving the desire of common people to gain information and recreation at the same time. This does not mean that print journalism is all about feeding the "popular imagination." Often, newspapers are (or at least have been) the vehicle that comes forward to influence public opinion and to bring about radical social changes. However, newspapers also serve the broader recreational function that other print materials have served since the Roaring Twenties. It is this function that is of particular interest here (not the loftier journalistic one).

A Newspaper Timeline

1620: *Corantos*, the first news sheets, are published in northern Europe.

1640s: *Diurnos*, the first daily newspapers, are published in England.

1644: English poet John Milton calls for freedom of speech in his pamphlet titled *Aeropagitica*.

1690: Boston printer Benjamin Harris publishes the first American newspaper, *Publick Occurrences, Both Foreign and Domestick*.

1735: Freedom of the press is defended when a jury rules in favor of printer Peter John Zinger, who had criticized the government in print and who had been charged with libel.

1783: The first daily newspaper in the United States, the *Pennsylvania Evening Post and Daily Advertiser*, is published.

1789: Freedom of the press is enshrined in the U.S. Constitution by the enactment of the First Amendment.

1827: The first African American newspaper, *Freedom's Journal*, makes its appearance.

1828: The first Native American newspaper, the *Cherokee*, makes its debut.

1833: The penny press era is ushered in with the publication of the *New York Sun*, costing only one cent.

1848: Six newspapers form the Associated Press and begin relaying news stories around the country via telegraphy.

1860: The *New York Morning* reaches a circulation of eighty thousand, showing that newspapers have become an integral part of mass communications.

Origins and Spread

Handwritten newssheets posted in public places in the ancient world are considered to be the forerunners of newspapers. The earliest was the Roman *Acta Diurna* (*Daily Events*), which was widely distributed starting in 59 BCE. The world's first print newspaper, a Chinese circular called *Dibao*, was produced using carved wooden blocks around 700 CE. The first regularly published paper-based newspaper in Europe can be traced to Germany in 1609. The newspaper business expanded considerably throughout Europe in the seventeenth and eighteenth centuries. By the late 1800s, newspapers had become popular reading materials, as competing newspa-

1883: Joseph Pulitzer buys the *New York World*, ushering in the era of yellow journalism (inaccurate, exaggerated reporting).

1895: William Randolph Hearst enters newspaper publishing and adopts sensationalistic techniques, further promoting yellow journalism.

1896: Adolph Ochs buys the *New York Times* and makes responsible journalism its primary objective.

1914: The first Spanish-language paper in the United States, *El Diario/La Prensa*, is founded in New York City.

1917: The Pulitzer Prize is established at Columbia University to reward achievement in journalism and other areas.

1920s: Newspaper chains spring up, leading to a decline in the number of daily metropolitan newspapers.

1930–1934: Hundreds of syndicated columns start up.

1972: The Watergate scandal stimulates a new era of investigative journalism.

1980: Ohio's *Columbus Dispatch* is the first newspaper to go online.

1982: *USA Today* is launched, the first newspaper modeled after television.

1998: The *Dallas Morning News* is the first newspaper to break a major story on its website instead of its front page. Increasing use of the Internet leads to the development of blogs, discussion groups, and the like, which take on many of the functions of traditional print newspapers.

2000s: By 2003, thousands of newspapers offer some kind of online news service.

pers in large cities tried to outdo each other with sensational reports of crimes, disasters, and scandals.

Not until 1690 was anything resembling the early European newspapers printed in the American colonies. *Publick Occurrences, Both Foreign and Domestick*, a three-page newspaper, was published that year in Boston, but it was suppressed by the government after one issue. The first true newspaper appeared slightly more than a decade later, in 1704. It was called the *Boston News-Letter*. It contained financial and foreign news and also recorded births, deaths, and social events. In 1721 James Franklin founded the *New England Courant* in Boston. His younger brother, Benjamin Franklin, went to Philadelphia in 1723 to found the *Pennsylvania Gazette* and the *General Magazine*.

Although these publications failed, Franklin nevertheless gained fame as a writer, editor, and publisher because of them.

The first New York City newspaper, the *Gazette*, was founded in 1725. It was soon followed by the *New York Weekly Journal*, edited by John Peter Zenger, who published acerbic critiques of the British colonial governor of New York and his administration. As a consequence, Zenger was arrested and jailed on charges of libel. He was tried and found not guilty. This trial created the crucial precedent for the tradition of a free press in America.

In 1783, the first daily newspaper in the United States, the *Pennsylvania Evening Post and Daily Advertiser*, was launched in Philadelphia. Until the 1830s newspapers were concerned almost entirely with business and political news, appealing primarily to the privileged classes. All that changed in 1833, when Benjamin Henry Day published the first issue of the *New York Sun*, creating a "penny press" revolution. The *Sun* included reports of crime and violence and entertainment all in the same issue. The modern newspaper, designed to appeal to a mass audience, was thus born, and it cost a single penny. Pop culture was just around the corner. With the advent of the first telegraph line in 1844, news could be transmitted quickly across the nation. In response to this development, an amalgamation of newspapers called the Associated Press was formed in 1848. The AP was not seen as biased toward any one part of the nation. Consequently, it was impelled to present news in a nonpartisan, objective manner, a standard that is still pursued today (at least in theory). A decade and a half later, during the Civil War, newspapers gained widespread popularity because they brought graphic accounts of battlefront developments to a mass audience of readers and also because of the unexpected appeal of their advertising sections.

As newspapers competed more and more with each other to increase circulation rates, a different type of journalism surfaced, developed cleverly by Joseph Pulitzer and William Randolph Hearst. Pulitzer made sensational and scandalous news coverage, catchy art design, and comic strips integral parts of popular journalistic style and content. Hearst published color comic sections that included a strip called *The Yellow Kid*. The term *yellow journalism* (alluding to the strip) emerged to describe Pulitzer's and Hearst's approach. Yellow journalistic style spread, and by the last decade of the nineteenth century it had helped to turn newspapers into popular reading materials.

Yellow journalism soon led to the *tabloid* genre, which gained wide popularity in the 1920s, heralding the emergence of newspapers as pop culture props. The tabloid was smaller and its reports were more condensed and sensationalistic, focusing on the occult, the weird, and the bizarre (from alien creatures to miraculous cures), and on celebrities and their "private lives." To this day, tabloids are seen more as part of recreational culture than of serious journalism.

Newspapers depend for survival on quickly and efficiently distributing as many copies of an issue as possible. Ironically, as popular as the newspaper is today, high operating expenses, especially the rising cost of labor and newsprint, have driven many out of business. Few cities now have competing dailies. In those that do, rival publishers typically print their papers on the same presses to reduce costs. Financial problems have hit major metropolitan newspapers the hardest, in part because they face strong competition from suburban newspapers and from television newscasts. Some big-city newspapers now publish morning and afternoon editions in an effort to gain wider readership.

In 1980, the *Columbus Dispatch* (of Columbus, Ohio) launched the first electronic newspaper in the United States. In addition to printing a regular edition, the *Dispatch* began transmitting some of its editorial content to computers in the homes, businesses, and libraries of a small number of subscribers. Today, most newspapers have followed suit, offering online versions of their regular editions and even entire issues. However, as in the case of books, this has not brought about the end of paper-based newspapers. People still seem to want to read such newspapers as they ride on public transport vehicles, as they wait for appointments in offices, as they sip coffee in coffee shops and in their homes, and in many other locales. Newspapers will continue to be bought by consumers as long as they remain cheap, entertaining, and topical.

Reading Newspapers

Why are newspapers so popular? Since their inception, they have been perceived to be many things at once—sources of relevant information about the world, agents of change, and sources of entertainment. One of the foremost examples of the power of the press came in 1974 when President Richard Nixon resigned from his office after revelations about the Watergate scandal pointed to his administration. The scandal had been brought to public attention by the *Washington Post*. Watergate gave rise to investigative reporting as a separate genre in the newspaper field. Newspapers are, in fact, a stage for showcasing public issues. But that stage also displays other "acts," much like the vaudevillian stage discussed in the first chapter. Indeed, to cope with the competition of instant news reports on radio, television, and websites, newspapers have become more and more entertainment props. People buy newspapers not only for their news content and editorial commentaries, but also (if not more so) for their advertising content, for the comics section, for the crossword puzzle, for sports gossip, for classified information, for entertainment news, for reviews of books and movies, for portraits of exceptional individuals, and for other such "variety acts" that rival television for entertainment value. Newspapers open up a silent (non-vocal) polyphonic dialogue, as Bakhtin would claim (see chapter 2).

Needless to say, different types of newspapers attract different kinds of audiences. They are thus perceptibly different in how they stage their acts, in what kind of language they use on their particular version of the vaude-villian stage. Some newspapers, such as the grocery store tabloids, are intended to have a crass appeal; others, like the *New York Times*, are designed to have a much more sophisticated appeal. A comparison of the two genres highlights the difference clearly.

Reading tabloids is akin to reading circus and carnival posters; reading newspapers like the *New York Times* is akin to reading reference manuals and literary exposés. Tabloids serve the same function as gossip and small-town sensationalistic storytelling. As the American poet e. e. cummings (1894–

Table 3.1. Style Differences between Tabloids and Sophisticated Newspapers

Tabloids	*Sophisticated Newspapers*
Headlines are large, informal, and sensationalistic: *Bodies Found Decapitated!*	Headlines are formal and restrained: *Gruesome Murders Discovered!*
Writing style is colloquial and characterized by slang features: *The headless bodies are like part of a horror movie.*	Writing style is more refined and sophisticated: *The headless bodies revealed a horrific scene.*
Reporting is sensationalistic and graphic: *There were gory pools of blood splattered all over the place.*	Reporting is subdued and rational: *Blood was found all around.*
Bawdy and occult topics and features are included: horoscopes, ads for sexual services, apocalyptic prophecies, items on "freaks" and "outcasts" (bearded ladies, obese individuals, etc.).	Bawdy and prurient topics are avoided, although some occult features such as horoscopes may be included.
Advertising is blunt: *If you've got a problem having sex, get Viagra.*	Prurient topics and advertising are treated with discretion and prudence: *Sexual satisfaction can be increased with Viagra.*

1964) aptly put it: "The tabloid newspaper actually means to the typical American what the Bible is popularly supposed to have meant to the typical Pilgrim Father: a very present help in times of trouble, plus a means of keeping out of trouble via harmless, since vicarious, indulgence in the pomps and vanities of this wicked world" (cited by *Vanity Fair*, December 1926). Tabloids entertain audiences by adorning their narrations with sensationalism and exaggeration. They do this by treating such bizarre topics as UFOs, alien visitations, and religious apparitions alongside melodramatic exposés of celebrity love affairs, sexual scandals, and the like. Due to its popularity, the tabloid style has spread somewhat to all newspapers, including sophisticated ones like the *New York Times*. Some newspapers have even blurred the line between the tabloid genre and the serious genre completely, mixing elements of both in their content and overall style of presentation. The most famous of these hybrid newspapers is *USA Today*, which began publication on September 15, 1982. With its admixture of tabloid-like features and traditional journalism, *USA Today* is a perfect example of how carnivalesque tendencies in pop culture are more and more leading to subconscious patterns of groupthink. Modeled in its structure after television newscasting, *USA Today* is quickly becoming Americans' default newspaper, which indicates that the blurring of lines between so-called high and low culture, through pastiche, is becoming the norm. Overall, the popularity of newspapers—in tabloid, sophisticated, or eclectic form—bears witness to the fact that the carnivalesque form of representation has broad appeal, especially when intermingled with the sacred (in this case, the more formal and noble aspects of print journalism).

Advertising

Arguably, advertising would not be the big business it is today without its early partnership with newspapers. The two go hand in hand and, indeed, the rise of modern-day newspapers and modern-day persuasive advertising occurred in tandem. On average, newspapers devote almost half of their space to advertising. Many people read a daily newspaper specifically to check the ads for information about products, services, or special sales.

More than three hundred years ago, the *London Gazette* became the first newspaper to reserve a section exclusively for advertising. So successful was this gamble that by the end of the seventeenth century several agencies came into existence for the specific purpose of creating newspaper ads for merchants and artisans. In general, these agencies designed the ads in the style of classifieds, without illustrative support. Nonetheless, the ads had all the persuasive rhetorical flavor of their contemporary descendants. The ad makers of the era catered to the wealthy clients who bought and read newspapers, promoting the sale of tea, coffee, wigs, books, theater tickets, and the like. The following advertisement for toothpaste dates back to a 1660 issue of the *Gazette*. Particularly captivating is the fact that its rhetorical style is almost identical to the one used today for the promotion of this very same type of product (cited by Dyer 1982: 16–17):

> Most excellent and proved Dentifrice to scour and cleanse the Teeth, making them white as ivory, preserves [cures] the Tooth-ach [toothache]; so that being constantly used, the Parties [people] using it are never troubled with the Tooth-ach. It fastens the Teeth, sweetens the Breath, and preserves the Gums and Mouth from cankers and Impothumes . . . and the right are only to be had at Thomas Rookes, Stationer.

Exaggerated style—such as "most excellent," "proved," "preserves the Tooth-ach," and so forth—and persuasive pitches are used throughout as subtle hints that bad breath is socially harmful, while the maintenance of a beautiful mouth is portrayed as socially advantageous. The grammar of English may have changed, but the use of rhetorical persuasion has not, and it remains central to newspaper advertising to this day.

Newspaper advertising spread throughout the eighteenth century in both Europe and America, proliferating to the point that the writer and lexicographer Samuel Johnson (1709–1784) felt impelled to make the following statement in *The Idler*: "Advertisements are now so numerous that they are very negligently perused, and it is therefore become necessary to gain attention by magnificence of promise and by eloquence sometimes sublime and sometimes pathetic" (cited by Panati 1984: 168). As advertising became a fixture of newspaper content, ad creators began paying more attention to the design and layout of the ad text itself. Layouts with words set in blocks and contrasting type fonts became widespread. New language forms (words and phrases) were coined regularly to serve the persuasiveness of the ad text. As a consequence, newspaper advertising was surreptitiously starting to change the very structure and use of language and verbal communication, as more and more people became exposed to newspaper advertising. Everything from clothes to beverages was promoted through ingenious new verbal ploys such as strategic repetitions of the product's name in the composition of the ad text, the use of compact phrases set in eye-catching patterns (vertically, horizontally, diagonally), the use of contrasting font styles and formats, and the inclusion of slogans and neologisms designed to highlight certain qualities of the product, alongside supporting illustrations. These techniques remain basic to advertising craft to this very day.

As the nineteenth century came to a close, advertising style became more colloquial, personal, and informal, frequently using humor to attract attention to a product. So persuasive had advertising become that, by the early decades of the twentieth century, it started to influence daily conversation, as ad slogans and catchy phrases entered the everyday lexicon. Newspaper advertisers had, in effect, become the new wordsmiths for the larger society.

MAGAZINES

The pulp fiction magazines discussed previously were critical in ushering in and spreading popular print culture. Magazines in general have always quickly blended in with all areas of the pop culture landscape, simultaneously becoming both conveyors of pop culture trends and props within it.

Origins and Spread

The earliest magazines published were the German *Erbauliche Monaths-Unterredungen* (1663–1668), the French *Journal des Sçavans* (1665), and the *Philosophical Transactions* (1665) of the Royal Society of London. These were essentially collections of essays on issues and trends related to art, literature, philosophy, and science. In a similar vein, *essay periodicals* followed in the early eighteenth century. Among the most widely read of the essay periodicals were the British publications *The Tatler* (1709–1711) and *The Spectator* (1711–1714)—creations of the renowned essayists Richard Steele (1672–1729) and Joseph Addison (1672–1719)—and *The Rambler* (1750–1752) and *The Idler* (1758–1760), founded by Samuel Johnson (1709–1784). In the latter part of the century, such periodicals developed into general-purpose magazines. With the publication of *The Gentleman's Magazine* (1731–1907) in England, the modern-day magazine materialized. This event also marked the first use of the word *magazine*. Deriving from the French word *magasin* (through Old Italian *magazzino* and Arabic *mahazin*), which meant *storehouse*, the magazine was a veritable literary storehouse, including essays, stories, poems, and reports of political debates.

A Magazine Timeline

1731: The first magazine, *The Gentleman's Magazine*, is published in England.

1732: *Poor Richard's Almanack* by Benjamin Franklin is published in the United States.

1741: Colonial magazines appear in Boston and Philadelphia.

1821: *The Saturday Evening Post* is launched.

1836: Sarah Josepha Hale becomes the first editor of *Godey's Lady's Book*, the first true women's magazine.

1846: *Harper's Weekly* begins publication.

1879: The Postal Act of 1879 lowers the postal rate for magazines, allowing distribution to thrive.

1880s: The advent of linotype and offset lithography lower the cost of magazine production.

1900: Muckraking style becomes highly popular.

1922: *Reader's Digest* is launched.

1923: *Time*, founded by Henry Luce, starts publication.

1936: *Life* starts publication.

1953: *TV Guide* is launched.

1954: *Sports Illustrated* begins publication.

1967: Rock-and-roll gets its own magazine with the launch of *Rolling Stone*.

1969: *The Saturday Evening Post* succumbs to specialized competition.

1974: *People* magazine starts publication.

1980s–1990s: Magazines for all kinds of tastes and hobbies proliferate.

2000s: E-zines and other magazine genres start proliferating in online versions.

By the mid-nineteenth century, magazine publication proliferated considerably, and the contemporary periodicals both mirrored and dictated social trends. *Godey's Lady's Book*, for example, with its colorful fashion illustrations, was vastly influential in setting the style in women's clothing, manners, and taste. *The Illustrated London News* (1842), *The Fortnightly Review* (1865–1954), *Punch* (1841) in England, *L'Illustration* in France (1843–1944), *Die Woche* (1899–1940) in Germany, and *Leslie's Illustrated*

Newspaper (1855–1922) and *Harper's Weekly* in the United States became staples of an emerging affluent middle class of readers. *Youth's Companion* (1827–1929) and later *St. Nicholas* (1873–1940) were among several children's magazines published in the same era that became highly popular for imparting literacy skills to children. Family magazines such as *The Saturday Evening Post* (1821–) also became vastly popular. A new era had begun in which certain days (such as Saturday) could be set aside for entertaining, informative, and wholesome reading.

With the publication of *Cosmopolitan* (1886–), the modern fashion and lifestyle magazine for women came into being. Between 1902 and 1912, this genre became very popular. In addition to *Cosmopolitan*, female readers could choose from *Ladies'* (later *Woman's*) *Home Companion* (1873–1957), *McCall's Magazine* (1876–2001), *Ladies' Home Journal* (1883–), *Good Housekeeping* (1885–), and *Vogue* (1892–) to while away the leisure hours. These magazines brought to the forefront the ever-growing role of women in pop culture. A publication written by women and designed for female audiences would have been unthinkable just a few years previously.

In 1922 the pocket-sized *Reader's Digest* began publication, confirming that people had increasingly little time to read entire books. With the summaries that this magazine regularly published, readers could indulge their need for narrative and, at the same time, make an informed decision regarding whether to buy and read an entire book. Since the 1950s, this periodical has had a monthly circulation in the millions. Two other significant developments, dating from the 1920s and 1930s, were the establishment of weekly news magazines such as *Time* (1923) and *Newsweek* (1933) and the emergence of weekly and biweekly magazines such as *Life* (1936–1972, revived as a monthly in 1978), *Look* (1937–1971), and *Ebony* (1946–), which focuses on issues of interest to African Americans.

Today, magazine publishing is a worldwide phenomenon, and the industry caters to specialized tastes. For example, *National Geographic* (1888–) contains information from the worlds of science, history, and travel; *Consumer Reports* (1936–) offers comparative evaluations of consumer products; *GQ* (1957–) focuses on issues of concern to urban males; *Rolling Stone* (1967–) is devoted to pop music; *Ms.* (1970–) deals with topics of interest to women; *People* (1974–) features stories on celebrities; *Discover* (1980–) is a general science magazine; and *Wired* (1993–) looks at issues pertaining to digital culture.

Predictably, in today's Digital Galaxy the magazine has converged with other media. E-zines (magazines published on the Internet) are proliferating and boast various advantages over paper-based magazines. For examples, e-zines can be distributed much more quickly and updated regularly, allowing readers to keep constantly abreast of current events. Moreover, given the hypertext capacities of e-zines, they can be linked with other sources of information. The Internet also hosts magazine chat rooms. In early 2000, *Vogue* and *W* magazines created one of the first magazine chat websites, Style.com, where people can get the latest gossip about the fashion industry. Such sites have now become commonplace.

Reading Magazines

Magazines, like newspapers, present content in the form of collage. Paradoxically, magazines are not perceived by readers as fragmentary, but rather as thematic. Perhaps this is not surprising, since we take from the reading process what we want to get from it, even though we actually remember little of what we have read. We thus experience the reading of *Time*, *Sports Illustrated*, or *Vogue* as a polyphonic dialogue with the magazine itself, and we select from the polyphony only those themes that are relevant to us. It is arguably for this Bakhtinian reason that magazines are highly popular as devices of mass communication and leisure.

At a literal textual level, a magazine is a collection of articles or stories, often supported by illustrations, photos, and the like. Some cover current events; others are designed just to entertain; still others provide professional information and counseling to those working in certain areas of employment. Magazines are intended to be kept much longer than newspapers. For this reason, most have a smaller page size and are printed on better paper. In content, magazines often show less concern with daily, rapidly changing events than do newspapers. Most have a cover featuring a photograph or a drawing rather than news stories. Writing of different styles—ranging from factual or practical reporting to a more personal or emotional style—is a basic characteristic of the magazine text. Some of the best writers have contributed either occasionally or regularly to magazines. And many well-known authors published their early works in them.

Of particular interest to the study of pop culture is the lifestyle magazine, because it has been amalgamated with pop culture since its appearance onto the social scene. Consider, as a case in point, *In Style* magazine. *In Style* was founded in 1994. Its circulation is estimated at three million readers, one-third of whom live outside of the United States. It is popular and very well-designed in typical carnivalesque style (as a collage of images, fonts, styles, and so forth). Like any lifestyle magazine, it offers its readers a pastiche of items on celebrities, lifestyle, cosmetics, and fashion trends along with numerous ads, which are targeted at upper-middle-class women. Each monthly issue is organized in a set pattern that strategically superimposes continuity between the products it advertises, its articles, and its website.

Each issue of *In Style* features a celebrity on the cover, and the relevant article about the celebrity is found a few pages from the back of the magazine, inducing the reader to peruse various fashion articles, including commentaries on current clothing trends donned by certain celebrities. Each issue also provides the reader with advice on where to find fashion items, how to maintain a healthy figure, how to enhance beauty through cosmetics, and the like. The magazine rarely diverges from this format and these contents. It intersperses ads of perfumes, automobiles, and clothing, which are integrated thematically with the articles. *Textual convergence* (the technique of linking ads and magazine content thematically) creates a syntax of sense between products and magazine content, which compels us to read the magazine fluently—that is, without seeing the ads as invasive or disruptive. Textual convergence constitutes the main structural characteristic of many current magazines, both lifestyle magazines and those of other genres. For example, a photography magazine attracts camera fans who will undoubtedly find its ads helpful in choosing certain photographic equipment and who, thus, will be receptive to seeing the ads as a consistent and continuous part of the magazine's text. Advertisers of such equipment can therefore reach many potential customers through the magazine by integrating their ad texts with the magazine's contents—that is, each ad will follow (or precede) an article that is thematically similar. Needless to say, the type of product connected syntactically to the contents must reflect the themes of the magazine and the interests of its readers. For instance, ads for Chanel products are inserted into women's lifestyle magazines and linked to their contents logically; ads for Nike shoes are inserted into trendy magazines for adolescents and young adults in a similar way; ads for Audi and BMW are integrated structurally into upscale magazines; and so on. The ads complement the articles in a textually fluid fashion.

Women's lifestyle magazines also bring out another key theme in pop culture study—the power of the female form (discussed in chapter 2). A simple perusal of covers selected from recent issues of *Cosmopolitan* shows clearly that this magazine highlights women's physique. Much like the statues of ancient goddesses, these cover models emphasize the power of female sexuality, not only to sell magazines but also to encourage readers to attain an (unattainable) ideal of beauty. It is because their looks are meant to inspire that the models (usually celebrities) are shot photographically straight on, gazing directly at the readers. This pose makes them more "human." Typically, inside the covers, we find that the celebrities have blemishes and experience travails, much like the reader. Clearly, this technique of bringing the goddess down to earth is carnivalesque, invoking caricature and parody of the goddess. Such women's lifestyle magazines consist of a blend of fantasy and carnival, the imaginary and the real. It is this very blend that defines pop culture generally, from print to electronic fare.

COMICS

The *comics* have become a target of great interest among pop culture analysts and stand out as an overarching symbol of pop culture itself. The predecessors of comics are the caricatures of famous people that became popular in seventeenth-century Italy. Caricature art spread quickly throughout Europe shortly thereafter. In the early nineteenth century, the art was expanded to include speech balloons, giving birth to the comics.

Comics (or *comic strips*) are narratives told by means of a series of drawings arranged in horizontal lines, strips, or rectangles, called *panels*, and read like a verbal text from left to right. They usually depict the adventures, exploits, or lifestyles of one or more characters in a limited time sequence. Dialogue is presented as written words encircled by a balloon, which issue from the mouth or head of the character speaking. Movement is illustrated largely through the use of lines of different sizes. For example, long thin lines trailing a running horse show speed. Short broken lines trailing a frog indicate jumping

Origins and Spread

One of the first American works with the essential characteristics of a comic strip was created by Richard Felton Outcault and appeared in the series *Hogan's Alley*. It was published on May 5, 1895, in the New York newspaper *Sunday World*. The setting depicted squalid city tenements and backyards filled with dogs and cats, tough-looking characters, urchins, and ragamuffins. One of the urchins was a flap-eared, bald-headed, Oriental-looking child with a quizzical, shrewd smile. He was dressed in a long, dirty nightshirt, which Outcault often used as a placard to comment on the cartoon itself.

Other early comic strips included *The Little Bears* by James Guilford Swinnerton, which first appeared in the *San Francisco Examiner* in 1892, *The Katzenjammer Kids* by Rudolph Dirks, which first appeared in *The American Humorist* in 1897, and *Mutt and Jeff*, which first appeared as *Mr. A. Mutt* in a November 1907 issue of the *San Francisco Chronicle*. Newspaper syndicates introduced *Mutt and Jeff* to a wider audience, turning it into the first successful daily comic strip in the United States. It became so popular that, to satisfy demand, newspapers published collections of the individual strips. A 1911 collection was the first such collection and lead to an independent comic book publishing industry. In 1933, a number of comic books, based on well-known newspaper comic strips such as *Joe Palooka* and *Connie*, were even given out as premiums with certain merchandise.

While the Sunday newspaper comic strips were originally designed primarily for children, the daily comic strips were intended to attract adult audiences. Harry Hershfield's *Abie the Agent*, first published in 1914, was the first truly adult American comic strip, capitalizing on the popularity of the pulp detective and mystery genre of the era. One of the earliest and most influential contributors to the genre's evolution was Roy Crane, who created *Wash Tubbs* in 1924. The adventure genre began with the publication in 1929 of *Tarzan* and *Buck Rogers*—the former adapted from the novels of writer Edgar Rice Burroughs (1875–1950). Adventure comic strips became instantly popular and have remained so to this day for a simple reason—their characters never age. There have been exceptions to this pattern—starting with *Gasoline Alley* by Frank O. King where the characters aged day by day—but, by and large, the appeal of the comic genre is its timelessness. For someone reading a comic strip, time stands still, at least in the world of fantasy.

The adventure genre has always been among the most well-loved of comic strip and comic book genres. Great impetus was given to the comic book industry by the phenomenal success in 1938 of *Action Comics*, of which the principal attraction was the *Superman* comic strip, which was later published in separate *Superman* comic books. *Superman* also spawned a series of comic book hero clones in the early 1940s—the decade that saw the debuts of *Batman*, *The Flash*, *Green Lantern*, *Wonder Woman*, and *Captain America*.

Like the pop culture they reflect, it is impossible to dismiss comics as just "entertainment texts." A number of strips have, in fact, found a devoted following among intellectuals. *Krazy Kat*, for instance, has been regarded by many as one of the most amusing and imaginative works of narrative art ever produced in America. The art of Charles Schulz (1922–2000) also falls into the category of thought-provoking comics. His comic strip *Peanuts*, which was originally titled *Li'l Folks*, debuted in 1950 and became one of the most popular comic strips in history, appearing in more than two thousand newspapers and translated into more than twenty-four languages. Its characters—Charlie Brown, his sister Sally, his dog Snoopy, his friends Lucy, Linus, Schroeder, Peppermint Patty, and Marcie, and the bird Woodstock— have become icons of pop culture. The characters are all children, but they seem to have much more insight into life than do adults, who are relegated to the margins of the strip. Its tone is one of subtle sadness, a veiled angst that begs the readers to ask the great questions of philosophy: Why are we here? and What is life all about?

Starting in the 1970s, many individuals and small companies began competing with the larger publishers. "Indie" or alternative artists experimented with new styles, more sophisticated formats, and stories suited to adults. For example, they are responsible for the *graphic novel*, which is a book-length comic book that tells a single story for adults. The most celebrated examples of this genre are *Maus: A Survivor's Tale* (1986) and *Maus II* (1991) by Art Spiegelman. They recount the artist's relationship with his father and the experiences of his father and mother during the Holocaust.

Early on, comics appealed broadly because they became mixed-media narratives for the modern world, both reflecting modern life and helping to mold it. Before the advent of television, they set the style for clothing, coiffure, food, manners, and mores. They have inspired plays, musicals, ballets, motion pictures, radio and television series, popular songs, books, and toys. Everyday language is replete with idioms and words created for the comics. For example, the code word for the Allied Forces on D-Day was *Mickey Mouse*, and the password for the Norwegian Underground was *The Phantom*. Numerous contemporary painters and sculptors have incorporated comic book characters into their art works; motion picture directors have adapted techniques of the comics into their films; and of course, Bugs Bunny (with his *What's up, Doc?*), Homer Simpson (with his *D'oh*), Rocky and Bullwinkle (with their wry humor), the Grinch, the Flintstones, Fat Albert, Popeye, Scooby-Doo, Arthur, Winnie the Pooh, Mr. Magoo, Felix the Cat, Yogi Bear, Mighty Mouse, Batman, Woody Woodpecker, and Tom and Jerry, to mention just a few, have become household names.

Today, there are many online e-toons, most of which are ironic or satirical in intent. There is *Gary the Rat* (www.mediatrip.com), which (in its original version) is about a ruthless New York lawyer who gets turned into a huge rat, in obvious parodic imitation of Franz Kafka's (1883–1924) horrifying novella masterpiece *Metamorphosis*. The rat is hated by his landlord, who wants to evict him, and chased by an exterminator who is out to eliminate him. Yet Gary is adored by his boss because clients are eager to work with him. *Queer Duck* (www.icebox.com) satirizes the gullibility of people today. It is about a gay duck and his animal pals who are frequent crank callers to a well-known radio psychologist. *The God and Devil Show* (www.entertaindom.com) is a cartoon talk show hosted by a bearded ruler of heaven and a sexy leader of hell. Other early popular online e-toons are: *The Producer* (www.thethreshold.com), which parodies media producers and production; *Kung Fu 3D* (www.entertaindom.com), which is a web animation update of the American television series that starred David Carradine (1972–1975); *The Critic* (www.shockwave.com), which features an animated film critic who comments satirically on current movies and actors; and *Star Wars Network* (www.atomfilms.com), which spoofs the subculture spawned by the *Star Wars* movies of the 1960s and 1970s. At the time of publication of this book, these online toons may have disappeared and been replaced by others. The point to be made here is that e-toons have become almost completely ironic in focus, perhaps inspired by the success of *The Simpsons*. Irony is a basic mindset of the carnivalesque, and thus it comes as no surprise to find that it is now defining the theatrical mode in cyberspace.

Reading Comics

Their very name, *comics*, suggests much about their original nature and about how we read them—in a comedic frame of mind. Comics were initially meant to bring about laughter through mockery and parody. This is why they were called *the funnies*. The 1933 *Funnies on Parade*, a magazine-format compilation of newspaper comic features, clearly showed this medium's pointedly humorous basis—the early funnies were just that, funny in a lampooning way. The extension of the comic genre to include all pulp fiction themes occurred after the publication in 1938 of *Superman*.

The superhero genre is as popular today as it was in the 1930s. The reason is that, as Barthes argued (elaborated in chapter 2), it recycles an ancient code—the code of the hero. This code includes, among other features:

- **A life-saving journey in infancy**: Superman had to leave his home planet of Krypton, to avoid being destroyed along with the planet.

- **An obscure childhood**: Little is known about the early lives of most superhero characters. Occasionally, flashbacks are used to enlighten the current situation.
- **Orphanage**: Some superheroes, like Batman, Captain Marvel, Black Panther, and Cyclops, have lost their parents, as had many of the ancient mythic heroes.
- **Superhuman powers**: In one way or another, and to varying degrees, superhuman powers (be they physical or intellectual) are possessed by all fictional superheroes. These are sometimes gained in unusual ways. Spiderman, created in 1962, has special powers that he developed after being bitten by an irradiated spider gone berserk. This, combined with his unusual blood type, leaves him with superhuman strength and reflexes, a spider sense (which warns him of impending danger), and a spider's adhesive shooter (with which he can climb walls and ceilings).
- **A fatal weakness**: Whether it be exposure to kryptonite, blindness (Daredevil), or psychological problems of various kinds (the Hulk and most contemporary superheroes), the fatal weakness is a basic feature of the hero code—Achilles had a weak heel, Samson's strength depended on his long hair, and so on.
- **Selfless dedication to the public good:** Usually at the expense to their own personal lives, the heroes of ancient myths and the superheroes of comic books exist to help common folk.
- **A magic weapon**: Many ancient heroes had a magic weapon at their disposal. For example, the Norse god Thor had a powerful hammer. Similarly, Spiderman has his web shooters, spider-tracers, and a versatile belt; Hellstorm has a trident that can shoot out fire; Iron Man has a sophisticated suit of armor; Batman has a sophisticated car and an array of gadgets; and so on.

The superheroes have also evoked their share of moral panic (a concept discussed in chapter 2). In the 1950s concern over violence in comics led to Senate hearings, which led, in turn, to "underground comics" in the 1960s. Underground comic artists referred to their strips as *comix* to distinguish them from mainstream comics. However, as moral panic theory suggests, public outrage and concern about comics was to last only a brief period of time. By the early 1970s, society came to see comics not only as simple forms of entertainment but also as mementos of a previous, supposedly more innocent period. By the middle part of the decade, DC and Marvel revived their superheroes, and new ones came onto the scene.

Of particular interest to the development of the comic book genre is the fact that comic book heroes are now crossing over to the movies and vice versa, indicating a true convergence of media stages in this domain of pop culture. *Watchmen*, for example, has been referenced in the television series *Lost* and *Buffy the Vampire Slayer*. *V for Vendetta*, *From Hell*, and *The League of Extraordinary Gentlemen* have all led to movie versions. *Watchmen* (released in 1986) is particularly interesting. It is about Rorschach, a demented vigilante with a morphing inkblot mask (hence his name) who investigates the murder of a character called the Comedian. Rorschach and the Comedian are parodies of superheroes. As Richard Reynolds (1992: 107) has remarked: "While the Comedian is in part a satirical reworking of the state-sponsored, nationalistic breed of superhero most notably exemplified by Captain America or Nick Fury, Rorschach is a version of the night-shrouded hero embodied by characters from Batman through Daredevil." In carnival theory, parody and irony reign supreme and—therefore, it comes as no surprise that a comic book has come forward to satirize the comic book genre itself.

Comics have broad appeal because they constitute a perfect example of how fantasy, the comedic, and the grotesque are intertwined in pop culture materials and spectacles. No wonder they are so appealing. People today look at the comic books of their childhood with a great sense of wistfulness. During the latter half of the twentieth century, comics became very popular items for collectors. Today the comic book is still popular, but the genre has crossed over almost completely to the movie medium, where Superman, Spiderman, the Fantastic Four, Batman, and many other comic book heroes now reign supreme. The form has also crossed over to the television sitcom, from *Beavis and Butthead* to *The Simpsons* and *South Park*, where it has reacquired its comedic and parodic functions. But perhaps comics' most critical crossover has been online. Webcomics, also known as online comics, are offering the whole range of comic genres, from the funnies to adventure superheroes and beyond, to new generations of readers across the globe.

It is also noteworthy that comics have started to change in step with broader social changes. For instance, Batwoman, who was introduced in 1956, has become a lesbian in her new incarnation. Black Panther is the king of a fictitious African nation. And the Great Ten are a team of Chinese heroes, including Mother of Champions, who can give birth to as many as twenty-five super-soldiers. Already in 1988 DC Comics published *The New Guardians*, which included an aboriginal girl, an Eskimo man, and an HIV-positive gay man as its superheroes. The great white male hero story of traditional adventure comics has finally been deconstructed and a more expansive story is now being told in its place.

4

RADIO

Captured by the radio as soon as she or he awakens, the listener
walks all day long through the forest of narrativities.

Michel de Certeau (1925–1986)

The *War of the Worlds* radio broadcast incident on Halloween night of
1938, mentioned briefly in chapter 2, showed how representation can
blur the line between fiction (fantasy) and reality. It was the famous actor
and director, Orson Welles (1915–1985), who transformed H. G. Wells's
novel into a radio drama, frightening many listeners into believing that Martians had landed and invaded New Jersey. Welles was able to bring about
this reality-simulating effect with a series of "on-the-spot" news reports
describing the landing of Martian spaceships. An announcer would remind
the radio audience, from time to time, that the show was fictional. Even so,
many listeners went into a state of panic, believing Martians had actually
invaded the Earth. The police and the army were notified by concerned
citizens; people ran onto the streets shouting hysterically; and some even
contemplated suicide. The reaction took Welles and his acting company by
surprise. They did not expect that people would take the show seriously—
after all, it was just that, a *show.* The actors and producers had forgotten or
ignored Plato's warning that representation and reality are almost impossible
for people to separate psychologically, especially when the former simulates
the latter.

The *War of the Worlds* incident is now famous in the annals of media
and pop culture history, and it underscores the powerful role that the first
electronic stage, *radio,* played in promoting pop culture and ensconcing it
in the mainstream. By the 1930s radio had become the primary locus for
the performance and spread of pop culture fare. That medium is still around,

97

although it has lost much of its former supremacy. This chapter will look at the electronic venue through which pop culture thrived for many years and through which it still finds a niche that attracts large audiences.

RADIO BROADCASTING

In 1837, the telegraph became the first electronic system of international communications. It soon became obvious, however, that the telegraph was relatively inefficient because it depended on a complex system of receiving stations wired to each other along a fixed route. In 1895, the American engineer Guglielmo Marconi (1874–1937) transmitted an electronic signal successfully to a receiving device that had no wired connection to his transmitter, thus demonstrating that a signal could be sent through space so that devices at random points could receive it. He called his invention a *radiotelegraph* (later shortened to *radio*) because its signal moved outward in all directions (that is, *radially*) from the point of transmission. Thus radio was introduced into the world.

As a mass communications device, at first called appropriately the *wireless*, the radio changed the world when, in 1901, Marconi developed an alternator appliance that could send signals much farther and with much less background noise. This advance led, about two decades later, to the development of commercial technology that established the radio as the first electronic pop culture medium, shaping trends in music, lifestyle, and society generally. Radio could reach many more people than print, not only because it could span great distances instantly, but also because its audiences did not have to be print-literate. Programming could thus be designed with mass appeal. Radio was therefore pivotal in spreading pop culture—a culture for all, not just the literati and the cognoscenti.

Historical Sketch

Evidence of a plan for radio broadcasting to the general public can be found in a 1916 memorandum written by David Sarnoff (1891–1971), an employee of Marconi's U.S. branch, American Marconi, which would eventually become the Radio Corporation of America (RCA). In the memo, Sarnoff recommended that radio be made into a "household utility." This plan was not given any serious consideration by management at first. After World War I ended in 1918, however, several manufacturing companies began to seriously explore Sarnoff's idea for the mass-marketing of home radio receivers, leading to mass-scale radio broadcasting.

In an effort to boost radio sales in peacetime, the Westinghouse Electric Corporation of Pittsburgh established what many culture historians consider to be the first commercially owned radio station, which offered a regular schedule of programming to the general public. It came to be known by the call letters KDKA, after it received its license from the Department of Commerce (which held regulatory power following the end of the war) in October of 1920. KDKA aired various kinds of popular programs, including recorded music, which was generated by a phonograph placed within the range of a microphone. The station did not charge user fees to listeners, nor did it carry paid advertisements. Westinghouse used KDKA simply as an enticement for people to purchase home radio receivers.

Other radio manufacturers soon followed suit. The General Electric Company, for example, broadcast its own programs on station WGY in Schenectady, New York. Seeing the rise of radio as a mass communications medium, RCA eventually gave Sarnoff permission to develop radio programming for home entertainment. Sarnoff opened stations in New York City and Washington, D.C., and in 1926 he founded the National Broadcasting Company (NBC), an RCA subsidiary created for the specific purpose of broadcasting programs via a cross-country network of stations. The Columbia Broadcasting System (CBS) radio service was established shortly thereafter in 1928 and became a dominant force in the American broadcasting industry over the subsequent fifty years. Already in 1922, AT&T began exploring the possibilities of toll broadcasting—that is, of charging fees in return for the airing of commercial advertisements on its stations. Fearing legal action, however, the telephone company sold its stations to RCA and left the broadcasting business. In return, AT&T was granted the exclusive right to provide the connections that would link local stations to the NBC network.

The sale of radios more than justified the expense to manufacturers of operating broadcasting services. According to estimates by the National Association of Broadcasters, in 1922 there were sixty thousand households in the United States with radios; by 1929 the number had topped 10 million. But vast increases in sales of radio receivers could not continue forever. The sale of advertising time loomed, consequently, as the only viable solution for the economic survival of American radio broadcasting. The merger of advertising with radio programming was the event that, arguably, trans-

A Radio Timeline

1890s: Guglielmo Marconi develops the first radio transmitter.

1906–1910: Lee De Forest invents the vacuum tube, called the Audion tube, improving radio reception. Reginald Fessenden makes the first radio broadcast, from the Metropolitan Opera House in New York City.

1910: Congress passes the Wireless Ship Act, requiring ships to be equipped with wireless radio.

1912: Congress passes the Radio Act, the first piece of government regulation for radio transmission.

1916: David Sarnoff, the commercial manager of American Marconi, writes a famous memo, the radio music box memo, in which he proposes to his boss to make radio a "household utility."

1916–1920: Frank Conrad founds KDKA in Pittsburgh as the first radio station in 1916. The station's broadcast of the 1920 presidential election results on November 2, 1920, is generally considered to constitute the beginning of professional broadcasting.

1922: The first uses of radio for commercial purposes begin with the airing of the first advertisements, by AT&T on station WEAF. This causes an uproar, as people challenge the use of the public airwaves for commercial messages.

1926: The first radio broadcasting network, NBC, is launched by RCA.

1927: A new Radio Act passed by Congress creates the Federal Radio Commission. AM stations are allocated.

formed the nature of mass communications. Noncommercial broadcasting would play only a minor role in the United States and there would not be a coast-to-coast noncommercial radio network until the establishment of National Public Radio (NPR) in 1970. In Great Britain, on the other hand, radio owners have always paid yearly license fees, collected by the government, which are turned over directly to the publicly run British Broadcasting Corporation (BBC).

Radio broadcasting reached the pinnacle of its popularity and influence during World War II. In that period, American commentator Edward R. Murrow (1908–1965) changed the nature of news reporting permanently with his sensational descriptions of street scenes during the German bombing raids of London, which he delivered as an eyewitness from the rooftop

1933: FM radio is introduced.

1934: The Federal Communications Commission (FCC) is created by an act of Congress.

1938: Mercury Theater of the air broadcasts *The War of the Worlds*, demonstrating how a mass medium can cause public panic.

1947: Radio starts to lose audiences to television.

1948: The DJ radio era takes off.

1949: *Red Hot 'n Blue* becomes one of the first radio rock-and-roll shows.

1955: Top 40 radio becomes the most popular type of radio format, indicating that radio is becoming more and more a marketing arm of the recording industry. Rock-and-roll enters the scene in the mid-1950s. It will dominate pop music radio until the early 1990s.

1970s: FM radio stations gain popularity, transforming radio into an increasingly specialized medium.

1971: National Public Radio starts broadcasting with *All Things Considered*.

1979: Sony engineer Akio Morita invents the portable Walkman.

1987: WFAN is launched as the first all-sports radio station.

1990s: Talk radio becomes popular. Old and new music genres, from country to gospel to opera, attract niche audiences.

1996: Congress passes the Telecommunications Act, allowing consolidation of radio ownership across the United States.

2000s: Satellite and web-based radio programs emerge in 2002. File-sharing, online radio programs, and the like become highly popular.

of the CBS news bureau there. In the same time frame, American president Franklin D. Roosevelt utilized radio as a propaganda device for the first time. The radio allowed him to bypass the press and directly address the American people with his "fireside chats" during the Great Depression. Roosevelt knew that the emotional power of the voice would be much more persuasive than would any logical argument he might put into print. The chats continue to this day as part of the American presidency. Adolf Hitler, too, saw the radio as a propaganda medium and used it to persuade millions to follow him in his quest to conquer the world. Also, the radio appeal from Japanese emperor Hirohito to his nation for unconditional surrender helped end World War II following the atomic bombings of Hiroshima and Nagasaki.

Radio broadcasting dramatically changed social life wherever it was introduced. By bringing information, critical commentary, and the arts directly into homes it democratized argument and aesthetics more than any other medium in the history of civilization. Historically a privilege of the aristocracy (or the cognoscenti), the arts could now be enjoyed by members of the general public, most of whom would otherwise not have access to venues such as the concert hall and the theater. The parallel growth of network radio and Hollywood cinema, both of which were launched as commercial enterprises in 1927, created an unprecedented mass culture for people of all social classes and educational backgrounds. While it is true that the democratization of culture was started in the domain of print (as mentioned in the previous chapter), it would not have become as widespread without radio for the simple reason that radio could reach more people, print-literate or not, solely for the initial (one-time) cost of a radio receiver.

In the Internet Galaxy, radio has shown itself to have remarkable staying power. It is estimated that there are about 2 billion radio sets in use worldwide, with more than half concentrated in North America, the European Union countries, and Japan. In developing societies, too, most citizens

From the 1920s to the early 1950s, radio broadcasting was society's primary medium of information, arts appreciation, and leisure.

©iStockphoto.com/Kati Neudert

own or have access to a radio. Radio is also technologically adaptive. All-digital satellite radio stations, such as XM and Sirius, are springing up regularly. In sum, the radio is not yet a relic in the Internet Galaxy. It may have come down from its top perch, but it continues, nevertheless, to be an integral part of mass communications and a promoter of pop culture fare.

Genres

At first, radio was no more than a new audio medium for delivering print and theatrical forms of pop culture. For example, it adapted the various genres of traditional stage drama, transforming them into radio dramas. It took the material of pulp fiction and converted it into action serials, situation comedies (or *sitcoms*), and soap operas. It looked to vaudeville to garner and adapt material for its comedy-variety programming. And it modeled its news coverage on the format of daily newspapers—early announcers would, in fact, often simply read articles from the local newspaper over the air. Because of its capacity to reach large numbers of people, from the 1920s to the early 1950s radio broadcasting evolved into society's primary medium of information, arts appreciation, and, above all else, leisure. Only after the advent of television in the 1950s did radio's hegemony begin to erode, as its audiences split into smaller, distinct segments. Today, radio is primarily a medium that people listen to in automobiles (during drive time) and at workplaces (while working). Because radio executives are aware of their audience's typical patterns of listening, stations generally present news and traffic information interspersed at regular intervals throughout their broadcasts and/or present uninterrupted stretches of music during certain periods of the working day. Many radio stations offer programming for niche audiences (sports stations, talk stations, and so on).

Despite the obvious differences between radio and television, the development of programming for both broadcast media is best understood as a single history comprised of two stages—that is, two pop culture venues and also two periods of time. Early radio broadcasting was dominated by adaptations of pulp fiction and vaudevillian genres. The sitcom, for example, was adapted from an improvised form of vaudevillian comedy that, itself, traced its roots back to the *commedia dell'arte*—a comedy form that emerged in Italy in the sixteenth and seventeenth centuries, characterized by the enactment of a standard comedic plot outline and stock characters. The commedia became a highly popular form of *street theater*, as opposed to the literary drama of the court and the academies that was performed on court stages. Common folk came in flocks to attend performances. Commedia troupes set up their makeshift stages in piazzas in much the same way as traveling circuses set up their tents in market squares. The script consisted of a *scenario* (an outline of a basic plot) and the actors wore masks to emphasize their character profile. The same actor always played the same role, adapting it through improvisation to the unfolding performance and the reactions of the audience. Most of the farcical plots dealt with love affairs, illicit or otherwise. Some of the characters, like Harlequin the clown and Pantaloon the old man, became so popular that their masks were worn by people at carnival time.

Radio sitcoms were descendants of the commedia genre that were adapted to new social realities. Like the commedia scripts, the sitcoms explored life, love, and romance in the home, the workplace, and other common locations in a comedic and often farcical manner. The sitcom became, consequently, very popular across audiences. The most highly rated sitcom was *Amos 'n' Andy*, in which actors performed the stereotypical roles of African American characters in outrageous caricature. The series premiered on NBC in 1928 and ran for twenty years on radio before moving to television, where it ran from 1951 to 1953. Similarly, *The Goldbergs* (1929–1950), *Life with Luigi* (1948–1953), and other ethnic family sitcoms successfully exploited the vocal character of the radio medium, as actors used thick immigrant accents and malapropisms to carve out their roles and characters. Lucille Ball's radio show *My Favorite Husband* (1948–1951) was a notable exception to the standard radio sitcom fare, developing its comedic artistry considerably. *My Favorite Husband* transformed elements such as the battle between the sexes, arguments among neighbors, and other mundane conflicts into matters of social concern and reflection.

Variety shows and dramas were also popular genres of early radio. The former were taken directly from vaudeville. Many early radio stars, including Jack Benny, Fred Allen, and Edgar Bergen, were originally vaudeville actors and comedians. A radio comedy-variety hour typically consisted of short monologues and skits featuring the host. These were alternated with various acts, including singers, musicians, comedians, and the like. Radio drama also became highly popular early on. The genre was presented in one of two formats—*anthology* and *serial*. The former showcased individual plays, such as one would expect to see on stage or in motion pictures. Anthology drama became highly popular in the 1930s and 1940s. Programs included *Mercury Theater on the Air* (1938–1941), created by Orson Welles (mentioned previously), and *Theatre Guild of the Air* (1945–1954). However, serial drama, using recurring characters, situations, and settings, was even more popular. Subgenres in this format included urban police dramas, such as *Gangbusters* (1935–1957), private eye mysteries, such as *The Shadow* (1930–1954), and westerns, such as *The Lone Ranger* (1933–1955)—all radio adaptations of pulp fiction stories and characters. The radio narratives became quickly *textual coordinates* for an entire society—that is, they provided reference points to which people could turn in their everyday discourse ("Did you hear how cleverly the Shadow solved the mystery?"). Radio drama virtually disappeared by the mid-1950s as its biggest stars and most popular programs crossed over to television—the emerging pop culture stage of the era.

Another very popular radio genre was the soap opera, or daily serial drama, which was originally developed as a daytime programming format aimed specifically at a female audience. The genre was so named because soap and detergent manufacturers sponsored many of the dramas. Soap operas explored romance, friendship, and familial relations in emotionally involving narrative formats. The invention of the soap opera is credited to Irna Phillips, who began developing proto–soap operas for local radio broadcast in Chicago during the 1920s. However, the first true soap opera is generally thought to be *Painted Dreams*, which premiered in 1930. It was a flop because it included too much advertising. However, its themes of romance, betrayal, and sexual intrigue became the ingredients that made (and continue to make) soap operas such as *The Guiding Light*, *Backstage Wife*, and *The Romance of Helen Trent* popular and entertaining. The genre was well-liked, arguably, because of its carnivalesque admixture of sex, betrayal, and romance. From the 1930s to the 1950s soap operas constituted a modern-day morality play. Sin and violence, which always occurred in "offstage" situations, frequently affected the lives of characters negatively. However, as in the morality plays of old, good inevitably triumphed, or at the very least wrongdoing was properly punished.

In the area of news reporting, radio could offer its audiences live coverage of events—something that newspapers could not do. The immediacy with which radio news reached people redefined the role of news reporting in society. Print journalism became a supplemental medium, focusing on in-depth coverage and editorial opinion. Today, radio continues to be a primary source of news reporting. So-called drive time (7–9 A.M. and 4–7 P.M., when most commuters are traveling to and from work) has become radio's prime time. Programming during these hours includes traffic bulletins, weather reports, breaking and current news items, and time checks. Some stations have now adopted news-only formats, reflecting radio's evolution into a medium for specialized audiences. National Public Radio's *All Things Considered* (1971–) and *Morning Edition* (1979–), for example, were developed as morning and evening on-air newspapers for sophisticated audiences. The variety and tailoring of radio programs and stations illustrates once again that the pop culture stage has room for all kinds of acts, from the vulgar to the highly sophisticated.

Among the acts that radio has always showcased are music and talk. Radio has traditionally been a promoter of trends in pop music. The jazz, swing, rock, and hip-hop movements would not have become as dominant as they did without radio. Radio hit parades have always featured new and old tunes, spurring consumers to buy records. Today, a host of radio stations provide specialized pop music broadcasting, from adult contemporary to classical music to jazz. Radio has also historically been a medium for talk. The original talk shows were little more than commentaries on politics and current affairs. But this genre soon broadened to include gossip and "shock talk." The contemporary talk show is usually a pastiche of gossip and commentary. The emphasis on luridness by some talk radio hosts is not unlike the custom of burlesque emcees and actors to enter into salacious and prurient talk with audience members. *Interactivity* is not an invention of the Digital Age. It has always been part of the allure of pop culture performances.

THE RADIO STAGE

Since it took over the vaudevillian and pulp fiction genres and adapted them to a new medium for broader audience reception, promoting pop culture as a society-wide mode of culture in the first half of the twentieth century, radio can be singled out as perhaps the most important media stage in history. Its influence on society cannot be overstated. The German Jewish refugee Anne Frank (1929–1945) perceptively wrote the following about radio in her famous diary (from *The Diary of a Young Girl*, 1947, p. 45):

> The radio goes on early in the morning and is listened to at all hours of the day, until nine, ten and often eleven o'clock in the evening. This is certainly a sign that the grown-ups have infinite patience, but it also means that the power of absorption of their brains is pretty limited, with exceptions, of course—I don't want to hurt anyone's feelings. One or two news bulletins would be ample per day! But the old geese, well—I've said my piece!

The radio was the perfect stage for an engagement in fantasy. As former presidential speechwriter Peggy Noonan has aptly phrased it, "TV gives everyone an image, but radio gives birth to a million images in a million brains" (cited in *What I Saw at the Revolution*, 1990, p. 34). Hearing is a more powerful stimulus for fantasizing, Noonan suggests, than is seeing. One cannot but agree with this assessment. Nowhere did radio's image-producing power become more evident than in the partnership that radio formed with advertising—the maximal promoter of dreams and fantasies.

Radio and Advertising

The newspaper was the first medium to converge with advertising. The two still go hand in hand. The same kind of convergence story can be written for radio a little later in time. A radio genre—the soap opera—was even named for the type of advertiser that sponsored it. In the United States advertising agencies produced almost all network radio shows before the development of network television. Stations often sold agencies full sponsorship, which included placing the product name in a program's title, as in *The Palmolive Beauty Box Theater* (1927–1937) or *The Texaco Star Theater* (1948–1953). Entire radio programs became associated with products. The ratings system arose, in fact, from the sponsors' desire to know how many people they were reaching with their advertising. In 1929 Archibald Crossley launched *Crossley's Cooperative Analysis of Broadcasting*, which used telephone surveys to project daily estimates of audience size for the national radio networks. The A. C. Nielsen Company, which had been surveying audience size in radio since the mid-1930s, eventually became the dominant ratings service. The resulting projections, or *ratings*, helped determine the price of advertisements and, ultimately, whether the program would stay on the air or be canceled. Only public radio stations have remained exempt from the "ratings game," since they are financed by government subsidies, individual donations, and corporate grants.

Radio introduced onto the pop culture stage the *commercial*—a mini-narrative or musical jingle revolving around a product or service and its uses. The commercial became a highly successful form of advertising because it could reach masses of potential customers instantaneously through the persuasive capacity of the human voice—which could be seductive, friendly, cheery, insistent, or foreboding, as required by the nature of the product. Early radio commercials consisted of pseudoscientific sales pitches, satires of movies, and snappy jingles. These commercials became so familiar that public perception of a product became inextricably intertwined with the style and content of the commercials created to promote it. The commercial allowed for the first fictitious advertising personalities, from Mr. Clean (representing a detergent product of the same name) to Speedy (a personified Alka-Seltzer indigestion tablet). Commercials also became a source of dissemination of recognizable tunes throughout society, from "Mr. Clean in just a minute" (for the Mr. Clean detergent product) to "Plop, plop, fizz, fizz—oh, what a relief it is" (for the Alka-Seltzer stomach product).

From the outset, radio advertising both reflected and set social trends. A synergy thus quickly developed between advertising campaigns and general lifestyle trends, as advertisers attempted to keep in step with changing trends and, at the same time, shape them through their commercials. Commercials were designed to have great appeal and indeed became popular in themselves. Some jingles became well-liked tunes. Even today, people recognize tunes such as "I'd like to teach the world to sing in perfect harmony" without realizing that they started out as jingles for a product (in this case, Coca-Cola).

Radio programs and brand advertising today are totally integrated. Commercials are interspersed throughout a program, informing listeners of products that are relevant to audiences of the program. Radio advertising has the advantage that people can listen to commercials while doing other things, such as driving a car or working at home. Another advantage is that radio audiences, in general, are more easily categorized according to tastes and lifestyle preferences. For example, stations that feature country music attract different kinds of listeners than do those that play rock. Therefore, audience members can be more readily identified as probable consumers of certain types of beverages, automobiles, and the like. By selecting the station in this way, advertisers can intelligently target their commercials, using ad scripts psychologically and socially suited to their customer base.

Orality

Even in a television and online world, radio remains an effective media stage for a basic psychological reason—the emotional power of the human voice. When it was the main stage for promoting the broader spectacle of pop culture, people were mesmerized by radio and often listened together as they sat quietly around the radio after dinner (thus transforming the after-dinner period to what later came to be called *prime time*.) The deep voices that introduced horror programs such as *Inner Sanctum* frightened listeners, while it was in reassuring tones that the voices of commercial announcers came through the same "magic box" to promote products and services. The voices of sitcom actors turned them into household characters, recognized by one and all through their vocal timbres and particular phonetic manner- isms. And, of course, the sultry and seductive tones of actresses and the virile masculine tones of actors never failed to create sexual interest—an interest that has always been a basis of the appeal of pop culture spectacles. In vaude- ville, singers and comedians made their fame as much through quality of voice as through appearance. The ability to control and utilize the voice onstage has always been a basic theatrical skill. To this day, radio announcers are judged on the basis of their vocal qualities more than on the content of their discussions (which are mainly scripted) or on the beauty or handsome- ness of their appearance.

Radio revived orality as a mode of mass communication, complement- ing the print mode discussed in the previous chapter. Orality has great emo- tional appeal and reaches back into history. Before the advent of alphabets, people communicated and passed on their knowledge through the spoken word. Of course, early oral cultures had invented tools, which were invari- ably pictographic, for recording and preserving ideas in durable physical form. But pictography did not alter the basic oral nature of daily communi- cation, nor did it alter early societies' oral mode of transmitting knowledge and of entertaining people through storytelling. Storytelling is the oldest form of folk culture. Since people started to communicate with each other, children and adults alike have requested, "Tell me a story." Our familiar myths, legends, and fables all arose out of storytelling culture. Reading and writing activate linear thinking processes in the brain, because printed ideas are laid out one at a time and can thus be connected to each other sequen- tially and analyzed logically in relation to each other. Orality, on the other hand, is not conducive to such precise thinking, because spoken ideas are transmitted through the emotional qualities of the human voice and are, thus, inextricable from the subject who transmits them. Literacy engenders the sense that knowledge and information are disconnected from their human sources and thus that they have "objectivity." Orality does not impart this sense.

As the history of radio has shown, the social functions of orality have not disappeared from modern life. The spoken word comes naturally; liter- acy does not. Radio clearly highlighted the differences between literacy and orality. As an oral medium that reintroduced the art of storytelling to mod- ern audiences, it also restimulated interest in oral communication generally.

Our fascination with orality might explain why such seemingly inane genres as talk shows continue to attract large audiences. Like sermons and oratorical performances generally, radio's persuasive effects are due to the sensory qualities of the human voice. As Benjamin Franklin (1706–1790) so aptly put it in his *Autobiography* (1771–1790, p. 234), there is no denying the power of the voice to convince and entertain:

> Every accent, every emphasis, every modulation of voice, was so perfectly well turned and well placed, that, without being interested in the subject, one could not help being pleased with the discourse; a pleasure of much the same kind with that received from an excellent piece of music. This is an advantage itinerant preachers have over those who are stationary, as the latter can not well improve their delivery of a sermon by so many rehearsals.

THE BIRTH OF CELEBRITY CULTURE

Radio personalities were the first true pop icons. Radio names including Louis Armstrong, Bing Crosby, Milton Berle, Bob Hope, and Lucille Ball became as recognizable and important to Americans as those of presidents and writers. From this pattern a celebrity culture crystallized and spread broadly, becoming socially all-embracing.

The topic of celebrities is central in pop culture studies. Celebrity culture and pop culture are really one and the same. Andy Warhol (1930–1987) showed himself to be a perceptive observer of pop culture trends with his comment that today everyone can have his or her "fifteen minutes of fame." Warhol was the first artist to realize the intrinsic connection between celebrity culture and pop culture. He also realized that a celebrity need not necessarily be a real person but could be, instead, a product or a fictional character (for example, a cartoon character such as Mickey Mouse or Bugs Bunny, or a comic book superhero such as Superman or Spiderman). Warhol's artistic subjects included both famous commercial products, such as Campbell's soup cans and Coca-Cola soft-drink bottles, and human celebrities, such as Elizabeth Taylor and Marilyn Monroe.

Celebrities

Adopting Warhol's categories, a celebrity is a person, fictional character, or commercial product that garners a high degree of public and media attention by virtue of the fact that he or she (or it) is on the media stage. There is a difference between *fame* and *celebrity*. Politicians or scientists may be famous, but they are not necessarily celebrities, unless the interest of the general public and the mass media are piqued in tandem. A classic example is Albert Einstein, who was famous as a scientist but also became a celebrity through the attention paid by the media to his personal life. Like a movie star, Einstein has been represented in comic strips and on T-shirts, greeting cards, and many other paraphernalia associated with pop culture. But Einstein was an exception. It is mass entertainment personalities, such as soap opera actors or pop music stars, who are most likely to become celebrities, even if they deliberately avoid media attention. The inevitability of celebrity for entertainment stars became obvious in the radio era, when a famous radio actor would receive everyone's attention when simply shopping or walking down the street.

Celebrities who become extremely popular and symbolic of something are known as pop icons. The actress Marilyn Monroe (1926–1962) is an example of a pop icon. Marilyn's great beauty in movies made her an overnight sex symbol in the ever-expanding pop culture carnival of her era. But in spite of her success, Monroe had a tragic life and died at the age of thirty-six from an overdose of sleeping pills. Since her death, she has become one of the most written-about film stars in history. Elvis Presley (1935–1977) is another example of a pop icon. Elvis was one of the first American stars of rock music and perhaps the greatest in the genre. He gained popularity through the radio, as his songs constantly hit the top of the charts. His voice and his particular style of musical delivery became the standards of rock, as every Saturday hordes of teenagers listened to Top 40 radio to hear their hero excite them with his unique brand of singing. His popularity continued after his death and he has risen to almost legendary status, as in the case of Marilyn Monroe. Movies and programs about Elvis are made to this day, and his music continues to be re-released. As mentioned throughout this book, nostalgia is a powerful force in the preservation of pop culture through the ages. Highlighting the importance of nostalgia, Elvis has become an even more celebrated figure since his death. The devotion of his fans is almost religious in its intensity, although it is starting to diminish as they age or pass away. His home in Graceland has become a major shrine to his memory. Thousands of fans from around the world continue to make pilgrimages to Graceland, especially on the anniversary of his death.

Decoding Celebrity

The analogy between Elvis and religion is not purely figurative. It is intended to show the probable underlying rationale for the crystallization and spread of celebrity culture. Indeed, the use of the term *icon* in *pop icon* is appropriate on various counts. First, an icon is something that can be easily recognized (the word is used this way in the terminology of computers). Pop icons are clearly recognizable by virtually everyone. Second, the word has a religious sense. It can refer to a painting considered sacred in the Eastern Orthodox Churches, created according to rules established by church authorities, which are intended to emphasize the heavenly glory of the holy subjects portrayed. Pop icons are similarly imbued by the media stage on which they perform with a quasi-religious quality. As a consequence, they are idolized in ways that parallel the idolatry of religious figures.

Thus, pop culture's celebrity-making effect can also be called a *mythologizing* effect because the celebrities that it creates are perceived as mythic figures, larger than life. Like any type of privileged space designed to impart focus and significance to someone (for example, a platform or a podium), a media stage such as radio, cinema, or television creates mythic personages simply by containing them, suspended in a mythic world of their own. It is because of its mythologizing powers that the radio was called a "magic box." It was at first perceived as similar to the speaking boxes of childhood fantasies. Radio personages became infused with godlike qualities by virtue of the fact that they were heard emanating from the magic box. The same effect is created by all media stages. It is because of the "magic" of pop culture that meeting movie actors, sitcom stars, and the like causes great enthusiasm and excitement in many people. These stars are perceived as otherworldly figures who have stepped out of the magic box to take on human proportions, in the same way that a mythic hero such as Prometheus came into our human world to help us.

Early or tragic death often helps establish pop icon status. Marilyn Monroe and Elvis Presley both died relatively young and under tragic circumstances—Monroe apparently committed suicide and Elvis died of a drug overdose. Similarly, James Dean, Bruce Lee, Tupac Shakur, and Kurt Cobain (to mention but a few) have achieved pop icon status through their premature and tragic deaths. The assassination of John F. Kennedy transformed the young president into a pop icon as well. But pop icon status can also be achieved through longevity. Many still-living celebrities attain the status of pop icon if they are able to continue being popular across generations. Examples include the Rolling Stones, Cher, and Madonna—and also such fictional characters as Bugs Bunny, Superman, and Batman, and such products as Campbell's soup, Coca-Cola, and Pepsi. The earning of pop icon status is in contrast to the overnight assumption of *pop idol* status. The latter type of fame tends to be brief. The pop icon, on the other hand, like a mythic figure, is perceived to have left a lasting and indelible mark and attains an enduring place of recognition in society at large. It is because of their pop icon status that Elvis and the Beatles are represented on such public items as stamps, alongside the figures of presidents and scientists. Indeed, a poll of the best-known personages of the previous one hundred years, taken at the millennium (in 2000), showed that most were pop icons. It is amazing to ponder how many people today recognize the names of pop icons of the present and past, as I myself discovered in a 2006 survey of my own students at the University of Toronto (nearly one thousand students in total). Virtually all my students recognized the names I selected from my own recollection of pop culture history. From each of the various pop culture eras I chose four names (as they came to my mind), covering the whole spectrum of spectacles, from music to sports. Of course, some of these celebrities are still around. But even the names of those who have passed away were easily recognized.

The list could be expanded almost ad infinitum and, I am sure, it would still garner a high degree of recognition with people of all ages today. The reason is that many former pop icons (indeed, probably all) continue to have some form of fan basis or acknowledgment through reissues of their work or replays of the spectacles in which they starred. They are the *figures*

Table 4.1. Pop Icons Chosen Randomly

Era	Pop Icons
1920s	Rudolph Valentino, Charlie Chaplin, Mickey Mouse, Babe Ruth
1930s	Bing Crosby, Superman, Louis Armstrong, Greta Garbo
1940s	Humphrey Bogart, Judy Garland, Batman, the Lone Ranger
1950s	Marilyn Monroe, Elvis Presley, James Dean, Lucille Ball
1960s	the Beatles, the Rolling Stones, Bob Dylan, Aretha Franklin
1970s	John Travolta, the Grateful Dead, Bruce Lee, Burt Reynolds
1980s	Madonna, Michael Jackson, Tina Turner, Cher
1990s	Michael Jordan, Tiger Woods, Courtney Love, Tom Cruise
2000s	Britney Spears, Matt Damon, Angelina Jolie, Paris Hilton

(as the term *icon* implies) that have become part of pop culture nostalgia. Without them there would be no continuity in pop culture. There is no form of culture without history, and it therefore comes as no surprise that pop culture has generated its own historical personages and institutions, including museums, academic disciplines, and the like, which tend to perpetuate it.

Pop icons and celebrities influence society broadly. Their clothing styles, for example, are imitated, as are their speech mannerisms. I recall that many of my adolescent peers in the 1950s imitated the southern drawl of Elvis and in the 1960s the British accent of the Beatles—mainly in a subconscious fashion. Instances of such mimesis have occurred throughout pop culture history. During the 1920s, many young men wore patent leather hair, which they slicked down with oil in the manner of the movie star Rudolph Valentino. In the 1950s, many sported a crew cut, in which the hair was cut extremely short and combed upward to resemble a brush, in imitation of movie actors; while others sported a ducktail (with the hair long on the sides and swept back), in imitation of stars such as James Dean. During the 1960s, young men copied the haircuts of the Beatles, who wore long bangs that covered the forehead. Also, needless to say, imitation of the clothing styles, speech mannerisms, and overall demeanor of rap stars in the 1990s was evident across the youth spectrum, as was a "girl power" fashion and body style on the part of women, in imitation of Lara Croft, Xena the Warrior Princess, and others.

Of course, each country has its own celebrity system, with its own history of film, radio, television, and sports stars. In Italy, for example, names such as Marcello Mastroianni, Sofia Loren, Renato Carosone, and Totò evoke the same kinds of iconic responses as do American names such as Marlon Brando and Marilyn Monroe. A similar celebrity-based history of diverse pop cultures can be written for India, Germany, Japan, Spain, or France, to mention but a handful of nations. In the Internet Age, though, the celebrity-making stage has become truly international. The global village has even made it possible for people outside of the usual stage to gain celebrity status. Two well-known examples include the late Mother Teresa and Pope John Paul II. In the global village, the media spotlight is cast on anyone who is deemed to be newsworthy. The media spotlight similarly mythologizes both actors and saints. It also brings before the public eye the exploits of *dark celebrities*, as they may be called, including serial killers and ruthless businessmen such as Donald Trump. Even academics can gain celebrity status if their ideas are showcased by the media spotlight. The blurring of the lines of who and what is considered newsworthy, and eligible for celebrity status, is evidenced moreover in the tendency of evangelical preachers to take on the very personality features seen in celebrity culture, and to use the very props employed in pop culture (such as entertaining music and overall spectacle), to promote their version of Christianity. From Jimmy Swaggart to contemporary "celebrity preachers," it would seem that the search for celebrity status is, as Warhol suspected, a symptom of the modern world—a world that now writes its history using references to Marilyn Monroe and Elvis Presley alongside references to John F. Kennedy and Albert Einstein.

From its crystallization in early radio and movies, the celebrity culture in which we live today is part and parcel of the modern world, connected to economic, political, technological, and general cultural developments. As a consequence, the media now have developed a sector devoted to the documentation of celebrities. Magazines like *People* and various tabloids, talk shows, and entire channels and websites devote their full contents to celebrities and their private lives. These sources of news regarding celebrities have become templates for evaluating and assessing what life is all about. Celebrities are alternately portrayed as shining examples of perfection (when earning Grammy awards, Oscars, or Nobel prizes) and as decadent or immoral (when associated with sex scandals or criminal behavior).

The notion of celebrity has become self-reinforcing, even though it is ultimately vacuous. Many celebrities are famous not for their accomplishments but merely for their place in the spotlight. For example, Paris Hilton would not be a public figure without her wealth, which has gained her a place in that spotlight. Like other celebrities of the past and present, she is famous in a negative way, since her lifestyle is provocative to moral purists, as were the performances of Madonna. However, unlike Madonna, Paris Hilton offers very little substance in her performances. As with any starlet in the carnival hierarchy, her moment in the spotlight will quickly pass (if it has not already passed at the time of this book's publication).

THE IMPORTANCE OF RADIO IN POP CULTURE HISTORY

As the foregoing discussion has indicated, the radio stage has been crucial in spreading pop culture, especially from the Roaring Twenties to the early 1950s. Radio's spectacles were society's spectacles for three decades. Trends in radio complemented and spread trends in movies, music, and other domains of pop culture, either by showcasing them or simply by announcing them. The radio stage had a singular captive audience. There were no niche audiences in the golden era of radio. Stars on radio were known to everyone.

Radio also highlighted a basic tendency within pop culture—namely, the blending of high and low forms of culture. If one thinks of cultural spectacles, events, and products as lying on a continuum with "pure entertainment" at one end and "aesthetic engagement" at the other, then all one can say about pop culture is that any one of its events, products, or personages will fall somewhere along that spectrum. The movie *Amadeus* would fall on the engagement end, while the *Jackass* movies would fall near the other end. Most fall near the center. The amalgamative aspect of pop culture was evident on the radio stage from the very outset.

Entertainment vs. Engagement

Playing and promoting recorded music is, and always has been, at the core of radio broadcasting. Today, most stations specialize in one kind of music, such as rock, classical, country, rap, or jazz. Some stations broadcast several kinds of music. From the outset, radio showed that the lines between the two levels of culture were irrelevant. What counts is the popularity of the music. Popularity or enjoyability became and has remained the only criterion of taste. As mentioned in chapter 2, pop culture's democratization of taste has brought about its harshest critiques, from those of the Frankfurt School theorists to those of current culture industry critics. Pop culture has obliterated the traditional dividing lines between entertainment and engagement, becoming a culture for one and all. It is carnivalesque in the general sense of that word—promoting a world of fantasy where any pleasure can be indulged, from the sublime music of Beethoven (available on CDs and iPods) to the sounds of any garage band (similarly available on CDs or iPods). The Saturday afternoon NBC opera radio broadcasts from New York's Metropolitan Opera are as popular today as they were in the 1920s. Indeed, these broadcasts were responsible for making opera stars pop icons like any other celebrity. Tenors such as Enrico Caruso have become household names alongside other musical celebrities such as jazz great Louis Armstrong. Opera played a vital role in the first experimental radio broadcasts, which began around 1910, when Lee De Forest produced a radio program from the Metropolitan Opera House in New York City, starring Caruso.

Today, most radio stations that broadcast music have DJs (disc jockeys) who introduce and comment on the music, playing the role of ipso facto music critics. Although most of the music on the radio today is for the entertainment of niche audiences, from country to rap and even classical, it must not be forgotten that radio was once a powerful stage that showcased not only entertainment but also engagement. The radio brought into the living room not only the exciting new music of band leaders like Tommy Dorsey, Duke Ellington, Benny Goodman, Harry James, Guy Lombardo, and Glenn Miller, but also concerts from symphony halls.

In the golden age of radio broadcasting (from the 1920s to the 1950s) the radio was the major source of family entertainment. Every night, families gathered in their living rooms to listen to comedies, adventure dramas, music, and other kinds of radio entertainment. Children hurried home from school to hear afternoon adventure shows and woke up early on Saturday mornings to listen to children's programming until the noon hour. In the daytime, homebound people listened to soap operas. Golden age radio dramas included not only pulp fiction delights such as *Buck Rogers in the 25th Century, Gangbusters, The Green Hornet, Inner Sanctum, Jack Armstrong, All-American Boy, The Lone Ranger, The Shadow,* and *Superman,* but also plays by Ionesco and other contemporary dramatists. Radio soap operas such as *The Guiding Light, John's Other Wife, Just Plain Bill, Ma Perkins, One Man's Family, Our Gal Sunday,* and *Stella Dallas* were complemented by documentaries on issues of concern and programs on science. Comedians like Fred Allen, Jack Benny, Eddie Cantor, and Bob Hope and ventriloquists like Edgar Bergen and his dummy, Charlie McCarthy, shared the same spotlight as presidents and scientists who talked about the state of the world or the theory of atomic fusion. This pastiche of levels and discourse styles that characterized radio broadcasting became the defining characteristic of pop culture.

The radio also became a source for producing change in society. Radio's capacity to induce change was highlighted, for instance, by the popularity of *Amos ' n' Andy*, a situation comedy that was broadcast each weekday throughout the 1930s. While the program was being broadcast (from 7:00 to 7:15 P.M. Eastern Standard Time) many movie theaters stopped their films and turned on radios so the audiences could listen to the program. Some stores and restaurants played radios over public address systems so that customers would not miss it. The actors and actresses on the show were whites who portrayed blacks. Many people criticized the program for portraying African Americans as a stereotyped group. There is little doubt that the controversy stirred by that program led a few decades later to the civil rights movement, since it emblazoned in people's minds the inequities that existed between the races. Treatises and even newspaper articles could never quite have had the kind of broad impact that the radio stage had.

The radio stage was communal—everyone listened to virtually the same programs broadcast by the networks. As television took over in the 1950s, radio lost its communal status and became instead a source of individualized entertainment. With technology, however, radio is changing its character once again. In the late 1980s and early 1990s, digital audio broadcasting (DAB), a system that converts sounds to digital (numeric) code before transmission, made radio an enduring medium. DAB was introduced at a world conference in Spain in 1992. In 1998, the first commercial DAB operation began in the United Kingdom. Because DAB can carry multiple signals, radio programs are now supplemented by images, text, graphics, and other data.

Information Culture

The advent of DAB and other information-carrying devices highlights the fascination with information in the modern world. Radio was the medium that ushered in the Information Age, with radio news reporters becoming as well-known as entertainers. Early radio news reporters included Edward R. Murrow, Lowell Thomas, and Walter Winchell. Newscasts became especially important during World War II, when millions of people turned to radio every day for the latest news on the war. Murrow won fame during the war for his on-the-scene radio broadcasts describing German bombing attacks on London. His listeners in America could hear the bombs exploding in the background, giving them the illusion of being ersatz participants in the war. As a result, governments have since made widespread use of broadcasts for propaganda purposes. The Voice of America, an agency of the United States government, began broadcasting overseas in 1942 to inform the world of America's role in the war.

Aware of the growing importance of information, Franklin Delano Roosevelt, as mentioned previously, started a new trend in politics—the use of the media stage for political purposes. His radio fireside chats were instrumental in helping him gain support for his policies. Earlier presidents, beginning with Woodrow Wilson in 1919, had spoken on radio. Roosevelt, though, was the first to fully understand the great emotional power of the oral medium and the opportunity it provided to take government policies directly to the people. Other political leaders, including Winston Churchill of the United Kingdom and Charles de Gaulle of France, made similar use of radio to address their nations in times of crisis. In some ways, World War II was fought as much over the radio waves as it was on the battlefield. The fight was for people's minds in the former, and radio proved itself to be highly effective in this regard.

Today, we live in an ever-expanding information culture. Information is itself part of entertainment. Programs that provide information are among the most popular on radio, on television, and online. These include newscasts, talk shows, and live broadcasts of sports events. Newscasts are now broadcast at regular times—every half-hour or hour on some stations—a trend established during the golden age of radio. In addition, radio stations present on-the-spot news coverage of political conventions, disasters, and other issues of public importance. Radio stations also broadcast specialized information such as stock market indicators. Other information features include public service announcements about community events and government services. All of these informational uses of radio broadcasting have gained great entertainment value. Like pop culture in general, information programs emphasize variety. Some, such as Howard Stern's talk show, are pure carnival.

5

MUSIC

I am fond of music I think because it is so amoral. Everything else is moral and I am after something that isn't. I have always found moralizing intolerable.

Hermann Hesse (1877–1962)

As mentioned in previous chapters, pop culture would never have materialized in the first place without music to propel it onto center stage. Pop music and pop culture are virtual synonyms. Trends in pop music have defined each era of pop culture, eventually becoming descriptors of the eras (as in *the jazz era, the swing era, the rock era, the counterculture era*, and so on). From the Charleston of the Roaring Twenties to the swing music of the 1940s, the sock hop dances of the 1950s, and hip-hop videos of the 1990s and early 2000s, pop music has always attracted large audiences because it is fun and exciting. It is the heart and soul of pop culture.

Although different musical styles have been fashionable in different generations, there is little doubt that pop music has always constituted a means for each generation to define itself. But that is not all there is to the pop music phenomenon. Many pop music compositions have also risen (and continue to rise) to the level of what is traditionally called "musical art." As mentioned throughout this book, the inclusion of "high art" comes as no surprise to pop culture analysts, given the intermingling of sacred and profane modes of expression that has always characterized the constitution and evolution of pop culture. The jazz works of Louis Armstrong, the rock music of the Beatles and Procol Harum, the film scores of Phillip Glass, and the songs of Alicia Keys, to mention but a few, can certainly be classified as musical art under any definition of art. It is music that, once heard, never leaves us. The great British conductor Sir Thomas Beecham (1879–1961)

121

has aptly put it as follows (in the *London Sunday Times*, September 16, 1962): "Great music is that which penetrates the ear with facility and leaves the memory with difficulty. Magical music never leaves the memory."

This chapter will consider the role of music in pop culture. Pop music is a central target of analysis, not only because it has always been a source of entertainment, but also because it has been used as a mode of protest and a source for inciting social change. As Plato warned, music motivates people, spurring them on to action. This has been the explicit goal of some pop music genres, such as counterculture rock and early rap.

THE ADVENT OF POP MUSIC

Without technology, pop music would never have had the social impact that it has had throughout pop culture history. Its rise to center stage started in the late nineteenth century with the advent of sound recording technology. In 1877, Thomas Edison (1847–1931) invented the first phonograph (record-player). A decade later, in 1887, the German-born American inventor Emile Berliner (1851–1929) improved Edison's model, producing the flat-disk phonograph, or gramophone, which was used shortly thereafter for recording and playing back music. About 1920, Berliner's mechanical technology was replaced by electrical recording and reproduction technologies, whereby the vibrations of the phonograph needle were amplified by electromagnetic devices. Pop music had found its technological medium for widespread diffusion.

Historical Sketch

By the 1920s, the cheapness and availability of mass-produced vinyl records had led to a true paradigm shift in musical art—the entrenchment of pop music as mainstream music. New musical styles and idioms, such as jazz, spread quickly because they appealed to mass audiences and because recordings of the music could be bought for very little money, as could gramophone machines.

Many historians of music trace the origin of pop music to late-eighteenth-century America, when catchy tuneful music was composed by professional musicians for performances in parks in front of large gatherings of people (generally on Sunday afternoons). By the early nineteenth century, Italian opera had also become popular throughout America, influencing the

A Timeline of Pop Music Recordings

1877: The phonograph is invented by Thomas Edison.

1887–1888: Emile Berliner develops the gramophone, which can play sounds imprinted on mass-produced discs.

1920s: The jazz era is born. The Charleston brings about moral panic.

1930s–1940s: The big band era spreads trends in lifestyle and fashion.

1947: Magnetic audiotape is developed by 3M. Wynonie Harris records "Good Rockin' Tonight," the first true rock-and-roll song.

1948: 33 1/3 records are introduced by Columbia Records and 45 rpm records are introduced by RCA Victor.

1955: Top 40 radio becomes a marketing arm of the recording industry. Rock-and-roll enters the mainstream in the mid-1950s, dominating the recording industry until the early 1990s.

1956: Stereo recordings are introduced.

1962: Cassette tapes are introduced.

1960s: Rock music is linked with social protest, spearheading the counterculture movement.

1967: The Beatles release *Sgt. Pepper's Lonely Hearts Club Band*, the first true concept album.

1979–1980: Rap emerges out of hip-hop clubs in New York City.

1981: Music Television (MTV) is born, becoming a new arm of the recording industry.

1982: Compact discs (CDs) are introduced. Rock fragments into many genres, from disco to punk, grunge, and techno. Rap and hip-hop dominate the pop music scene until the early 2000s.

1997: DVDs make their debut, offering more storage space than CDs and making music videos popular.

1998: Music download sites proliferate on the Internet.

2000: MP3 technology shakes up the music industry as Internet users share music files on Napster. Napster is eventually ordered to stop unauthorized file-sharing.

2000s: Rap and hip-hop remain popular but lose their market domination.

2001: Peer-to-peer Internet services make music file-sharing even more popular.

2003: Apple Computer's iTunes music store makes its debut, making it possible to buy music on the Internet.

Mid-2000s and continuing: Devices such as Apple's iPod enhance access to and availability of music.

development of a soft, sentimental type of singing known as *crooning*, which became widespread. Before the advent of sound recordings, the primary medium for disseminating such music was printed sheet music. At the threshold of the twentieth century, the growing popularity of the new pop music idiom created a flourishing music-publishing business centralized in New York City, in an area of lower Manhattan called Tin Pan Alley. The first Tin Pan Alley song to sell one million copies, "After the Ball" (1892) by Charles K. Harris, inspired rapid growth in the music-publishing industry. Tin Pan Alley constitutes the first chapter in pop music history.

The crooning and Tin Pan Alley songs were simple, memorable, and emotionally appealing to large audiences. Vaudeville included them as part of its variety show fare. At about the same time, *ragtime* pieces written by professional composers such as Scott Joplin (1868–1917) also became popular, introducing a new and powerful creative force into music composition that would influence the development of mainstream pop music permanently—African American musical art.

A small cadre of composers and lyricists based in New York City produced the best-known songs of the 1920s and 1930s. In most cases, the composers worked in pairs (George Gershwin and Ira Gershwin, Richard Rodgers and Oscar Hammerstein, Richard Rodgers and Lorenz Hart, and so forth). Their songs were popularized by Broadway musicals, by well-known singers accompanied by dance orchestras, and above all else by recordings and radio play. Singers such as Bing Crosby and, later, Frank Sinatra became pop icons overnight through the medium of recordings and the radio broadcasts that promoted their music.

The African American influence on mainstream popular music became particularly evident during the so-called Jazz Age, which preceded the Great Depression of the 1930s. In 1935, white jazz musician Benny Goodman boosted the popularity of the style with his band's recordings of jazz works. From 1935 to 1945, the dominant type of popular music was big band *swing*, a genre modeled on the style of black jazz orchestras. The "big band" era ended after World War II, but the influence of swing music could still be heard in the "jump band" rhythm and blues and swing music of the 1940s.

Important shifts in popular music after World War II were tied even more to social and technological changes. The massive migration of Southern musicians and audiences to urban areas and the use of the electric guitar were particularly influential in shifting the paradigm in American pop music. These factors set the stage for the hard-edged Chicago blues of

Muddy Waters, the honky-tonk or "hard-country" style of Hank Williams, and in the mid-1950s the rise of rock-and-roll music.

Rock grew out of the intermingling of several converging streams of postwar styles, including rhythm and blues, the songs of "shouters" such as Big Joe Turner, gospel-based vocal styles, boogie-woogie piano blues, and honky-tonk music. Promoted by entrepreneurs such as Alan Freed—who introduced the term *rock-and-roll* as a commercial pop music category—and recorded by small independent labels, rock was an unexpected success, attracting a newly affluent youth audience in the mid-1950s. The pioneers of rock came from varied backgrounds. The star of Bill Haley and the Comets, whose "Rock Around the Clock" (1955) was the first rock song to gain wide popularity through the medium of records, was a country-and-western bandleader; Fats Domino was a rhythm and blues artist; Chuck Berry was a hairdresser; and Elvis Presley was a truck driver. The golden era of rock-and-roll—defined by the exuberant recordings of Haley, Berry, Domino, Presley, Little Richard, Jerry Lee Lewis, and Buddy Holly—lasted from 1954 to 1959. The most successful artists of the era wrote and performed songs about love, sexuality, adolescent identity crises, personal freedom in youth, and other issues that were (and continue to be) of central concern to teenagers and, increasingly, to everyone living in a "forever young" society.

In the early 1960s most of what the music industry promoted as new rock-and-roll was no more than an imitation of the original form. But in the same period the development of distinctive regional styles emerged, such as the sound of the southern California band the Beach Boys; the Greenwich Village urban folk movement that included the art of Bob Dylan, the Kingston Trio, and Peter, Paul, and Mary; and the rugged sound of Northwest groups such as the Sonics. Audiences for crooning music, jazz, and other pop music forms were in decline. Rock was becoming the musical voice of larger and larger segments of society. In one short decade, it had made its way to center stage.

Rock's rise became especially noticeable when the "British Invasion" began in 1964 with the arrival of the Beatles in New York City, and as the "rock group" emerged as an artistic phenomenon. British pop bands, raised on the influence of blues, rhythm and blues, and early rock-and-roll, invigorated mainstream popular music, in part by reinterpreting the early classics of American rock. Each group developed a distinctive style: the Beatles incorporated Chuck Berry's guitar-based rock-and-roll into a sophisticated new style; the Animals amalgamated blues and rhythm and blues styles to produce a hard-driving musical idiom of their own; and the Rolling Stones incorporated aspects of Chicago urban blues into their distinctive, thrusting sound.

The late 1960s was a period of corporate expansion and stylistic diversification in the record industry. Pop music was being defined more and more as music for young people. Styles included not only the influential experiments of the Beatles, but also San Francisco psychedelia, guitar rock by Jimi Hendrix and Eric Clapton, Southern rock, hard rock, jazz rock, folk rock, and other styles. Soul music, the successor to rhythm and blues, emerged with a wide range of highly popular styles, including the gospel-based songs of Aretha Franklin, the funk techniques of James Brown, and the soulful crooning of Marvin Gaye. Country music—firmly centered in Nashville, Tennessee—also produced a new generation of stars who combined elements of old country-and-western style with rock-and-roll. Johnny Cash, Waylon Jennings, and Patsy Cline helped contribute to the rising popularity of such music.

In the 1970s, a plethora of distinctive new styles—disco, glam rock, punk rock, new wave, reggae, funk, and so on—emerged and were pioneered by independent labels. As a consequence, by the end of the decade pop music had become highly fragmented and thus much less profitable for record companies to market to large homogeneous audiences. The pop music industry became cautious for the first time in its history, as sales of records dropped dramatically between 1978 and 1982. However, a number of factors contributed to the industry's economic revival in the mid-1980s. Among these were the advent of the music video; the debut in 1981 of Music Television (MTV), a twenty-four-hour music video channel; and the introduction in 1983 of the compact disc (or CD). The video-album *Thriller* (1982) by Michael Jackson became the biggest-selling artifact in pop music history up to that time and prompted a pattern in which record companies relied upon a few big hits to generate profits. Popular musicians of the period included Bruce Springsteen, the working-class bar-band hero; the artist known as Prince, whose 1984 single "When Doves Cry" was the first song in decades to have topped both the mainstream pop charts and the black music charts; and Madonna, the iconoclastic performer from a working-class background who transformed herself into a controversial "sex kitten" and pop icon.

Audiences for pop music became even more fragmented by the 1990s, although several main trends rose to the surface. Bands such as Blur, Oasis, Pearl Jam, R.E.M., and Radiohead continued the tradition of counterculture rock music. However, rap and hip-hop dominated the scene. Today, it is becoming increasingly clear that each new pop music style comes and goes more quickly than ever before. Unlike the music of classical composers, and perhaps of some jazz greats such as Louis Armstrong (1901–1971), pop music generally has a very brief "musical battery life," so to speak. This is not meant to imply that today's pop music lacks highly influential and important art forms. However, the commercialization of such forms dictates that they have a short life span, so that the economics of music recordings can be profitable. Simply put, most pop music is not designed to last. It is a variable in the law of supply and demand.

For this reason, it is mind-boggling to think that jazz and even classical music made an unexpected comeback in the 1990s. Many newly formed record labels devoted themselves to reissuing the classical music repertoire on CD. Their success was fueled in large part by the repeated use of classical music by the movies. Labels such as Naxos and Chandos, for instance, became more profitable than labels promoting new pop music trends. The renewed interest in jazz was highlighted by a brilliant ten-part documentary on American PBS, by director Ken Burns, in early 2001. The main point made by the program was that the jazz phenomenon not only dictated all subsequent pop music trends but also functioned as a mirror of twentieth-century musical art. The television program was followed by a coffee-table book, a DVD boxed set, a five-disc CD companion set, and a special series of compilations of the works of twenty-two essential jazz artists.

In sum, the history of pop music is the history of pop culture. Since the 1920s, pop music styles have been simultaneously perceived both as a source of entertainment and leisure for mass audiences and as a part of contemporary musical art traditions. Inevitably, as pop music styles proliferated throughout the twentieth century, so did the tendency for audience fragmentation. Today, with so much musical fare available through recordings in different digital formats and on different kinds of recording and playback devices, such as cell phones and iPods, musicians and producers know full well that their music will appeal primarily to niche audiences. As with modern-day print media and radio audiences, the fragmentation of music audiences is a salient characteristic of pop culture in the Internet Age.

Decoding Pop Music

By and large, pop music styles come and go and are loved primarily by the generation of people with whom they were once popular. Whatever the style, music has great significance to people, because it speaks to them emotionally. Music is meaningful to people when they are young, and the same music continues to be important to them as they age—hence the prevalence of infomercials on television promoting compilations of songs from the fifties, the sixties, and so on. Music from one's youth stimulates strong feelings of nostalgia. For example, when someone who was young in the 1950s hears songs by the Platters and Roy Orbison, he or she tends to be particularly moved by them. Their inner beauty seems to have become more conspicuous with the passage of time, which provides indirect evidence of the power of music to sway people. The philosophers of classical Greece believed that music originated with the gods Apollo and Orpheus, and that it reflected in its melodic and harmonic structure the laws that rule the universe. They also believed that music influences human thoughts and actions, because each melody possesses an emotional quality that listeners experience directly. In some African societies music is considered to be the faculty that sets humans apart from other species. Among some Native American cultures it is thought to have originated as a way for spirits to communicate with human beings.

The question of what constitutes musical art is not easy to answer, because music appeals to our feelings more than to our intellect. However, one thing is for certain—only those works that are genuinely meaningful to one and all will remain. Beethoven's *Missa Solemnis* and his last string quartets, to mention but two examples, will remain because they convey, through sound, a profound inner quest for meaning in life. Rummaging through the pop music experiment of the last fifty years does not produce anything that comes close to the Beethovenian standard. As Greil Marcus put it in 1976, in the end most rock music will likely fade away because it "is a combination of good ideas dried up by fads, terrible junk, hideous failings in taste and judgment, gullibility and manipulation, moments of unbelievable clarity and invention, pleasure, fun, vulgarity, excess, novelty and utter enervation" (Marcus 1976: 18). The same comment could also be applied to most other genres of pop music. Unless they have that "Beethovenian standard," they will evanesce into obscurity when the nostalgia factor disappears with the loss of specific generations of music aficionados.

All of this might sound elitist to the reader. But it is not. Mozart wrote music that he intended for the enjoyment of common folk—not just the cognoscenti. The operas of Verdi and Rossini, too, were "populist" forms of musical art. The idea of "classical music" as an elitist form of art is a modern one. It is a myth that simply needs to be dispelled once and for all. We are lucky to live in an era in which the music of a Mozart or a Beethoven need not lie dormant. It can be heard for the price of a CD or an online download. These composers' musical art cannot be so easily managed by the entrepreneurs of taste. It will exist regardless of the economic system in place in a given society in a particular era of time. It is also ironic to reflect on the fact that the greatest composers were very young when they composed some of their best works. And they died at ages that would certainly be considered premature today. Mozart died at the age of thirty-five, Chopin at thirty-nine, and Schubert at thirty-one. But their music was, and continues to be, ageless and timeless. There are various jazz, rock, and rap works that have as much aesthetic validity as do the great works of classical music. But they are few and far between. One such modern masterpiece is undoubtedly *The White Album* by the Beatles, which reverberates with great melodies and harmonies and yet remains essentially simple in texture, much like the music of the great musicians. Similarly, the music of the Platters and Procol Harum, to mention but two groups, is bound to live beyond the nostalgia syndrome.

When all is said and done, however, it is the profane nature of pop music that gives it such emotional power. Whether showcasing a primal, pagan-like form of frenzy (as in some heavy metal songs) or a subdued, romanticized form of swooning (as in rock love ballads), pop music is essentially about the carnivalesque. It engages us both corporeally and emotionally and is theatrically subversive in its overall intent. The lyrics of the 1950s ranged from portraying love as infatuation (for example, in Paul Anka's "Puppy Love") to portraying love as sexual activity (for example, in Jerry Lee Lewis's "Breathless"). In the 1960s, the lyrics of rock stars urged sweeping social changes, turning rock temporarily into music with a subversive subtext. But love and sex did not disappear from the counterculture rock scene. Indeed, sex was practiced openly at rock concerts, which added to the subversiveness of that scene. Gone from mainstream rock was the puppy love element, probably once and for all, although it occasionally resurfaces in tween-directed music (as it did, for example, in the early music of the rock ensemble Wham! in the 1980s and in current tween bands such as the Cheetah Girls). Like other aspects of the pop culture carnival, much of pop music consists of mock theater. It is for this reason that pop music is largely ineffectual in bringing about radical social changes. Take rap as a case in point. Initially denounced as a threat to America's moral fiber, rap has gradually become tame and sanitized for larger audiences. This transformation of rap into a generic musical art style shows what pop culture is all about. It is all about theater and spectacle. There are, of course, notable exceptions—

for example, the music of Alicia Keys, to mention but one. However, for the most part, pop music is part of the vaudevillian variety show, entertaining its audiences through its corporeality and mock transgression.

Genres

Although music genres, recording stars, and hit songs change constantly, strong continuities can be detected within the history of popular music. Many genres of music today draw upon the smooth, romantic vocal style of Tin Pan Alley; others continue the strong rhythms and emotional intensity of original African American jazz, gospel, and blues music; and so on. The transgressive or subversive theater evident in punk bands and in cross-dressing performers such as Kiss and Marilyn Manson might seem to be unique. But it is not. Transgression has always been implicit in pop music styles, from the Charleston and jazz to swing and early rock.

The spread of multiple music genres is also a basic tendency within pop culture, due to the increase of options brought about by changing technologies. Today, everything from rock and jazz to classical and gospel have niche audiences, each with its own record labels, radio stations, websites, accompanying magazines, and so on and so forth.

In addition to the largely American-based typology of genres, the musical styles of other countries have also started gaining widespread appeal through recordings, radio, satellite television, and of course the Internet. The Argentine tango, for instance, gained worldwide popularity in the 1910s, initiating a craze for Latin ballroom dancing in Paris, London, and New York City. Its carnivalesque sexuality was revived by Shakira in her "Assassination Tango" video in which she cleverly "demasculinizes" the dance form, shifting the focus to the power of the female form in dance. The Cuban rumba also became popular around the world in the 1930s, primarily through recordings and radio. In the post–Top 40 era, such styles have made a comeback, becoming popular with new audiences across the world. Another emerging pop music genre is Indian film music, which is produced in studios in New Delhi and Mumbai. Although it gets very little attention from the mainstream Anglo-American media, it nevertheless has a very large audience worldwide, including a growing fan base in America. African music too is popular in today's diverse global village, attracting all kinds of audiences. It includes a number of distinctive regional styles, such as the *juju* music of Nigerian bandleader King Sunny Adé; central African *soukous*, a blend of indigenous songs and dance rhythms with Afro-Cuban

Main Music Genres Today

Adult contemporary: a mix of oldies and softer rock hits (Celine Dion, the Backstreet Boys, il Divo, Andrea Bocelli, Mariah Carey)

Contemporary hit radio: mostly current hits, usually a mix of pop, rap, rock, and otherstyles (Madonna, Shakira, Nelly Furtado)

Country: subdivided into *traditional country* (Hank Williams, Dolly Parton), *urban country* (Dixie Chicks, Lee Ann Womack), and *rock country* (Shania Twain, Garth Brooks)

Alternative rock: various forms of rock, including hard rock (Hole, Korn), industrial rock (Marilyn Manson), grunge (Nirvana), and punk (Green Day)

Disco: classic disco from the 1970s and 1980s (the Bee Gees, KC and the Sunshine Band) and more recent disco styles (techno, house)

Rap and hip-hop: works by rap and hip-hop stars (Ludacris, Jay-Z, 50 Cent, Eminem)

Oldies: 1950s and early 1960s rock (Elvis Presley, Neil Sedaka, Little Richard, the Supremes)

Classic rock: rock songs of the mid- to late-1960s (the Rolling Stones), 1970s (the Cars, Pink Floyd), and 1980s (Elvis Costello, The Police)

Rhythm and blues: rhythm and blues music by classic and contemporary performers (Tina Turner, Luther Vandross)

Experimental: music styles promoted mainly by college and university radio stations

Latin: music composed and performed by Hispanic artists (Pepe Aguilar, Ricky Martin, Christina Aguilera, Jennifer Lopez)

Classical: music intended for lovers of the great composers (Bach, Mozart,Beethoven, Chopin)

Jazz and blues: jazz and blues music intended to appeal to lovers of both current (Herbie Hancock) and traditional (Louis Armstrong) jazz and blues artists

Gospel: gospel music intended to appeal to lovers of both current (Kirk Franklin) and traditional (Mahalia Jackson) gospel performers

Opera: mainly from the Romantic era (operas by Rossini, Verdi, Puccini, Bizet)

Retro: any form of music that looks back and recycles music from previous eras using new stylistic details music; and South African *isicathamiya*, the Zulu choral singing style performed by Ladysmith Black Mambazo.

The list of new trends for niche audiences could go on and on. Never before has music of all types been so readily available to those who want to listen to it. From classical music and jazz to the latest musical craze, pop culture has literally brought music to the people. The expressions and themes that pop music expounds quickly pass into nostalgia, and the clothing fashions that pop musicians wear quickly become general fashion trends, only to be replaced by newer ones. Music has also become highly integrated with other media stages for pop culture. It is an important element in many movies and some television programs. For instance, the fast-paced *William Tell* overture by the eighteenth-century opera composer Gioacchino Rossini has become so closely linked with the *Lone Ranger* radio and television series of the 1940s and 1950s that the two are hardly ever perceived as separate by those who grew up in that era. Similarly, another Rossini overture, which he composed for the opera *The Barber of Seville*, has become so broadly associated with a famous *Bugs Bunny* cartoon episode that the two are now inseparable in many people's minds.

THE ROCK ERA

The swing music that became the rage between 1935 and 1945 appealed mainly to the young people of the era, who saw it as a way to cope with the stark economic realities of the post-Depression era and the moral ravages of world war. In 1942, Frank Sinatra wowed "bobby-soxers" at the Paramount in New York, giving America a foretaste of the teenage hysteria that was just around the corner. The marriage of pop music with teenagers was officially consummated a little more than a decade later when *rock-and-roll*, the very name of which clearly suggested the sexual impulses connected with adolescence, emerged as a music designed to appeal exclusively to teenagers. Today, rock is a matter of nostalgia. In its heyday, though, it showed the essence of what pop music was all about.

Historical Sketch

The first true rock songs were composed in the 1940s and early 1950s and reflected a blend of popular musical forms of previous eras—the *blues*, the gospel-based vocal-group style known as *doo wop*, the piano-based

All-Time Favorite Rock Albums
(from a 2002 *Rolling Stone* poll)

1. *Revolver*, the Beatles (1965)
2. *Nevermind*, Nirvana (1991)
3. *Sgt. Pepper's Lonely Hearts Club Band*, the Beatles (1967)
4. *The Joshua Tree*, U2 (1987)
5. *The White Album*, the Beatles (1968)
6. *Abbey Road*, the Beatles (1969)
7. *Appetite for Destruction*, Guns N' Roses (1987)
8. *OK Computer*, Radiohead (1997)
9. *Led Zeppelin*, Led Zeppelin (1971)
10. *Achtung Baby*, U2 (1991)

rhythmic style known as *boogie woogie*, and the country-music style known as *honky tonk* (made popular by Hank Williams). The early songs were recorded and released by small, independent record companies and promoted by controversial radio disc jockeys such as Alan Freed, who used the term *rock-and-roll* to help attract audiences unfamiliar with the fledgling music style. Incidentally, it seems that Freed's term was used by the Boswell Sisters in 1934 in their song titled "Rock and Roll," although in their usage

Ten of the Best-Known Twentieth-Century Musical Icons

1. Elvis Presley
2. the Beatles
3. Bob Dylan
4. James Brown
5. the Rolling Stones
6. Madonna
7. Stevie Wonder
8. Chuck Berry
9. Michael Jackson
10. Kurt Cobain

the term referred to the back-and-forth movement of a rocking chair, not to the meanings it developed in 1950s youth culture. By the time Elvis Presley recorded "Good Rockin' Tonight" in 1954, as a remake of Wynonie Harris's 1948 rendition of the song, rock had established itself as a powerful new trend in pop culture. Harris's song, a rhythm and blues number, triggered the use of the word *rock* shortly thereafter. After Bill Haley and the Comets recorded "Rock around the Clock" in 1955, the term was appropriated by teenagers to describe a music they could call exclusively theirs. "Rock around the Clock" was part of the theme music for *The Blackboard Jungle*, a 1955 motion picture about teenagers coming of age in the 1950s.

The link between rock-and-roll and adolescence was visible from the outset. Changes in rock music became sources of change in teen lifestyle. The two went hand in hand. The success of rock caught the attention of media moguls and the culture industries generally. Hollywood jumped on the teen bandwagon early and produced, in addition to *The Blackboard Jungle* and *Rebel without a Cause*, a slew of rock movies that were, in effect, forerunners of the rock video. The 1956 movie *Rock, Rock, Rock*, for instance, included acts by rock stars and groups of the era. It also featured an appearance by Alan Freed. Similarly, in *Rock, Baby, Rock It* (1957) and *Go, Johnny, Go!* (1958), the finest rock musical talents of the period were featured. The rock stars of the era—Chuck Berry, Elvis Presley, Little Richard, and Buddy Holly, to mention but a few—have become emblazoned in the annals of pop culture history as pioneers of social and cultural trends. Elvis Presley's "Hound Dog" (1956) and "All Shook Up" (1956), Little Richard's "Tutti Frutti" (1955) and "Lucille" (1957), Chuck Berry's "Maybellene" (1955) and "Johnny B. Goode" (1958), and Buddy Holly's "Peggy Sue" (1957) catapulted rock music to the forefront of American society. It was "in your face" music. Teens loved it; parents hated it. As the 1958 song by Danny and the Juniors put it rather prophetically, rock-and-roll was "here to stay."

In the 1960s, rock changed its homogenous complexion, fragmenting into diverse styles—Motown, California surfer rock, folk rock, and so on. The so-called British Invasion, as mentioned above, began in 1964 with the arrival of the Beatles in New York City—a key moment in the history of pop music and pop culture generally since, arguably, it gave momentum to a then-fledgling counterculture movement. By 1967, with *Sgt. Pepper's Lonely Hearts Club Band*, which was rock's first "concept album," the Beatles established new standards for studio recording and carved out the image of the rock musician as a creative artist, in the idealistic sense of the Romantic era—an image that remains intact to this day.

The most famous style came to be known as counterculture rock. It emerged in San Francisco around 1966 and was associated with the use of hallucinogenic drugs, psychedelic art, light shows, peace, and public displays of sexuality without moralistic censure. Counterculture musicians such as Jerry Garcia of the Grateful Dead experimented with long, improvised stretches of music called *jams*. It was clear that this new type of rock was vastly different from golden-era rock in that it was spearheading and sustaining a political youth movement, the objectives of which were to reject the traditional bourgeois goals of consumerist society. This new form of rock also reflected how much teens had changed in a decade. They were now "rebels with a cause" who denounced the corrupt business, military, and political establishment as the cause of all social ills. Musicians and musical groups such as the Who, Jim Morrison (of the Doors), Frank Zappa, and Jimi Hendrix, among many others, were known not only for their music but also for their political views. The rock concert became a *happening* of great ideological impact, spurring youths on to social activism and to engagement in subversive acts. It was a tribal ritual that showcased elements of the profane implicit in rock's overall subtext. At concerts such as Monterey Pop (1967) and Woodstock (1969), drugs were used to heighten the aesthetic experience of the music, and sexual activities were displayed openly, in obvious defiance of adult moralism. In a bizarre way, what Plato (c. 427–347 BC) feared most about music millennia ago had come about in the counterculture world of the 1960s. As the Greek philosopher astutely pointed out: "The introduction of a new kind of music must be shunned as imperiling the whole state; since styles of music are never disturbed without affecting the most important political institutions." Counterculture rock certainly seemed to imperil the modern state.

However, the counterculture movement faded by the early 1970s. Various analyses have been put forth to explain its demise—the end of the Vietnam War (which had been a major reason for youth protest in the 1960s and early 1970s), effective social changes brought about by the movement itself, and so on. In my view, though, it faded simply because the adolescents became older and because the adult establishment itself forged a tacit merger with the rock stars who, despite their anti-establishment attitudes, nevertheless signed lucrative contracts with major recording companies. The mainstreaming of rock music set the stage for it to enter the realm of nostalgia, where it could be tamed and relegated to pop culture lore.

As mentioned previously, by the mid-1970s a number of distinctive new styles had appeared—disco, glam rock, punk rock, new wave, reggae, and funk—showing that audiences for pop music were fragmenting more and more into distinctive aesthetic communities and even subcultures. Initially associated with the gay lifestyle of New York City, disco drew upon black popular musical styles of the past, attracting a large teen following. Although despised by many segments of the teen population, disco had a substantial impact on pop music, especially after the release of the motion picture *Saturday Night Fever* (1977) and its hugely successful soundtrack featuring the Bee Gees. Around 1976, punk rock originated in London and New York as a reaction against the commercialism of disco and the artistic pretentiousness of 1960s rock. Punk rock was raw, abrasive, and rude. In its original intent, it was a throwback to the golden era of rock. However, unlike the golden era rockers, early punk bands such as the Sex Pistols and the Clash eliminated melody and harmony from their music, transforming it into an angry, shrill, brutal style. Eventually, with such bands as the Ramones, Blondie, and Talking Heads, punk adopted a softer and more melodic style, called new wave. The original punk style, though, has not disappeared from the pop music radar screen. It is still around in *neo-punk pop* forms (such as in the music of Green Day). Also in the mid-1970s, reggae—developed by musicians in Jamaica—began to attract attention among a sizable number of teens, especially after the release of the 1973 film *The Harder They Come*, which starred reggae singer Jimmy Cliff in the role of an underclass gangster. The superstar of the style was, however, Bob Marley, who by the time of his death in 1981 had become one of the most popular musicians in the world.

As mentioned previously, by the end of the 1970s, pop music sales had plummeted. At least for a little while, it appeared that the final chapter on rock history had been written. However, technology and the media came to the rescue. The invention of video recording technology, the debut in 1981 of MTV, and the introduction onto the market of the compact disc revived interest in rock music. A new generation of "video rock stars," such as Michael Jackson, Bruce Springsteen, Prince, and Madonna became the new icons of "TV teens." The astronomical success of Michael Jackson's 1982 album *Thriller* contributed greatly to demonstrating the promotional value of video rock, as did the videos of heavy metal bands, such as Van Halen, AC/DC, and Metallica.

The success of video rock highlights the role that the media have played in the propagation of rock (and more recently hip-hop). Rock-and-roll became popular across the teen world after Elvis Presley appeared on *The Ed Sullivan Show* in 1956. The same program catapulted the Beatles

Highlights of the Partnership between Rock and Video

1957: Dick Clark's *American Bandstand* is launched, spreading new trends in music, fashion, and dance.

1967: The Who include explosives in their musical act on *The Smothers Brothers Comedy Hour*, introducing "crudeness" into rock performances long before the advent of punk rock.

1968: Elvis Presley makes a comeback with his special on NBC, leading to the entrenchment of an "Elvis subculture" after his death in 1977.

1975: *Saturday Night Live* introduces rock musical acts into its programs, spreading rock music even more into the mainstream.

1981: MTV is launched with the video "Video Killed the Radio Star," by the Buggles.

1983: The *Motown 25* special features Michael Jackson's first "moonwalk."

1984: Madonna shocks audiences by appearing in a wedding gown singing "Like a Virgin" on the MTV Video Awards.

1985: The *Live Aid* concert airs on ABC and MTV, rekindling interest in rock as a vehicle of political and social commentary.

Early 1990s: MTV starts its own reality television program, called *The Real World*, which attracts viewers from early adolescents to thirty-somethings.

Mid- and late 1990s: Rap and hip-hop are showcased on MTV, in movies, and in other media.

Early 2000s and continuing: The World Wide Web becomes the new video stage for pop music generally. File-sharing and video-sharing spread throughout the online world.

to fame in 1964. An estimated 73 million people watched the Beatles' first appearance on the show. Arguably, without television, rock would have remained confined to the teen world. Its crossover to the musical mainstream was fostered and nurtured by media such as radio and television. These continue to be major players in the spread of new music. In a book titled *If It Ain't Got That Swing* (2000), Mark Gauvreau Judge argues that "adult pop music" has been gradually marginalized since the advent of rock in the 1950s. He suggests, however, that the "rock experiment" may have run its course. Judge may be right. Rock appears to be increasingly an object of nostalgia. In 1995, for instance, the Rock and Roll Hall of Fame opened in Cleveland, Ohio—a sure sign that rock may have become "museum music." Also in the 1990s, several major television documentaries were produced on the history of rock-and-roll, and historical box-set recordings were reissued featuring rock artists from the past—further signs that rock music may have indeed become more a part of pop culture history than anything else.

Decoding Rock

There is little doubt that rock was and, continues to be, an important act on the vaudevillian pop culture stage. From deafening amplification and onstage performances that come across as pure corporeal spectacle, to dance trends, fashions, and lifestyles they initiated, rock musicians have been a part of that stage for over fifty years. The panic always brought about initially by rock trends, from Elvis's hip-swinging to punk fashion, now appears quaint to us. However, in its early forms, rock was certainly perceived as dangerous music. Evangelical zealots labeled it "the devil's music," because it was sexually suggestive and profane. The implication of danger was imprinted into the style and delivery of the music itself. It was louder and more intensely rhythmic than any of its predecessors. When compared to, say, crooning music, it stood out blaringly (pun intended).

The instrument that truly set rock apart from all previous pop music styles was the electric guitar. Rock-and-roll guitarist Chuck Berry first showed the phallic power of the electric guitar with his "electrifying" performances (again, pun intended). The electric guitar remains a powerful symbol within pop music to this day. Beginning in the late 1960s a new

Table 5.1.   Characteristics of Crooning Music and of Early Rock Music

Crooning Music	Early Rock Music
Soft and tender	Loud and rough
Restrained rhythms	Hard-driving rhythms
Flowing melodies	Hard-edged melodies
Romantic lyrics	Lyrics tinged with allusions to sexuality
Accompanied by traditional instruments	Accompanied by electric instruments with the capacity to amplify the music significantly

generation of rock guitarists, including Jimi Hendrix, Eric Clapton, and Carlos Santana, experimented with amplification and various electronic devices, extending the musical potential of the instrument considerably. Other instruments commonly used in early rock music included the stand-up bass, the electric bass guitar, keyboard instruments, and the drum set. But the guitar was the heart and soul of early rock and gave the music its phallic nature. Like the phallotropes of carnival mockers, the guitar stood out in obvious mockery of hypocritical moralism, as it was caressed and stroked sensually by male rock musicians. Only in the 1980s when women started using the instrument in bands such as Blondie did the guitar start losing its phallic symbolism. In the early days it was a major carnivalesque prop in rock performances, employed in the same way that phalluses were used by carnival actors, simultaneously to excite audiences sexually and to deride male sexuality.

The carnivalesque nature of rock became even more evident in the 1970s with the emergence of punk rockers, who made the ritualistic violation of social symbols and the glorification of indecency part and parcel of their stage act. Like carnival jesters, punk rockers were "lords of misrule," celebrating everything viewed as unconventional and vulgar, and parodying

The electric guitar remains a powerful symbol within pop music.
©iStockphoto.com/Pascal Genest

social norms through their dress, language, and overall demeanor. Although these carnivalesque elements were subtly implicit in early rock stars such as Little Richard and Jerry Lee Lewis, they became intentionally explicit in punk rock. Punks aimed to confuse, parody, and satirize the mainstream, and to glorify vulgarity, in much the same way as did commedia dell'arte characters in public squares, and as did jesters or clowns at carnival time. Rage, horror, and comedy were united in punk and continue to be part of specific subtexts within pop culture, from cartoon sitcoms such as *South Park* to goth culture and slasher movies like the recent *Saw* films. Early punk bands, such as the Sex Pistols, sang about the grotesque nature of bodies. One of their slogans was "F★★★ Forever!" alluding to sex as a simple animal act. They also vomited onstage, wore garbage bags held together with safety pins, and exalted other gross forms of spectacle, such as urination, defecation, drunkenness, and so on. After the death of bassist Sid Vicious in 1979, the band sported T-shirts bearing the words *Sid Lives*. Such profane rituals are theatrical put-downs of sacred images that are understood as authoritarian and rigidly moral. The Sex Pistols made fun of the British monarchy and government, the human body, multinational corporations, and other forms of rock. The same kinds of carnivalesque patterns can be found today throughout the pop culture spectrum. The function of such performances was, and continues to be, that of purification. Through crude, bawdy, and vulgar performances and rituals the grotesque within us is sublimated, as Bakhtin often pointed out (elaborated in chapter 2). Such performances are innocuous. The impulses represented become dangerous only if they are repressed. Thus, while punk rock created moral panic, it never really had a disruptive impact on the social mainstream. After purification, the sacred is restored.

Much of pop music (and pop culture generally) allows for the grotesque within us to be purified. The profane and the sacred complement each other, and every healthy society needs them in a state of balance. The profane (often expressed in comedy) and the sacred (often expressed in tragedy or in profoundly beautiful art) complement each other, and every healthy society needs them in a state of balance. This topic will be revisited in the final chapter. Suffice it to say here that seriousness has always gone hand in hand with play, the prince with the fool, tears with laughter, reflection with instinct. Rituals throughout the ancient world were designed to maintain this balance. Alongside their sacred pagan rituals, the ancient Romans also held a festival called Saturnalia, in honor of Saturn, the god of agriculture, to give expression to the profane instinct. It constituted a time of general merriment similar to the medieval carnivals and to contemporary Mardi Gras. Even slaves were given temporary freedom to do as they pleased. Similar rituals existed throughout the ancient world.

Considering carnival theory, it becomes understandable that women's bodies have always played a central role in pop music and in pop culture generally, from the suggestive movements of early "girl bands" on stage to the more blatant "booty shaking" of women in rap videos. Many religious people see the exposure of the female body, or its sexually suggestive movements, especially at carnival time, as sinful and dangerous. However, carnival incorporates the female body simply as part of its transgressive spectacle, so as to stimulate *hysteria*—a word derived from the Greek for *womb*. Emphasis on the female body is everywhere in pop culture, from hip-hop videos and erotic movies to advertising and everyday fashion shows. This emphasis charges the social atmosphere sexually, giving it a constant tinge of carnival. It is no wonder that Sigmund Freud's analysis of hysteria as sublimated sexuality draws on festive images that are similar to those enacted by female actors in medieval carnivals.

THE HIP-HOP ERA

Since the mid-1980s, the rock carnival has given way to a new set of actors. In that era, the word *rock* started being used less and less to refer to pop music. Ironically, rock superstars, such as Peter Gabriel, David Byrne, and Paul Simon, played an unwitting role in bringing about this shift by introducing the works of different musical styles to audiences in the United States and Europe. Paul Simon had released two albums that showcased music from other continents—*Graceland* (1986) featured musicians from Africa and *The Rhythm of the Saints* featured musicians from South America. At about the same time, a new style called *rap* seemed to come out of nowhere to attract the attention of the new generation of teens. Rap emerged as a genre in which vocalists performed rhythmic speech, usually accompanied by snippets of music, called samples, which either were culled from previously recorded material or newly created for the rap song. The first rap records were made in the late 1970s by small, independent record companies. Although rapper groups such as Sugarhill Gang had national hits during the late 1970s and early 1980s, the rap musical style did not enter the pop culture mainstream until 1986, when rappers Run D.M.C. and the hard-rock band Aerosmith collaborated on the song "Walk This Way," cre-

A Hip-Hop Timeline

1979: DJ Flash recruits local emcees and records the first socially conscious rap hit, "The Message." In the same year, a trio created by the owner of Sugar Hill Records, called The Sugarhill Gang, improvises the first hip-hop smash, "Rapper's Delight," but then fades fast. Also in that year the charismatic rapper MC takes rap to national television.

1980: Blow's single "The Breaks" becomes rap's first gold record.

1981: Blondie records "Rapture," believed to be the first rap song that did not rely on samples from previously recorded music. It becomes rap's first number-one single.

1982: The first controversy associated with hip-hop comes to the forefront when rapper Ice-T records "Cop Killer." In the same year the Beastie Boys make rap more socially acceptable with their playful style.

1983: Run D.M.C. add hard rhymes and beats to rap. Soon afterward, Too Short makes pimping (displaying behavior that is imitative of pimps) a central theme in rap. Rap gets its first video on MTV—Run D.M.C.'s "Rock Box." Grandmaster Flash and Melle Mel release the anti-cocaine anthem "White Lines (Don't Do It)." Hip-hop fuses with jazz on "Rock It" by Herbie Hancock and Grandmaster DST.

1984: Rap takes a romantic turn with the music of LL Cool J. The first rap-only radio station, KDAY-AM in Los Angeles, goes on the air. Russell Simmons and Rick Rubin start Def Jam Records. The label and its artists—Run D.M.C., the Beastie Boys, Public Enemy—push rap closer into the musical mainstream.

1985: 2 Live Crew get into legal trouble because of their explicit lyrics.

1986: Run D.M.C. join Aerosmith to record "Walk This Way." Rakim adds lyricism to rap.

1987: DJ Jazzy Jeff and the Fresh Prince inject prurient comedy into rap, while Public Enemy uses explicit political messages in his lyrics. The group N.W.A. put gangsta rap on the map.

1988: Geto Boys spread gangsta rap. De La Soul adds an element of parody and goofiness by toting daisies. Queen Latifah challenges male rap hegemony with her overpowering presence and moving musical style. Public Enemy releases *It Takes a Nation of Millions to Hold Us Back*, which is widely regarded as rap's greatest album. N.W.A., featuring Ice Cube and Dr. Dre, record

Straight Outta Compton, the first gangsta album to become widely known.

1989: A Tribe Called Quest incorporate jazz into rap, paying homage to African-American musical history.

1990: Ice Cube translates black youth's rage into incisive, controversial lyrics. The erotic lyrics of 2 Live Crew's album *As Nasty as They Wanna Be* are declared obscene by a Florida judge, whose decision is overturned on appeal.

1991: Cypress Hill ignites hip-hop's so-called Stone Age. No Limit Soldiers accentuate machismo themes.

1992: Dr. Dre becomes infamous due to his purportedly sexist lyrics and starts Death Row Records with partner Suge Knight, an ex-con. The label releases *The Chronic*, which makes a star out of another ex-con, Snoop Dogg.

1993: The Wu-Tang Clan inject gothic themes into rap. Snoop Dogg continues his success with *Doggystyle*.

1994: Bone Thugs-N-Harmony spread a new melodic trend in rap. Meanwhile, the Fugees inject a soulful style.

1995: Eminem comes onto the scene as "the white rapper." His lyrics decry the social conditions of poor people and the dispossessed.

1996: Lil' Kim projects a powerfully sexual persona, spawning a horde of copycats. In his videos, Lil John uses images that appear to have been filmed in strip clubs or spliced in from pornographic movies.

1997: Puff Daddy (P. Diddy), Wyclef Jean, and Missy Elliott become icons by making rap more and more palatable, musically and lyrically, to the mainstream.

1998: Big Pun, Lauryn Hill, and Ja Rule turn rap into a multilayered spectacle of song and sex. 50 Cent adds a new version of gangsta swagger to rap.

1999: Lauryn Hill is the first woman to be nominated for ten Grammy awards in a single year. She wins five of them, thus legitimizing hip-hop as a musical art form.

2000: Ludacris incorporates pornographic imagery and lyrics into his videos, while Nelly Furtado rides sexual innuendo to stardom.

2001: Four hip-hop albums make VH1's list "The 100 Greatest Albums of All Time."

2003: The career of Kanye West epitomizes rap's evolution into big business as he becomes one of the most successful producers in rap history. Eminem's "Lose Yourself," from his film *8 Mile*, wins the Oscar for best original song.

2004: Tupac Shakur surpasses 37 million in total album sales, making

(continues)

him one of the top forty best-selling pop artists of all time. Eminem, Jay-Z, and the Beastie Boys surpass the milestone of 21 million albums sold.

2005 and continuing: Sales of individual rap CDs and videos start to diminish considerably, as fragmentation and diversification spread throughout rap music. Like all previous forms of pop music, rap becomes part of pop culture lore.

---

ating a new audience for rap among white, middle-class teens. By the end of the 1980s, MTV had launched a program dedicated solely to rap, and the records of rap artists such as M.C. Hammer and the Beastie Boys had achieved multi-platinum status.

Characterizing Hip-Hop

Rap and *hip-hop* are terms that are frequently used interchangeably. However, the former, which was spread broadly from a recording by Sugar-hill Gang called "Rapper's Delight" (1979), refers to the musical style itself, whereas the latter refers to the attendant lifestyle that those who listen to rap tend to adopt. The word *hop* has been around since the 1920s, when *Lindy hop* dancing, also known as *jitterbug*, was popular in Harlem. The word was also used to describe 1950s rock dancing, as captured by Danny and the Juniors in their 1958 hit "At the Hop." It is useful, if not necessary, to understand the history of the rap and hip-hop movement, at least in bare outline form, as one basic story line. The historical era of hip-hop starts in 1979. Only in the early 2000s did this powerful genre start to yield its rule over the pop music scene.

The rise of hip-hop in many ways parallels the birth of rock-and-roll in the 1950s. Both originated in African American culture and both were initially aimed at black audiences. In both cases, the new style gradually attracted white musicians, who made it popular among white audiences. For rock-and-roll that musician was Elvis Presley; for rap it was, as mentioned above, the band called Aerosmith. In the same year, a white group from New York City, called the Beastie Boys, released the rap song "Fight for Your Right to Party" (1986), which quickly reached the Billboard top-ten list of popular hits.

Rap vocals typically emphasize lyrics and wordplay over melody and harmony, achieving interest through rhythm and variations in the timing of the lyrics. Rap's themes can be broadly categorized under three headings: those that are blatantly sexual; those that chronicle and often embrace the so-called gangsta lifestyle of youths who live in inner cities; and those that address contemporary political issues or aspects of black history. Rap is not unlike the musical form of the late medieval era known as the *madrigal*—a composition for two or three voices in simple harmony, following a strict poetic form, developed in Italy in the late thirteenth and early fourteenth centuries. Early madrigals were sung with single voices, without instrumental accompaniment or harmonic texture, as were many early rap songs. The rhythm, rather than the melody, drove the music. Rap is pop culture's version of the madrigal. It was originally a voice of dispossessed black youth. However, by the mid-1990s it had turned into a form of theater for one and all. Rap artists borrowed from folk music, jazz, and other musical styles, developing an eclectic pastiche of sound that started to attract larger audiences and that became more and more melodious and traditional in its use of instrumentation.

Subversive Theater

In 1988 the rap group N.W.A. released the first major album of gangsta rap, *Straight Outta Compton*. Songs from the album generated an extraordinary amount of controversy because of their suggestions of violence. As a result they created moral panic, drawing protests from a number of organizations, including the FBI. So too did the early music of Ice-T, Dr. Dre, and Snoop Dogg. However, attempts to censor gangsta rap only served to publicize the music more widely, and, thus, to make it even more attractive to youths generally. The "in your face" attitude noticeable in hip-hop videos to this day, some of which appear to be little more than erotic videos, continues to be worrisome to parents, at the same time that it is highly attractive to many young people.

The lifestyle associated with rap music is called, as previously mentioned, hip-hop. It became a popular lifestyle in the mid-1990s. The salient features of this lifestyle include the practice of assuming a new name, known as a *tag*, and the related practice of etching the tag on the urban landscape—on bus shelters, buses, subway cars, signs, walls, freeway overpasses, mailboxes, and the like—with markers, spray paint, or shoe polish. There are two main forms of tagging, known as *throw-ups* and *pieces*. By the late 1990s, tagging art had become so interesting that some traditional art galleries even started putting it on display. In December of 2000, the Brooklyn Museum of Art organized an exposition of four hundred pieces of urban street art, called *Hip-Hop Nation: Roots, Rhymes & Rage*, reflecting several decades of hip-hop tagging art. In a city where nearly two thousand arrests for graffiti offenses were carried out in the same year, the art gallery had taken on the role previously relegated to the streets. This museum exhibit was evidence that hip-hop had indeed made it into the mainstream, despite efforts to suppress it.

Hip-hop is really all about subversive theater. It is a stage on which youths can enact their rage over social inequalities and racism. As with all previous forms of subversive theater, the rage against it soon subsided. Often criticized for its harsh lyrics and negative images, by 2000 rap music had started to garner a second reading from the mainstream, which started to see it as a legitimate artistic vehicle rejecting the racist inclinations of the past so that something could be done to change the situation once and for all. Given the overall lack of opportunity afforded to young African Americans in contemporary society, rap music came to be seen as a vehicle through which they could secure a voice and a place in the public sphere and, above all else, their own sense of history and tradition. It is for the sake of creating their own tradition that hip-hop artists spell their performance names differently—*Dogg* instead of *Dog*, *Sista* instead of *Sister*, and so on. This practice, though, is not an invention of hip-hop youths. It could already be found in the Roaring Twenties, as mentioned previously. In 1952, the African American musician Lloyd Price spelled his hit song "Lawdy Miss Clawdy," in obvious imitation of Black English Vernacular pronunciation.

Today the original rage in rap is being expressed less and less, providing testimony that nothing lasts in pop culture. Significantly, a *New York Times* 2002 survey found that most of the top rap artists at the time were "historical figures" in the rap movement—Dr. Dre, Warren G, Puff Daddy, Shaggy, SMX, Nelly Furtado, Ludacris, Coolio, Salt-N-Pepa, and Snoop Dogg. With its own magazines, movies, radio and television programs, footwear, clothing, beverages, and jewelry, hip-hop had become big business. Another sure sign that the rap movement was fading was the onset of nostalgia. By the mid-2000s rap and hip-hop had become more a matter of retrospective and taking trips down memory lane than of producing new and innovative material. However, one must not forget that through its subversive theatricality hip-hop has made a difference in society nonetheless. Take the song "Changes" by Tupac Shakur, an artist who was murdered at the age of twenty-five by unknown assailants. Tupac grew up in the ghettos of

New York and later moved to Los Angeles, where he spent the rest of his short life. His life was a paradigm for troubled young blacks. Although he spent time in prison, was acquitted of the charge of shooting a police officer, and was shot five times himself, he left the world some of the most moving lyrics and melodies ever written. With "Changes," Tupac emphasized the need for change to occur not only in the larger society, but also in black communities themselves. With lines such as "Tired of being poor and even worse I'm black, my stomach hurts so I'm looking for a purse to snatch," Tupac encapsulated the tragic irony of the situation facing many blacks. When basic survival needs such as food become unattainable, antisocial behaviors surface. Tupac suggested that there was a conspiracy in the higher echelons of mainstream society to make sure that black communities had access to guns and drugs so that they could destroy themselves: "First ship them dope and let them deal the brothas; give them guns, step back, and watch them kill each other."

EMERGING PATTERNS

"Memories Are Made of This" is the title of a popular pop song of the 1940s by crooner Perry Como. In the post–hip-hop era, this title has taken on prophetic dimensions. Pop music today seems, in fact, to have made a 180-degree turnabout, with traditional melodic lines and rhythms becoming again part of its code. The memories of the past have become the forms of the present. Although this pattern is not unexpected within the analysis of pop culture being put forward in this book, the withdrawal to nostalgia at earlier and earlier stages is. A second emerging pattern is that more and more individuals are jumping onto the pop music stage to grab a voice for themselves. While populism has always been at the basis of pop culture's allure, it is also true that today there just may be too many actors on the pop culture stage for any specific type of performance to catch on broadly. So, if there are any trends in pop culture and music today they are largely negative ones. Pop culture may be losing its hegemony. The pop culture experiment of the past 150 years either is on the verge of disappearing completely or else is morphing into a new form that will differ radically from its historical paradigm.

The Early Onset of Nostalgia

A look at the lyrics and forms of current musical styles reveals that certain things never seem to change. Sexuality and its sentimental counterpart, romance, still dominate new music. Also, as in the hippie 1960s, protest and a general critique of society still can be found in a variety of emerging musical genres. Laté 1990s groups such as Rage Against the Machine attempted to continue the tradition of Bob Dylan and Crosby, Stills, Nash, and Young, expressing rage against "the system." However, although such musical voices remain important vehicles for stimulating social awareness and protest, like all other things in contemporary pop culture they seem either to pass much too quickly from the public eye or else to have very little effect other than to get people to buy CDs and DVDs.

Several signs suggest, moreover, that almost the instant they come out, musical trends pass unnoticed into the realm of nostalgia. One sign is the current lack of moral panic with regard to the new trends. Another sign is the constant glorification of musicians from the past. The stars of yesteryear are as much in the limelight as are current ones. For example, in the past few years, no new artists have been hired to star at the halftime Superbowl show. On the contrary, this show has been headlined by names of the past such as Janet Jackson, Paul McCartney, the Rolling Stones, and Prince. A third sure sign is the constant recycling of previous trends. Bored with the onslaught of new musical fads, fleeting pop icons, and simply bad music, many people today seem to be turning away from new forms of pop music and opting to engage in nostalgic fads, such as ballroom dancing.

Indie Music

Today, virtually anyone with access to the Internet can express himself or herself musically. The result has been a proliferation of online pop musicians. While they may be garnering international attention, the attention is short-lived. Rarely does an indie musician cross over to the traditional media stages. And this, more than anything else—that is, the drawing of audiences' attention to numerous ephemeral musical and pop culture trends—may be spelling out the demise of pop culture. In some ways the online democratization process started with grunge music, epitomized by the band Nirvana. Although Nirvana became highly popular, successful enough to be considered a true indie band, its style of music inspired thousands of young people to pick up an instrument (whether they could play it or not) and start a band. Nirvana's music was simplistic and easy to play yet somehow had great appeal. It was interesting in itself, but it may have led to the eclecticism that now borders on randomness.

Pop music in general has caught the grunge virus, so to speak. Most of it has a do-it-yourself attitude. Online indie bands will use anything from kitchen utensils to highly sophisticated electronic instruments in tandem or in various combinations to make their largely aleatory music—which can be easily downloaded, free of charge. But trends from the online stage are going nowhere. To lovers of pop culture, the hope is that this pattern is ephemeral, nothing more than a contemporary form of bricolage. Perhaps the problem is that the online stage itself has not yet become the dominant new stage for pop culture. Only the future will tell. Needless to say, the current fragmentation and uncertain future of pop culture is a key topic in contemporary pop culture studies. This issue will be addressed again in the final chapter.

6

CINEMA AND VIDEO

The cinema, that dream factory, takes over and employs countless
mythical motifs.

Mircea Eliade (1907–1986)

The great French director Jean-Luc Godard (b. 1930) once wrote, "All
you need for a movie is a gun and a girl" (Godard 1992: 8). Godard's
witticism not only captures in microcosm the whole gamut of genres that
we associate with popular cinema but also highlights two key components
of pop culture entertainment generally—sex and violence. Perhaps no other
media stage has been as influential as cinema in spreading and ensconcing
sex and violence as part of the more generic pop culture spectacle. But that
is not all that cinema is about. For example, some of the first celebrities were
enshrined through their appearances on the silver screen; and fashion trends
spread from that screen to society at large (and still do). No other media
stage has stimulated so much artistic creativity as has that screen. And no
other art form has had the capacity to hold up a mirror to the contemporary
psyche as has cinema. As the Swedish director Ingmar Bergman, born 1918,
said in a 1991 interview in London: "No art passes our conscience in the
way film does, and goes directly to our feelings, deep down into the dark
rooms of our souls."

The purpose of this chapter is to discuss the role of cinema and (more
recently) video in the rise and spread of pop culture. Cinema is especially
important for understanding pop culture's dualism of entertainment vs.
engagement, since the film industry has produced outstanding examples of
both "trash" and "high art." Cinema is also the media stage that gave rise
to the style of artistic representation known as *postmodernism*. Film remains

the art form to which people today respond most strongly and to which they look for recreation, inspiration, and insight.

MOTION PICTURES

Photographic technology is the predecessor of cinematic technology. Photography dates back to the Renaissance, when the first crude camera, called a *camera obscura* (*dark chamber*), consisting of a box with a tiny opening in one side that allowed light to come in, was used mainly by painters as a sketching aid. In 1826 the French physicist Joseph Nicéphore Niépce (1765–1833) produced the first modern camera. Photographic machinery was developed shortly thereafter by French painter Louis J. M. Daguerre (1787–1851), who worked as Niépce's partner for several years, and the British inventor William Henry Fox Talbot (1800–1877). The first successful "moving photographs" were made in 1877 by Eadweard Muybridge (1830–1904), a British photographer working in California. Muybridge took a series of photographs of a running horse, setting up a row of cameras with strings attached to their shutters. When the horse ran by, it broke each string in succession, tripping the shutters. Muybridge's procedure influenced inventors in several countries to work toward developing devices for recording moving images. Among them was Thomas Edison (1847–1931), who invented the first functional motion picture camera in 1888, when he filmed fifteen seconds of one of his assistants sneezing. Shortly thereafter, Auguste Marie Louis Nicolas Lumière (1862–1954) and his brother Louis Jean Lumière (1864–1948) gave the first public showing of a "moving picture" film, in a Paris café in 1895.

Historians trace the origin of cinema to the year after the Lumière demonstration (1896), when the French magician Georges Méliès made a series of films that explored the narrative potential of the new medium. In 1899, in a studio on the outskirts of Paris, Méliès reconstructed a ten-part version of the trial of French army officer Alfred Dreyfus and filmed *Cinderella* (1900) in twenty scenes. Méliès is chiefly remembered, however, for his clever fantasies, such as *A Trip to the Moon* (1902), in which he exploited the movie camera's capacities to capture the emotional subtleties of human expression through close-up and angle techniques. His short films were an instant hit with the public and were shown internationally. Although considered little more than curiosities today, they are significant precursors of an art form that was in its infancy at the time.

American inventor Edwin S. Porter produced the first major American silent film, *The Great Train Robbery*, in 1903. Only eight minutes long, it was to have a great influence on the development of motion pictures because of its intercutting of scenes shot at different times and in different places to form a unified narrative, culminating in a suspenseful chase. With the successful production of D. W. Griffith's *The Birth of a Nation* (1915), small theaters sprang up throughout the United States. Cinema had become a mass entertainment art form. Most films of the time were short comedies, adventure stories, or filmed records of performances by leading vaudevillian actors of the day.

Between 1915 and 1920, grandiose movie palaces proliferated throughout the United States. The film industry moved gradually to Hollywood. Hundreds of films a year poured from the Hollywood studios to satisfy the cravings of a fanatic movie-going public. The vast majority were westerns, slapstick comedies, and elegant romantic melodramas such as Cecil B. De Mille's *Male and Female* (1919). After World War I, motion-picture production became a major business, generating millions of dollars for successful studios.

The transition from silent to sound films was so rapid that many films released in 1928 and 1929 had begun production as silent films but were hastily turned into sound films, or *talkies,* as they were called. Gangster films and musicals dominated the new "talking screen" of the early 1930s. The vogue of filming popular novels, especially of the pulp fiction variety, reached a peak in the late 1930s with expensively mounted productions, including one of the most popular films in motion-picture history, *Gone with the Wind* (1939). In the same era, many studios also started tapping into pulp fiction's successful foray into the realms of fantasy and horror, with films such as *Dracula* (1931), *Frankenstein* (1931), and *The Mummy* (1932), and their sequels and spin-offs. One of the most enduring films of the era was the musical fantasy *The Wizard of Oz* (1939), based on a book by L. Frank Baum—a children's movie with a frightful theme that reflected the emerging cynicism of society at large, namely, the sense that all human aspirations are ultimately make-believe, that the Wizard at the end of the road of life is really a charlatan. The fun of living is in getting to Oz, not finding out the truth about Oz.

One American filmmaker who crossed over to Hollywood from radio in 1940, transforming cinema into a veritable art form, was the writer-director-actor Orson Welles. Welles experimented with new camera angles and sound effects that greatly extended the representational power of film.

Film and Video Timeline

1877: Eadweard Muybridge captures moving images on film.

1888: Thomas Edison develops the first motion picture camera.

1889: Hannibal Goodwin develops technology that allows movies to be created.

1894: Thomas Edison opens up the first kinetoscope parlors with coin-operated projectors.

1895: The Lumière brothers show the first short films, in Paris.

1896: Thomas Edison invents the Vitascope, which is capable of large-screen projection.

1903: Edwin S. Porter's *The Great Train Robbery*, an early western, gains popularity, indicating that the era of cinema is just around the corner. *The Great Train Robbery* is the first violent film.

1907: Storefront movie parlors, called *nickelodeons* because the price of admission was five cents, begin to flourish.

1910s: Silent films become popular. The first movie celebrities emerge in the late 1910s and early 1920s.

1914: Movie palaces start opening up in New York City.

1915: D. W. Griffith's *The Birth of a Nation*, the first racist film, gains unexpected success.

1920s: The Big Five studios (Paramount, MGM, Warner Brothers, Twentieth Century Fox, RKO) and the Little Three studios (Columbia, Universal, United Artists) are founded in the late 1920s.

His *Citizen Kane* (1941) and *The Magnificent Ambersons* (1942) influenced the subsequent work of virtually every major filmmaker in the world. His efforts to make cinema a modern vehicle for art were also paralleled in other parts of the world. In Italy, for example, cinema achieved an intimacy and depth of emotion that has since become associated with the cinematic medium generally, starting with Roberto Rossellini's *Open City* (1945) and Vittorio De Sica's *The Bicycle Thief* (1949).

One of the most distinctive and original directors to emerge in post–World War II international cinema was Sweden's Ingmar Bergman (b. 1918), who brought an intense philosophical and intellectual depth to movie-making that has rarely been equaled, treating the themes of personal isolation, sexual conflict, and religious obsession in emotionally powerful ways. In his film *The Seventh Seal* (1956) he probed the mystery of life and

1922: The American movie industry establishes voluntary censorship.

1927: Soundtrack technology leads the way from silent films to talkies. The first talkie is *The Jazz Singer* (1927), starring Al Jolson.

1930s: The golden age of cinema arrives.

1946: Cinema becomes a major medium, as over 90 million people attend movies weekly.

1947: The House Un-American Activities Commission starts holding hearings on communism in Hollywood.

1957: In *Roth vs. United States* the Supreme Court sets community standards as the criteria for defining obscenity.

1968: MPAA movie ratings are introduced.

1976: VCRs are launched, creating a new movie rental and purchase industry. *Star Wars* initiates a new era of big-budget blockbusters.

1990s: Independent films become popular and successful.

1995: The first megaplex movie theater is built in 1995 in Dallas, leading to a wave of megaplexes and a new cinema-going culture. *Toy Story* is the first completely computer-generated movie, starting a new trend in movie production.

1997: DVDs come onto the scene in 1997, displacing videotapes.

2000s: Movies converge with the Internet, where trailers are shown and where even full features can be seen.

2005 and continuing: Movies start being viewed in new kinds of digital formats, including on cellphones and iPods.

spirituality through the trials and tribulations of a medieval knight playing a game of chess with Death. In *Wild Strawberries* (1957) he created a series of poetic flashbacks reviewing the life of an elderly professor. He then dissected the human condition starkly in a series of films—*Persona* (1966), *Cries and Whispers* (1972), *Scenes from a Marriage* (1973), and *Autumn Sonata* (1978)—which excoriated the futile penchant in the human species to search for meaning in existence.

Starting in the late 1950s, color movies gradually started replacing the black-and-white variety. But some filmmakers continued to prefer the latter, striving for "naked" realism. Such black-and-white films as Alfred Hitchcock's *Psycho* (1960), Peter Bogdanovich's *The Last Picture Show* (1971), Martin Scorsese's *Raging Bull* (1980) and *Zelig* (1983), Woody Allen's *Shadows and Fog* (1992), and Steven Spielberg's *Schindler's List* (1994) have become classics in the genre.

Of the many directors of the last few decades, perhaps no one has been more successful at exploiting the film medium as a versatile form of both art and entertainment than Steven Spielberg (b. 1947). Capitalizing on our profane instinct for horror, the occult, and the grotesque, Spielberg has successfully sanitized this instinct into a "family-friendly" form. His *Jurassic Park* (1993), for instance, taps into the same sense of fear as does the grotesque horror genre while at the same time rendering this fear palatable through characterization and implicit tinges of humor.

Types of Film

There are three main categories of film—*feature films*, *documentaries*, and *animated films*, also called *cartoons*. The feature film is a work of fiction, almost always narrative in structure, which is produced in three stages. The pre-production stage is the period when the script is procured. The script may be an adaptation of a novel or short story, a play, or some other print work; it may also be something written specifically for the screen. The production stage is the period when the filming of the script occurs. Finally, the postproduction (editing) stage is the phase when all the parts of the film, which have been shot out of sequence, are put together to make one cohesive story.

The documentary is a nonfiction film depicting real-life situations, in which individuals often describe their feelings and experiences in an unrehearsed manner to a camera or an interviewer. Documentaries are frequently shot without a script and are rarely shown in theaters that exhibit feature films. They are seen regularly on television, however. Documentaries can be shot on location or simply assembled from archival material.

Animation is the technique of using film to create the illusion of movement from a series of two-dimensional drawings or three-dimensional objects. The creation of an animated motion picture traditionally begins with the preparation of a *storyboard*, a series of sketches that portray the important parts of the story. Additional sketches are then prepared to illustrate backgrounds, décor, and the appearance and temperaments of the characters. Today, most (if not all) animated films are produced digitally on computers. The most popular film genres of today derive their ancestry from the various early and golden age eras of filmmaking.

Movies have revolutionized the delivery of mass entertainment and also traditional notions of art. Whereas in print fiction the author(s) can be easily identified as the creator(s) of the text, in films the question of authorship is much more complex, since a screenwriter and a director are involved in a partnership (although many times the two are one and the same person). The function of screenwriters varies greatly with the type of film being produced. The screenwriter may be called upon to develop an idea or to adapt a novel, stage play, or musical to the special requirements of the screen. But the writer is not the key individual in the production of the film—that role belongs to the director, the individual who visualizes the script and guides the production crew and actors in carrying out his or her vision. In theory, the director has artistic control over everything from the script to the final cut of the film, although in reality various circumstances compromise this ideal of the director's absolute artistic authority. Nonetheless, it is the director's sense of the dramatic, along with his or her creative visualization of the script, that transforms a story into a motion picture.

Alongside the screenwriter and director is the musical composer. For many feature films, composers are assigned the task of creating a musical score to accompany scenes in the story. The composer works with the director to enhance the dramatic content of the individual scenes, since music can establish a mood as well as conjure up any number of emotions. For example, music can identify a person as being suspicious when there is nothing visible on the screen to suggest this trait. Music can also function as a bridge from one scene to another to prepare the audience for an impending change of mood. One or two characters may also be associated with their own musical themes, either related to or separate from the main theme. Film music has become a genre of its own, and in some cases the score has eclipsed the film itself.

The Movie Theater

Throughout the first eighty years of its existence, the movie form was experienced as a communal event, inside a movie theater, complete with intermissions, food fare, and other accouterments of the traditional theater. On every corner of urban America one was bound to find a movie theater. It was often the central attraction of that part of town. But all that changed in the late 1980s with the advent of VCR technology, which threatened to make the movie-watching experience a more individualistic one and, thus, lead to the elimination of the movie theater. The new technology, combined with the advent of cable television, which featured relatively current films on special channels, seemed to seriously threaten the survival of movie theaters and created a climate similar to that of the early 1950s, when television began to challenge the popularity of motion pictures. As a result, film companies increasingly favored large spectacles with fantastic special effects in order to lure the public away from home videos and back to the big screen. Despite the challenge from video, the traditional movie theater has remained as popular as ever—a testament to the power of cinema as a social art form. Digital video discs (DVDs), invented in the 1990s, have stimulated even more interest in movies. Although they make it possible to enjoy movies in the home with all the technological splendor offered by movie theaters (given the right equipment), DVDs too are in fact further entrenching movie-watching in social life, not replacing it.

Today, the threat to the traditional movie theater is coming from the same sources that are threatening traditional paper book culture—cyberspace and new electronic devices. It remains to be seen whether the social function of movie theaters will be transferred to other locales–that is, whether movie-going can or will be replaced. So far the advent of videos, DVDs, movie channels, and other new devices for receiving movies has actually fostered a much wider audience for movies. All kinds of films, past and present, are now available in different media and formats; rentals and sales of movie-carrying devices are providing new revenue for motion-picture companies (in some cases, more revenue than the companies earn from theatrical releases); and advance sales of video and other media rights enable small production companies to finance the creation of low-budget films. With television cable networks as additional sources of revenue, and functioning in some cases as producers themselves, a substantial increase in independent feature-film production has ensued.

Additionally, movie theaters have shown themselves to be resilient by becoming more and more part of the overall pop culture experience. Indeed, to emphasize their entertainment function, today's megaplexes feature not only movies and the usual fast food fare but also video game sections, restaurants, and other recreational accouterments. The movie theater itself has become a variety show.

Genres

The study of movie genres is central within pop culture studies. Early filmmakers drew upon traditional novels, pulp fiction, vaudeville, the circus and other early entertainment sources for their film scripts, projecting cinema directly into the evolutionary momentum that pop culture was gaining in other entertainment domains at the turn of the twentieth century. But

Table 6.1.   Early Movie Genres

Genres	Examples
Crime drama	*Little Caesar* (1930)
Science fiction (sci-fi)	*A Trip to the Moon* (1902)
Animation	*Snow White and the Seven Dwarfs* (1937)
Comedy	*It Happened One Night* (1934)
Character drama	*Citizen Kane* (1941)
Historical drama	*Intolerance* (1916)
Documentary	*Nanook of the North* (1921)
Detective	*The Maltese Falcon* (1941)
Suspense	*M* (1931)
Monster	*King Kong* (1933)
Horror	*Nosferatu* (1922); *Dracula* (1931)
Musical	*Flying Down to Rio* (1933); *The Wizard of Oz* (1939)
War	*Birth of a Nation* (1915); *Wings* (1931)
Action/adventure	*Thief of Baghdad* (1921)
Film noir	*Double Indemnity* (1944)
Western	*The Great Train Robbery* (1903)
Romance	*The Sheik* (1921)
Melodrama	*The Perils of Pauline* (1914)

they also created their own genres, which still greatly influence film production. Current films, television series, made-for-TV movies, miniseries, and even new forms of video and online multimedia productions often follow the genre formulas of early cinema—crime stories, mystery, romance, and adventure, often including violence and sex. From the outset, movies were able to enter the world of mass pop culture easily because they made fiction available to large audiences, including those who previously had restricted access to print works of fiction due to illiteracy. The central objective of all such early film genres was to take the subject matter of pulp fiction and convert it into movie form.

Given the breadth of artistic possibilities that cinema affords, it should come as no surprise that film has spawned its own pastiche of genres, from slasher to "beach party" to "jackass." "Chick flicks" deal with the plight of modern womanhood, and girl power movies feature a fearless heroine. All of these genres tap into general trends within pop culture itself. The chick flick (exemplified by the *Bridget Jones's Diary* series) is especially revealing in this regard because, unlike traditional love stories or romances aimed at primarily female audiences, this new genre highlights the difficulties facing the "liberated woman." Chick flicks constitute a new site in the struggle for women to come to grips socially with their new sense of freedom. In con-

Table 6.2.   More Recent Movie Genres

Genres	Examples
Youth rebellion	*The Wild One* (1954); *Rebel Without a Cause* (1955)
Spy adventure	James Bond series
Intrigue	*Mission Impossible* series; *The Da Vinci Code* (2006)
Romantic comedy	*Pillow Talk* (1959)
Science fiction (sci-fi)*	*The Matrix* (1999)
Slasher	*Friday the Thirteenth* (1980); *I Know What You Did Last Summer* (1997); *Saw* series
Pop music	*Jailhouse Rock* (1957); *A Hard Day's Night* (1964); *Spice World* (1998)
Martial arts	Bruce Lee movies
Rap/hip-hop	*8 Mile* (2002); *Barbershop* (2004)
African-American	*Superfly* (1972)
Hispanic	*El Mariachi* (1992)
Coming-of-age	*The Breakfast Club* (1985)
Antiwar	*Apocalypse Now* (1979)
Sword and sorcery	*Conan the Barbarian* (1982); *Lord of the Rings* series (2001–2003); *Harry Potter* series (2000–2007)
Disaster	*The Towering Inferno* (1974); *The Perfect Storm* (2000)
Apocalyptic thriller	*Lost Souls* (2000); *Left Behind* (2001)
Fear	*Jaws* (1975); *Jurassic Park* (1993)
"Dumb" or "jackass"	*Dumb and Dumber* (1994); *Jackass II* (2006)
Chick flick	*Bridget Jones's Diary* series
Girl power	*Lara Croft*

*The genre of science fiction existed in early film history but has been greatly enhanced by digital techniques.

trast to the fantasy world portrayed in previous romance films targeted at women, the universe of the chick flick challenges traditional views of women as passive beings. It is noteworthy that, although this genre appears to portray womanhood in a new way, it traces its roots to the works of great writers such as Virginia Woolf and Daphne Du Maurier, and to movies such as *The Thornbirds* and *Gone with the Wind*, which were far ahead of their eras.

This type of representation of modern, liberated womanhood is somewhat in contrast to the showcasing of femininity in the broad tradition of the "sacred feminine" or the "Gaia myth," wherein the goddess of the earth, Gaia, is purported to exercise power over Nature and mankind (literally: *man*kind). More than any other filmmaker, Walt Disney (1901–1996) tapped into these mythic views of femininity, with representations that have been both controversial among early feminists and yet strangely popular among women. Using mythology theory as a framework (elaborated in chapter 2), it becomes clear that Disney's popularity is likely due to his sense of the mythic power of womanhood in human life. Nowhere was this idea more evident than in his first great full-length animated feature of 1937, *Snow White and the Seven Dwarfs*. This movie, based on (but significantly differing from) the original 1810 story by the Grimm brothers, has become one of the most popular films in cinema history. Why is this so? According to early feminist theory, the movie was broadly embraced because it portrayed women as passive creatures waiting for their Prince Charming to come along. However, post-feminist criticism and other models of interpretation have counter-proposed an opposing view. According to these theories, the power of women can be seen in the movie when one probes beneath the textual surface. First, the only truly powerful characters in the story are two women—Snow White and the evil queen. The men either are dwarves serving their newfound mistress faithfully, or else they play a perfunctory role (such as providing an anonymous kiss). Snow White is a ruler of Nature. All respond to her command, from the animals to the dwarves and the prince, who is beckoned to her side by an implicit natural instinct. Disney further explored the power of womanhood with similar motifs in *Cinderella* (1950) and *Sleeping Beauty* (1959). For example, like Snow White, Cinderella talks to the animals as part of the way in which she exercises her mystical force over Nature.

As mentioned, some early feminist critics saw the movies as portraying a patriarchal view of womanhood, which revolved around romance, but post-feminist thinking has rejected this narrow interpretation. In the characters of Snow White, Cinderella, Sleeping Beauty, and Tinkerbell (from *Peter Pan*) many now see the emergence of a powerful form of femininity and a deconstruction of patriarchy. The theme of the deconstruction of patriarchy has been further explored by the Disney Studio starting with its 1989 feature *The Little Mermaid*, modeled after the Shakespearean story of Ariel, a mischievous spirit. Ariel's departure to the world above her father's Sea Kingdom saliently showcases the fading power of the patriarchal system. Similarly *Beauty and the Beast* (1991) entails a clever reversal of roles, wherein it is the accursed prince who has to wait for his rescuer princess to come by and save him (Phoca and Wright 1999). Belle has carved out a model for a generation of women to follow in taking charge of their own identities. Two similar movies from the Disney Studio followed in the 1990s, *Pocahontas* (1995) and *Mulan* (1998), in which the heroines are portrayed as being physically and intellectually superior to any of the films' males. At the same time, the characters Pocahontas and Mulan possess the "feminine mystique" of predecessors like Snow White.

Pinsky (2004: 77) claims that movies such as *Snow White* are "archetypal female rescue fantasies with essentially passive fantasies." However, as discussed here, I read a different story in the Disney movies. Snow White, Cinderella, and Sleeping Beauty are hardly passive. They are wise and kind, but not submissive. They motivate those around them, even to the extent that others are at their beck and call. At least in my view, they are strong, feminist characters who at the same time are accepting of others. One cannot overstate the influence of Disney and the Disney Studios on the evolution of contemporary American womanhood and on current representations of femininity in characters such as *Lara Croft* and *Xena*. Despite early feminist misunderstandings of the Disney mythological subtext, it has become clear that cinema was, and continues to be, a powerful force in shaping belief systems and in changing the world, especially in deconstructing views of gender. As the contemporary Czech writer Milan Kundera (b. 1929) has aptly put it (Kundera 1991: 43):

> Woman is the future of man. That means that the world which was once formed in man's image will now be transformed to the image of woman. The more technical and mechanical, cold and metallic it becomes, the more it will need the kind of warmth that only the woman can give it. If we want to save the world, we must adapt to the woman, let ourselves be led by the woman, let ourselves be penetrated by the *Ewigweiblich*, the eternally feminine!

Disney was among the first cinematic geniuses to ensconce the principle of Ewigweiblich into the mindset of pop culture. In so doing, he created a true modern "fairy-land" run by the Tinkerbells of the human imagination. As Fishwick (2002: 61–62) has observed, "Walt Disney wedded art and mass media, revitalizing fantasy for our times."

The Thriller

A genre that has stimulated great interest among pop culture analysts recently is that of the thriller. The thriller is probably the most popular of all genres today—which Dan Brown clearly understood when writing *The Da Vinci Code* (2002). The early director most closely associated with the thriller is Alfred Hitchcock (1899–1980), noted for his technically innovative and psychologically complex treatments of the genre. Hitchcock entered the movie-making business in 1920 as a designer of silent-film title cards and worked as an art director, scriptwriter, and assistant director before directing his first picture, *The Pleasure Garden*, in 1925. It was Hitchcock's third picture, *The Lodger* (1926), about a man suspected of being Jack the Ripper, that thrust the thriller genre into cinematic center stage. In 1929, Hitchcock made his first talking film, *Blackmail*, which was acclaimed for its imaginative use of sound in evoking suspense and a feeling of "creepiness." The term *spine-chiller* became widespread shortly thereafter to describe movies that induced the same kinds of reactions. In *Blackmail*, Hitchcock used a continually clanging shop bell to convey the heroine's feelings of guilt, making her situation a chilling one, both aurally and psychologically. During the 1930s and 1940s Hitchcock gained international fame with a series of immensely popular suspense thrillers, including *The Man Who Knew Too Much* (1934), *The 39 Steps* (1935), *The Lady Vanishes* (1938), *Suspicion* (1941)—about a woman who imagines that her husband is a murderer— *Shadow of a Doubt* (1943), and *Notorious* (1946).

Hitchcock embarked upon the most creative period of his career in the 1950s. In rapid succession, he produced and directed a series of inventive films, beginning with *Strangers on a Train* (1951) and continuing with *Rear Window* (1954), a remake of *The Man Who Knew Too Much* (1956), *Vertigo* (1958), *North by Northwest* (1959), *Psycho* (1960), and *The Birds* (1963). The plots of these pictures have been likened to surreal nightmares that take place in daylight—a small town appears calm on the surface but reveals dark tensions underneath; an innocent man finds himself suddenly the object of suspicion; a wholesome-looking motel clerk is actually a psychotic killer who impersonates his dead mother; and so on. Hitchcock's movies are also notable for their techniques, which were clearly influenced by the montage experiments of Russian director Sergey Eisenstein, such as the use of a series of quick shots to evoke strong emotions in the viewer. In addition to employing montage, Hitchcock manipulates his audience with unusual camera angles and carefully placed sound effects. He meticulously planned each shot and sound segment, creating the impression that nothing in the film had been put there by chance.

So effective was Hitchcock's cinematic art that all subsequent thriller movies are now cast in his shadow. Every new thriller movie is either implicitly or explicitly compared to his work, and the adjective *Hitchcockian* has entered the movie lexicon permanently. The formula *Hitchcock film* = *thriller* is now part of pop culture lore and a prominent page in pop culture's historical evolution. The American Film Institute's 2001 listing of the one hundred most popular thrillers of all time, voted on by 1,800 cinema-goers, ranked Hitchcock's *Psycho* as number one. Two other Hitchcock films made the top ten: *North by Northwest* at number four and *The Birds* at number seven.

A recent film that falls into the category of Hitchcockian thriller, meriting comment here because of its popularity among cinema buffs and theorists alike, is the 2001 film *Memento*, written and directed by Christopher Nolan and based on a short story written by his brother Jonathan Nolan ("Memento Mori"). The plot is both chilling and spine-tingling in true Hitchcockian style. The main character, Leonard, is forced to live entirely in the present, unable to create new memories after suffering a head injury, as he seeks revenge for the rape and murder of his wife. Leonard writes notes on his body, takes Polaroid photos, and keeps pieces of paper so that he can remember what he has discovered—hence the title *Memento* to indicate that his memory is a series of mementos, which he is unable to connect in any coherent way to create a true sense of reality. The narrative's time sequence is presented in reverse, so the audience is denied the key clues of which the protagonist is also deprived, due to his amnesia. Much like the protagonist in *North by Northwest*, the viewer is projected directly into the horror of having lost memory. Fragmentation and dislocation in the narrative lead to doubt about the reality of consciousness.

We know at the very start that Leonard's wife was killed. Leonard was apparently hit on the head during the intruder's commission of the brutal act, and he is consequently left without short-term memory. He carries with him a picture of the man he suspects of the murder. The death of the man in the picture, and the inference that Leonard killed him, ends the tale. Leonard goes on to write a letter, in the style of previous mementos, perhaps to himself, knowing that he would otherwise forget what happened.

As in many of Hitchcock's thrillers, surreal symbolism is used by Nolan to evoke a sense of mystery and the unknown in viewers. The movie is replete with symbols of time—alarm clocks ringing, a wristwatch, and so forth. However, the movie destroys the sure sense of time normally evoked by such artifacts by showing the plot in both forward and reverse time, distinguishing the two sequences by black-and-white and color cinematography respectively—color sequences show what actually happened; black-and-white ones what Leonard believes happened. The first color scene, in which Leonard shoots and kills Teddy (the suspected murderer of Leonard's wife), is chronologically the last scene of the narrative. In that clip we see a Polaroid undeveloping, a bullet flying back into the barrel of a gun, and Teddy coming back to life. This sequence is followed immediately by a black-and-white scene of Leonard in a motel room talking to an anonymous person on the phone, explaining his circumstances.

To make the movie even more thrilling and spine-chilling, Nolan intersplices the parallel story of a man named Sam Jenkins. As an insurance investigator, Leonard came across a medical claim from Sam Jenkins, who eerily had the same memory problem that he has now. Leonard investigated the case and denied Sam the money he sought because he believed that Sam was faking his condition. Sam's wife also wasn't sure if her husband was faking. So, she came up with a memory test. She had diabetes and it was Sam's job to administer shots of insulin to her. If, in a short time frame, she repeatedly asked for the shots and he repeatedly gave them, she would be able to prove that his condition was real. To her dismay, Sam administered the shot each time she requested it, forgetting that he had just given her one. Eventually, she slipped into a coma from the overdoses and died, leaving Sam a patient in a mental institution. The Sam Jenkins subplot creates a surreal sense that Leonard may, himself, be a patient in a mental institution, and that he himself may have killed his wife.

Why do we get so much pleasure from thrillers, ranging from childhood stories of unknown spirits haunting us to modern-day tales of espionage and horror? The great Greek philosopher Aristotle (384–322 BCE) saw the narrative form itself as the source of this bizarre pleasure, which, he claimed, is motivated by our engagement with fear of the world and with a hidden sense of pity. Narrative allows these feelings to become sublimated through the cathartic effect it produces in us. It is likely the anticipation of evil and the anxiety of impending danger that it creates in us that makes the thriller narrative a pop culture favorite, as Aristotle anticipated. We sense fear whenever the main protagonist of a story is threatened; we experience pity when the character actually experiences harm; and with the release of inner fears and pity through the narrative, we experience *catharsis* (an inner cleansing). In the Hitchcockian thrillers and in movies like *Memento*, catharsis is suspended and not allowed to be released, owing to the lack of any real resolution at the end of the movie. The films end up providing a thrill just for the heck of the thrill. Perhaps that is why we find them intriguing, as we search for catharsis outside of the movie context and in our own lives.

Horror Movies

The sense of horror that thrillers create in us is subliminal. In the horror genre, however, that sense becomes visually concrete, projected right before us on the screen in the form of monsters and terrifying situations. Horror movies serve a similar function to that of carnival freak shows. Like P. T. Barnum's (1810–1891) sideshows, exhibiting "monsters" of Nature such as Siamese twins, bearded ladies, eight-foot wrestlers, and eight-hundred-pound individuals, the horror movie puts on display the feared grotesque in the form of fictional monsters such as Frankenstein and King Kong.

The horror genre has been popular ever since it came onto the pop culture scene through the pulp fiction medium. It is still a staple of current movie fare. From the zombie films of the 1950s and 1960s to present-day bloody movies like *Hostel* (2004) and the *Saw* series of films, the horror movie provides a cathartic relief from inner fear. Not all critics would agree with this assessment, however. Many pop culture critics have understood the monster movie *King Kong* (1933) in terms of how the ape's predicament parallels that of exploited groups, such as African Americans. Do such movies legitimize exploitation by allowing it to become sublimated in fictionalized form and thus purge people of the guilt that they bear? Another reading of the horror genre is that it caters to men's scopophiliac instinct (the pleasure of viewing women as erotic objects). In this interpretive frame, the heroine who falls for King Kong is seen as the true victim, succumbing to masculine voyeurism. Again, do horror movies legitimize this form of exploitation? Or are both types of interpretation really no more than vehicles for expressing particular views of the world on the part of certain critics with a hidden agenda of their own? Neither theory seems to really get at the roots of the appeal of a movie such as *King Kong*, as neither theory considers this genre's basis in folkloric traditions. The use of grotesque images throughout the ages, especially in performances of marionettes and puppetry, suggests a deeper motivation for the appeal of horror stories that is not purely social or scopophiliac. Considering a more fundamental, historically continuous reason for this genre's popularity is helpful to our understanding, especially since a large part of the audiences for such movies consists of African Americans and women. Whereas Disney allowed viewers to escape into a fantasy world of beauty and surreal mythic images, horror allows us to escape to the "other side" of fantasy—the dark, horrific side. Put differently, Disney flicks are to sweet dreams what horror flicks are to nightmares. There is more to the viewing of horror movies than social or scopophiliac interpretive schemes suggest.

No director has shown a greater understanding of the deep roots of the genre of horror than the Canadian David Cronenberg. In his classic *Video-*

drome (1983), Cronenberg suggests that the only horror is the video medium itself. In the film, a video "virus" emits infectious rays that induce hallucinations (a television screen, for example, becomes a huge pair of lips, and a video cassette is forced into a woman's genitals). At the end, the protagonist mutates into a videocassette, prepared to bring about hallucinations in others. The movie is both a warning against and a parody of modern-day censorious critiques of horror such as the two discussed above. As Cronenberg himself phrased it: "Censors tend to do what only psychotics do: they confuse reality with illusion" (Cronenberg 1992: 134).

The first true horror story, *Frankenstein* (1818), was penned by a woman, Mary Shelley (1797–1851), contrary to what scopophiliac theory would anticipate. It is also noteworthy that the word *Frankenstein* was taken from the monster created by the Swiss physician Frankenstein from parts of corpses. Frankenstein's monster has, in a sense, destroyed its creator. And that may be the true subtext of the entire horror genre—the search for a creator and the need to destroy that creator for having given us life in all its horror. As British film critic Robin Wood (1979: 23) aptly observes, "One might say that the true subject of the horror genre is the struggle for recognition of all that our civilization represses and oppresses"—especially the recognition of our own probable purposelessness.

Horror movies are fantasies taking place in the dark side of human nature, which symbolize this dark side through ghosts, vampires, zombies, the undead, serial killers, slashers, and the like. As the French psychoanalyst Jacques Lacan (1901–1981) suggested, horror films are really about our fear of and fascination with the "dark instincts" of the body. In *The Texas Chainsaw Massacre* (1974), a hitchhiker slits his hand open just for the thrill of it. Onlookers recoil in horror, except for the invalid Franklin, who realizes that what lies between the body and the outside world is really only a small membrane of skin, protected merely by a social taboo against its violation. The gap between inner and outer worlds is blurred by horror movies through what Lacan calls *glissage*, whereby the inner body "spills out" into the world, becoming nothing but matter. The appeal of the slasher movie lies, arguably, in its visual depictions of the body's inner organs (brains, intestines, eyeballs, and so on) falling out into the world. But slasher movies were not the first to make explicit this glissage of the body. It has been a central feature of horror movies since Tod Browning's 1932 film *Freaks*, which included a brief shot of an armless, legless man crawling with a knife between his teeth and emerging from under a circus wagon like a gigantic worm. As sideshow oddities, freaks at circuses and carnivals epitomized horror. At the end of the movie *Freaks*, in an improbable horrific act, the high-wire artist is somehow transformed into a chicken with the head of a woman.

Many horror movies have simply updated the circus horror show to fit contemporary social themes. In *The Exorcist* (1972) it is parent-child relationships that provide the context for the satanic horror (Reagan's parents are divorced and her father neglects her, and Father Karras's mother dies in poverty). If the family can survive the crisis together in spite of everything, the evil entity will die; if the family collapses, the evil will have successfully destroyed the moral system at the heart of society. In *Dawn of the Dead* (1978), Ridley Scott's *Alien* movies (1978, 1986, 1992, and 1997), and John Carpenter's *The Thing* (1982), aliens serve as metaphors for the dark side of the psyche. In these films, the aliens invade our most private spaces, impressing themselves more and more indelibly on us. These movies' subtext is transparent: the ultimate threat to humanity comes from within the human mind itself.

POSTMODERNISM

Consideration of the appeal of horror movies brings us to the topic of *postmodernism*, a movement in the arts that gained a foothold in Western society in the 1980s and 1990s. The Hitchcock movies in particular were fundamentally postmodern, especially in that they presented no solutions to the mysteries and various puzzles faced by human beings.

The term *postmodernism* was coined originally by architects in the early 1970s to designate a style that was meant to break away from an earlier modernist style (including skyscrapers, tall monolithic apartment buildings, and so on) that had degenerated into sterile and monotonous formulas. Postmodern architects called for greater individuality, complexity, and eccentricity in design, along with architectural allusions to historically meaningful symbols and themes. Shortly after its adoption in architecture, the notion started to catch on more broadly, becoming a more general trend in philosophy and the arts.

To understand the roots of this movement it is instructive to step back in time to the origins of modernism, to the belief that science was the means for answering life's great questions. Modernism (in this sense) can be traced to the Renaissance, when scientists like Galileo started arguing that science was as effective as religion for gaining insights into the structure of the world, if not more so. Modernism received its greatest impetus after the Enlightenment movement in the eighteenth century came forward to emphasize the use of reason to scrutinize previously accepted doctrines and traditions. In the subsequent nineteenth century, the dizzying growth of technology and the constantly increasing certainty that science could eventually solve all human problems further entrenched modernism into Western groupthink. At mid-century, Charles Darwin (1809–1882) introduced the controversial notion of natural selection, which posed the most serious challenge ever to traditional religious worldviews. By the end of the century, the now famous assertion that "God is dead," made by the German philosopher Friedrich Nietzsche (1844–1900), expressed in a nutshell the radical change in worldview that modernism had brought about in Western society. Postmodernism in philosophy and the arts was a reaction against the modernist perspective. In postmodernism, nothing is certain, and even science and mathematics are seen as constructs of the human imagination, as subject to its vagaries as are the arts. The essence of postmodern technique in the arts was, and continues to be, irony and parody of the modernist belief in scientific certainty. The technique has been expanded to encompass destructive critiques of society itself. As the sociologist Zygmunt Bauman (1992: vii–viii) has perceptively remarked, postmodernism constitutes "a state of mind marked above all by its all-deriding, all-eroding, all-dissolving destructiveness."

Nowhere in pop culture has postmodernism received more room in the limelight than in the movies. Without the silver screen it is unlikely that postmodernism would have become so embedded in popular culture and in society generally. That screen is the medium through which postmodern techniques were first displayed and through which philosophical themes about existence and the "state of the world" have been brought to the attention of countless common folk, not just philosophers and religious thinkers. Several movies merit commentary in this regard, since they show the various aspects of cinematic postmodernism and the phases through which it has gone. These will be discussed below. To my mind, they are significant texts for understanding the recent orientation of pop culture toward postmodern modes of representation, as witnessed in television sitcoms like *The Simpsons*.

I should mention from the outset, however, that postmodern representation in pop culture did not originate in cinema, although it has received its most powerful staging on the screen. Its pop culture origins can be traced to the theater of the Irish-born playwright and novelist Samuel Beckett

(1906–1989), a leading figure of the movement known as *the theater of the absurd*. In his novels and plays, Beckett focused on the wretchedness of existence, exposing the essential frightfulness of the human condition, which he ultimately reduced to the solitary Self. His late 1940s play *Waiting for Godot* is a remarkable work of "proto-postmodern" drama. People reacted strongly to the play, which became an instant classic of the Western theater soon after its debut on television in 1951. *Waiting for Godot* appeals to the modern imagination because, like the two tramps in it, many people have become skeptical about the presence of any purpose to human existence. The play challenges the age-old belief that there is a meaning to life, insinuating instead that all our structures and systems of meaning (language, religious concepts, and so forth) are no more than illusory screens we have set up to avoid the truth—that life is an absurd moment of consciousness on its way to extinction.

Future Worlds

The fear of the future on the basis of the present has been a target of postmodern movie-making since the early 1970s. One of the first postmodern movies that played on this fear is *A Clockwork Orange*, the 1971 cinematic masterpiece of Stanley Kubrick (1928–2000). The setting for the movie is Britain in the future (which many critics claim foreshadowed the world as we know it today). A teenage thug, Alex De Large, lives a life of wanton and reckless crime and sex. Caught and imprisoned for murder, he volunteers to undergo an experimental shock treatment therapy designed to brainwash him to become nauseated by his previous lifestyle. However, Mr. Alexander, one of Alex's victims, traps him, with the aim of avenging himself. He hopes to drive Alex to commit suicide to the strains of Beethoven's Ninth Symphony. But Alex is supported by the media and soon afterward is released and restored to health through therapy.

The movie ends in typical postmodern fashion with no true resolution. The film's showcasing of senseless, aimless violence perpetrated by a teenager and glorified by media attention is a typical postmodern portrait of contemporary life. As mentioned in chapter 2, Alex is a goalless and ruthless adolescent trapped in a dull, decaying world. His psychic escape is through intimidation and crime. He is a ticking time bomb ready to explode at any instant. Alex feels an acute and urgent need to change—indeed to "save"— the world. But he does not know how to save it or what to save it from! The rage in Alex's eyes is the rage shown by contemporary street youths.

The film's fragmented images of life on the streets reinforce the view that life is absurd, without a purpose, and that human actions are a montage of senselessness. Some of the scenic techniques of *A Clockwork Orange* were emulated by Ridley Scott in his 1982 masterpiece *Blade Runner*, based on the science fiction story "Do Androids Dream of Electric Sheep?" by Philip K. Dick (1928–1982). *Blade Runner* still attracts considerable interest from movie aficionados. Before discussing it, however, it is necessary to cover briefly the genre of science fiction, which was a forerunner of postmodernism's futuristic fiction.

Science fiction is so called because it deals with the potential effects of science on human beings. The genre has ancient roots—in his *True History* (160 CE) Lucian of Samosata described a trip to the moon; the seventeenth-century British prelate and historian Francis Godwin also wrote of travel to the moon; and the English statesman Sir Thomas More wrote about a futuristic world in *Utopia* (1516). However, science fiction as we now know it traces its origins to the period after the Industrial Revolution when, in her novel *Frankenstein* (discussed previously), the British novelist Mary Shelley explored the potential of science and technology for doing evil. With the publication of her novel, the science fiction genre emerged as a new form of popular fiction. An early writer specializing in the new genre was French author Jules Verne (1828–1905). His highly popular novels included *Journey to the Center of the Earth* (1864) and *Around the World in Eighty Days* (1873). The first major English writer of science fiction was H. G. Wells (1866–1946), whose *The Time Machine* (1895), *The Island of Dr. Moreau* (1896), and *The War of the Worlds* (1898) quickly became cult classics.

In the twentieth century the popularity of science fiction grew with the publication of *Brave New World* (1932) by Aldous Huxley (1894–1963) and *Nineteen Eighty-Four* (1949) by George Orwell (1903–1950). Interest in the genre was also spurred by the advent of sci-fi movie thrillers, starting with Méliès' *A Trip to the Moon* (1902), and by the rise of television science fiction programs such as *The Twilight Zone* (1959–1964, revived 1985–1987), *Lost in Space* (1965–1968), *Star Trek* (1966–1969), *Dr. Who* (1961–1991), and the *X-Files* (1993–2002), along with the birth of sci-fi television channels.

The movie *Blade Runner* was scripted in a 1980s style of science fiction writing known as *cyberpunk*. The target of cyberpunk writers was dehumanized societies dominated by technology and science. Their work especially emphasized the fallibility of scientists. *Blade Runner* deals with the following typical cyberpunk theme: What if we could bring machines to life? What would they be like? Would they be more "human" than humans?

Against the depressing backdrop of a contemporary choking urban landscape, Rick Deckard is one of a select few futuristic law enforcement officers, nicknamed *blade runners*, who have been trained to detect and track down *replicants*, powerful humanoid robots who have been engineered to do the work of people in space. The replicants need to be tracked down because they have run amok. They have somehow developed the mental characteristics of humans and have started to ask fundamental philosophical questions about their own existence, made all the more urgent by the limited lifespan programmed into them. A desperate band of killer replicants has made its way back to earth seeking to have their programs changed. They look desperately for the corporate tycoon responsible for their creation so that he can give them eternal life. Deckard's assignment is to find these runaway replicants and terminate them.

His search takes place in an urban wasteland where mutants control the streets while the pathetic inhabitants in endless blocks of gloomy high-rises remain glued to their television sets. Deckard relies on a VCR, complete with stop action and precise image-enhancers, to follow the replicants through dark alleys abandoned to the forces of anarchy.

The method used by Deckard to identify a suspect as being either human or replicant is reminiscent of the classic Turing test used by artificial intelligence theorists. The British mathematician Alan Turing (1912–1954) suggested, shortly before his untimely death, that one could program a computer in such a way that it would be virtually impossible to discriminate between its answers and those contrived by a human being. His notion has become immortalized as the *Turing test*. It goes somewhat like this. Suppose a human observer is placed in a room that hides a programmed computer on one side and, on the other, another human being. The computer and the hidden human being can only respond to questions in writing on pieces of paper that are passed back and forth from the observer to the computer and human being through slits in the wall. If the observer cannot identify, on the basis of the written responses, who is the computer and who the human being, then he or she can only conclude that the machine is "intelligent." It has passed the Turing test. Deckard's detection technique rejects the validity of the Turing test because he focuses on the reactions of his interviewee's eyes, not on the simple content of their answers. The eye is a symbol of humanity, and its expressiveness can never be replicated artificially. The replicants and the various mannequins seen in the movie are, clearly, icons of the human form. One of the replicants is even killed by a mannequin. Human-like toys are also seen from time to time. But there is one feature that differentiates human anatomy from artificially made anatomies—the eye. Replicants use their "eyes" exclusively to see; humans also use them to show feeling. Aware of the mysterious power of the human eye, the replicants kill their maker by poking out his eyes. Interestingly, we are never sure throughout the movie if Deckard is a human or a replicant himself, since the camera never provides a close-up of his eyes!

In this postmodern world the replicants, paradoxically, are more "human" than the human characters. Deckard even falls in love with one of them, Rachel, whose name has obvious intertextual connections with the biblical character of the same name. She helps him track down his prey and falls in love with him (or so it seems). The film makes many other references to the Bible. For example, near the end, the replicant Roy, wearing only a white cloth around his waist, in obvious allusion to the scene of Christ's crucifixion, saves Deckard's life at the cost of his own. The white dove that appears when Roy "expires" is reminiscent of the dove that was sent to Noah's ark in the midst of torrential rain to help the ark find a safe place away from the deluge—a symbolic quest for a safer future. Soon after Roy's demise, Deckard and Rachel succeed in reaching safety, escaping the gruesome city scene by rambling off into the countryside. The dark, gloomy atmosphere suddenly clears up, the sun comes out, and a new day dawns. This scene's images call to mind the biblical Garden of Eden. This ending of the movie was not the original one but rather the one that the producers insisted upon. Nevertheless, in my view, it is as valid as is the version in the director's cut.

Blade Runner asks the fundamental questions of philosophy in a new way: What is a human being? What is real? Is there any purpose to existence? By making the replicants icons of human beings, and by transforming their struggle to survive and to know who they are into a reflection of our own struggle, the movie shows the sophistication possible in postmodern movie-making, which integrates pulp fiction style (*Blade Runner* is basically a detective thriller) with philosophical inquiry.

Images Over Words

Perhaps the most frequently discussed example of postmodern technique in cinema is Godfrey Reggio's brilliant 1983 film *Koyaanisqatsi*—a film without words that unfolds through a series of discontinuous, narrative-less images. On the one hand, the movie shows us how disjunctive and purposeless the twentieth-century world based on technology had become; on the other hand, it is an example of what postmodern art is all about. The film has no characters, plot, dialogue, or commentary—that is, it has nothing recognizable as a narrative. The camera juxtaposes contrasting images of cars on freeways, atomic blasts, litter on urban streets, people shopping in malls, housing complexes, buildings being demolished, and the like into a visual pastiche. We see the world as the television camera sees it. And it is a turgid, gloomy world indeed, with no identifiable purpose or meaning. People move around like mindless robots. To show the insanity of a world characterized by countless cars, decaying buildings, and crowds bustling aimlessly about, Reggio incorporates the mesmerizing music of Philip Glass (b. 1937) into the movie to act as a guide to understanding the images, interpreting them tonally. We can hear the senselessness of human actions in the contrasting melodies and rhythms of Glass's music. His slow rhythms tire us with their heaviness, and his fast tempos—which accompany a demented chorus of singers chanting in the background—assault our senses. When the filmic–musical frenzy finally ends, we feel an enormous sense of relief.

The whole film can be conceived of as a musical sonata with an opening part or exposition, a middle developmental section, and a final recapitulation with a coda. The film starts off with a glimpse into a vastly different world—that of the Hopi people of the southwestern United States. The Hopi have a holistic view of existence that does not separate humans from Nature through technology. Glass's choral music in this exposition is sacred and profound. It inspires reverence for the bond that links the human spirit to the physical world. This initial segment stands in dark contrast to the development of the filmic sonata—a cornucopia of dissonant images of a decaying, senseless, industrialized world. Then we are taken back, at the end, to the Hopi world. As in any recapitulation, the opening strains of the choir return, hauntingly, awesomely, and with a warning this time (the coda), which is projected onto the screen: "*Koyaanisqatsi* (from the Hopi language)—crazy life, life in turmoil, life out of balance, life disintegrating, a state of life that calls for another way of living."

Jean-François Lyotard (1984: xxiv) states that in postmodern art, "Narrative function is losing its functors, its great heroes, its great dangers, its great voyages, its great goal." However, in making Western culture more aware of its narrative presuppositions and its preoccupation with science and technology, postmodernism has engendered a serious reevaluation of belief systems. Today postmodernism may have run its course, as happens to everything in pop culture. Indeed, movies such as *Koyaanisqatsi* are no longer being produced, except perhaps by small, experimental production companies. Nevertheless, postmodernism has left its mark on cinema and on society. Recent examples of its legacy include *The Matrix* (1999) and its sequels, which struck a resounding chord with young audiences brought up in a world dominated by computers.

Another common postmodern theme, as discussed already with regard to *A Clockwork Orange*, is the role of violence in daily life. This theme is broached in *Fight Club*, directed by David Fincher, which is even more frightening in its implications about today's society than was *Koyaanisqatsi*. The film's protagonist is a successful young professional living in modern-day America, with a good job and a nice apartment, but suffering from insomnia. To get help for his problem he joins support groups for the terminally ill. He reasons as follows: "When people think you're dying, man, they really, really listen to you instead of just waiting for their turn to speak." His world changes with the entry into his life of a woman named Marla Singer, who is very much like him in outlook and demeanor. No longer able to go through his weekly cleansing rituals, he serendipitously meets a man named Tyler Durden while on a business trip. Tyler is everything the protagonist wishes he could be. Tyler encourages him to join a "fight club," where anything goes among the fighters, much like in a cockfight. Little by little, the fight club starts taking over the protagonist's life. Eventually he realizes that Tyler Durden is himself—a persona he takes on that is a creation of his own mind. It is only in the final stages of the movie that the protagonist comes to understand that the only reality is in the human mind. As Tyler puts it at the end: "We're the middle children of history, man. No purpose or place. We have no Great War, no Great Depression. Our Great War is a spiritual war. Our Great Depression is our lives."

THE BLOCKBUSTER

Blockbuster is a term that comes up often in cinema culture. The word derives from theater slang referring to a highly successful play; in film parlance it refers to a movie that earns an excessive amount of revenue or one that involves famous stars and captures public attention, even if the movie does not meet financial expectations. Blockbusters are of major interest within pop culture studies. Two directors who are particularly associated with the blockbuster are Cecil B. De Mille (1881–1959) and Stephen Spielberg (b. 1947).

Birth of the Blockbuster

Although it has come to the forefront as a major type of film since the mid-1970s, the blockbuster originated with Cecil B. De Mille, an early American motion-picture director and producer, whose spectacular historical epics and biblical film extravaganzas brought the blockbuster into existence. In the 1910s, De Mille made a number of distinctive silent films, including *The Warrens of Virginia* (1915), *Joan the Woman* (1916), and *The Whispering Chorus* (1918). In a short time, through his own personal lifestyle, he carved out the image of the dashing Hollywood director that continues to hold sway over the public's imagination.

In 1923, De Mille produced the first blockbuster with *The Ten Commandments*, an overblown spectacle that contained the blueprint for the blockbuster formula. The movie was enormously successful at the box office. De Mille followed this success in the subsequent decade with many others, including *The Sign of the Cross* (1932), *Cleopatra* (1934), and *The Crusades* (1935). Subsequently, De Mille's larger-than-life, big-budget films became legendary with a string of pictures that included *The Plainsman* (1936), *The Buccaneer* (1938), *Union Pacific* (1939), *Northwest Mounted Police* (1940), *Reap the Wild Wind* (1942), and *Samson and Delilah* (1949), plus a sensationalistic remake of *The Ten Commandments* (1958).

The blockbuster is to movie-making what P. T. Barnum's circus was to spectacle in general. It introduced sensationalism into movies. In fact, one of De Mille's most insightful blockbusters was the 1952 epic about the circus called *The Greatest Show on Earth*.

Entrenchment of the Blockbuster

There is very little doubt that De Mille's successors are Steven Spielberg and George Lucas. Spielberg began making movies at the age of twelve, and by the time he finished college he had at least eight amateur filmic works to his credit. His earliest commercial efforts were TV movies, among which *Duel* (1971), a suspense film about "road rage," brought him wider recognition. *Sugarland Express* (1974), Spielberg's first theatrical feature film, was an expertly crafted variant of *Duel*. He followed it up with

Jaws (1975), a thriller based on American author Peter Benchley's novel of the same name. *Jaws* proved such a tremendous success that Spielberg became a household name.

Jaws marked a turning point in the fortunes of the American film industry. Blockbuster-type films had already become part of the Hollywood production mix, as mentioned above, but *Jaws* rewrote the formula and, above all else, proved that in conjunction with effective marketing strategies a movie release could produce unprecedented revenues. Although it was based on a best-selling novel, *Jaws* lacked big-name stars; it had, instead, the frightening special effect of a mechanical monster shark. The movie also impressed upon Hollywood that the most important segment of the movie-going audience was young people. The importance of young people to the movie industry was further corroborated by the film that surpassed *Jaws* at the box office, George Lucas's *Star Wars* (1977), a science-fantasy block-buster film that, in scenes of space flight, displayed the most spectacular special effects ever seen in cinema up to that time.

The *Star Wars* phenomenon showed that blockbuster movies allowed for family-based rituals, attracting children and parents together to the movie theater. Family outings to the movies would have been unthinkable in the early and golden eras of cinema. Why was (and is) the family experience of going to movies so popular? Mythology theory can be fruitfully enlisted again. The *Star Wars* series of six movies, which wrapped up in 2005, entails a sophisticated pastiche version of several pulp fiction genres, including the superhero tale and the sci-fi story. Like pulp fiction, the *Star Wars* movies are steeped in mythological narrative traditions. For example, in a Greek tragedy the story begins typically with a prologue or monologue that explains the tale's topic. Each episode of *Star Wars* begins in the same manner through the use of rising text against the background of space: "A long time ago in a galaxy far, far away . . ." The *Star Wars* saga is also divided into individual episodes, released in a sequence that starts in medias res, with the fourth episode being the first one put out. Homer's *Iliad* is structured in exactly this manner. The unifying theme of all the *Star Wars* episodes is the universal mythic struggle between evil (the Dark Side) and good (the Force). The villains appear in futuristic white armor, but their leader, Darth Vader, stands out from the foot soldiers by dressing in black and speaking with a low, foreboding tone of voice. He is the leader, after all, of the Dark Side. As the story unfolds, Luke Skywalker, the last Jedi Knight left to fight against the Dark Side, discovers that his father was a Jedi Knight. Luke yearns to know who his father was. In line with the Greek tradition of tragic irony, as in the Oedipus myth, Luke learns that his father is the very person he has destroyed—Darth Vader.

The *Star Wars* saga reverberates with mythic oppositions. Some of these are as follows:

Table 6.3.   Mythic Oppositions in *Star Wars*

Specific opposition	Possible extrapolated meaning
Young vs. old	Idealism vs. wisdom
Luke vs. the emperor	Common person vs. authority figure
Nature vs. technology	Nature vs. culture
The Force vs. the Dark Side	Good vs. evil
Jedi vs. Sith	Democratic society vs. totalitarianism
Rebels vs. empire	Common folk vs. authority
Freedom vs. tyranny	Democracy vs. autocracy
Love vs. hate	Constructive behavior vs. destructive behavior

The twist given to the resolution of the oppositions in *Star Wars* is, of course, an American one. Only in America does youth win out over old age; only here do young people teach adults about love and goodness. As a modern mythic morality tale based on the good vs. evil opposition, *Star Wars* simply reframes this contest as a battle between the Jedi and Sith. Members of the Jedi Order have dedicated themselves for thousands of generations to mastering the Force. They have pledged their lives to fight against evil, living an austere life. By using the Force, the Jedi can manipulate the minds of the weak-willed, move objects telekinetically, peer into the future, move around at enormous speeds, and survive death with their consciousness intact. After a devastating battle, the fallen Jedi are banished and settle in a far-flung planet (Korriban), and this group becomes known as the Sith. Fueled by hatred and a never-ending thirst for power, the Sith and the Jedi clash constantly. The collateral damage from these battles has devastated entire star systems. As in the ancient myths, the setting is cosmological. Humans can only watch the titanic battle that is going on in the cosmic order, as with all mythic battles of religions and legendary traditions. The viewing in this case comes from a seat in the movie theater (or home theater).

Following the standard set by the *Star Wars* saga, blockbusters today usually consist of a series of movies (*Harry Potter* movies, *The Lord of the Ring* movies, and so on). The most popular series is, arguably, that of James Bond. The hero James Bond quickly became an integral part of pop culture after his introduction in 1953 in the novel *Casino Royale*, by writer Ian Fleming (1908–1964) (South and Held 2006). The character became a pop icon, however, only after his filmic debut in *Dr. No* (1962). As a modern-day superhero spy, he is adaptive to change and, yet, retains his essential character. The Bond blockbuster series achieves its appeal by virtue of being one consecutive ongoing narrative, complete with an opening sequence involving a gun barrel, scantily clad or nude women in silhouette, and a signature musical theme. But there is a difference between the James Bond set of blockbusters and the *Star Wars* movies. The *Star Wars* films do not involve audience interaction—in them, the audience is simply a spectator of the unfolding cosmological events. The James Bond movies, on the other hand, allow the audience to enter into a ritualistic thrill ride with the hero. Many of the car scenes come across as moments from video games. James Bond is, essentially, an early video game hero who, even before the advent of video games, could guarantee the audience "players" their thrills at winning the game through vicarious participation in the visual action.

VIDEO CULTURE

The late 1980s saw a revolution in the way people related to movies, with major releases being made available for home video viewing very soon after they left the movie theater. This development created a climate of uneasiness in movie studios. As a result, film companies started increasingly favoring the production of blockbuster-style movies with fantastic special effects in the hope of luring the public away from home videos and back to the big screen. The movie industry's fears, however, turned out to be unfounded. As in the early days of cinema, going to the movies is still perceived as a communal event, something that is to be shared with others, albeit in a strangely silent and uncommunicative way. Being at a movie theater is a social act. So, despite the challenge from video cassettes (and, more recently, DVDs, iPods, and the like), the traditional movie theater has remained as popular as ever. As mentioned previously, the cinema has become an overarching entertainment palace, including video games and restaurants as part of the overall spectacle.

Indeed, the video game, often available in movie theaters, has become a pop culture genre of its own. Today, some movies are adapted directly from video games' themes and characters.

The Advent of Video

The first home videotape recorder on the market was the Beta machine, invented by the Sony Corporation in the late 1970s. The popularity of that device was quickly eclipsed by the VHS videotape format, introduced into the market through clever advertising by the Radio Corporation of America.

The videocassette recorder (VCR), with its capacity to play pre-recorded videotapes that can be rented or purchased at video shops, and to record programs shown on television for later playback, at first made an inevitable dent in movie-going. So too, as previously mentioned, did the cable television systems that emerged at about the same time, which vastly expanded the number of channels available to the home viewer and provided access to recent movies via a pay-TV format. As these new technologies came into widespread use, movie studios were understandably worried. But it was all for naught. The studios had forgotten a major lesson of cinematic history—being in a movie theater with a real audience is part of the communal effect that cinema is intended to create.

Video Games

Video games played on a video console started out as arcade games, going perhaps as far back as the Roaring Twenties, according to some historians. A home video game is really an arcade game with expanded capabilities. In the early 1970s the electronic tennis game named Pong introduced the video-game industry in the United States. After this industry nearly collapsed in the mid-1980s, Japanese companies, especially the Nintendo Corporation, assumed leadership, improving game technology and introducing popular adventure games such as Donkey Kong and Super Mario Brothers, thus spawning a video game culture that is now blossoming into one of the most interesting of all contemporary pop culture spectacles.

The term *video game* is now used to refer to any electronic game, whether it is played on a computer with appropriate software, on a game console, on some portable device (such as a cell phone), or online. There are now genres of video games, and various formats in which they can be played. Particularly relevant to the present discussion is the genre of *role-*

playing, which gained popularity with the Dungeons & Dragons game. Participants pretend to be in a situation or environment, such as a battle or a newly discovered place; each situation has its own rules and each participant plays a specific role or character in the scenario. Occult and horror themes exploited by such games, along with related fantasy themes, highlight the fascination with the macabre and the grotesque that pop culture allows us to indulge. Rather than allowing filmmakers or others to create the horror and adventure, role-playing games let users do so themselves. The increase in the popularity of online gaming of this type has resulted in the formation of subgenres. One example is that of multiplayer online role-playing games, which, as L. Taylor (2006) has recently remarked, are designed as much for sociability and interaction as for the thrill of the game.

The structure of role-playing games is now fully conducive to having multiple players. Participants create a character, known as an *avatar,* by inputting descriptions of appearance and behavior into a communal online space for the game. Other characters have no way of knowing whether the character's traits correspond to the real physical appearance or personality of the player. In this way realism and fantasy mesh completely.

Video gaming has traditionally been intended as a social experience. It has also incorporated many of the popular film genres, from mythic (as in the game Dungeons & Dragons) to adventure, spy, war, and other pulp fiction genres. Sports themes are also highly popular. The question arises: Why are video games so popular? The probable answer is that they make the escapism provided by cinema even more powerful by taking the make-believe element from the screenwriter and director and putting it directly into the hands of the viewer. In video game scripts, the player is the scriptwriter, actor, and director at once. Playing a video game is virtual cinema. Video gaming has spawned its own culture, with attendant websites, blogs, magazines, and the like. With their fusion of music, three-dimensional techniques, and reality-simulating sounds and effects, video games are perfect for the technologically savvy audiences of the contemporary world. The industry's technology enables players to participate in the outcome of a story or plot, to explore its variables, and to take charge of the scene. The spectator is no longer a passive viewer of the spectacle but rather a participant in it. Only in carnivals (such as Mardi Gras in New Orleans, where festivities are essentially in the hands of the participants) does such a possibility exist elsewhere. Like any puzzle or game, the video format requires the player to use his or her creativity to carry out a story line or to win at something. Playing a video game is an engagement with the imaginary.

Video games incorporate many popular film genres, including mythic and fantasy, war, adventure, and science fiction.

©iStockphoto.com/slobo mitic

As with other forms of media and pop culture, opposition and censorship have targeted video games, especially those that involve macabre themes, violence, or sex. To a pop culture analyst such controversy comes as no surprise, for such elements of pop culture have always tended to engender moral panic. It is the usual suspects—namely, politicians, organized religious groups, and other special interest groups—who oppose this new form of "profane theater." Interestingly, recent surveys have shown that video games are attracting diversified groups, not consisting solely of the typical male teenager. Video gamers now include almost as many female players as males and many older individuals, especially for casual online and mobile phone games.

Video games give participants the feeling of being immersed in a simulated world that resembles the real world. The development of more interface features, which relay the sense of touch and other physical sensations into the virtual world, further connect video games to real experience. For example, the Nintendo Wii system features a controller that registers users' movements and transfers them to the game world; a user can "swing" the controller like a golf club and "hit" the virtual golf ball. The division between the imaginary and the real is becoming blurred. Living in Fantasy-land, it would seem, is much more exciting than living in Reality Land.

As Steven Johnson (2005) has cleverly argued, video games may be fostering new and more powerful form of consciousness and intelligence. Video games, Johnson claims, provide a locus for the same kind of rigorous mental workout required for mathematical theorems and puzzles. Video games improve abstract problem-solving skills. The complex plots and intricacies of video games are thus making people today sharper than at any other point in the history of civilization. Johnson sees in this phenomenon a "*Sleeper* curve." This term comes from Woody Allen's 1973 movie *Sleeper*, in which a granola-eating New Yorker falls asleep and reawakens in the future, where junk foods actually prolong life, rather than shorten it. According to Johnson, the subtext of the movie is clear: the most apparently debasing forms of mass diversion turn out to be nutritional after all.

We are a "problem-solving species," Johnson claims—hence the addictive power of video games. Johnson's argument may or may not be true. Will our next great scientific minds and artistic geniuses be addicted video game players? It is quite a stretch to say that video games enhance problem-solving skills and are essential to the future evolution of our species. One thing, though, is for certain—video games, like any other prop in pop culture, provide great enjoyment. If fun enhances cognition, so be it. The lesson to be learned from studying pop culture is not that it is intertwined with intellectual or cognitive growth but rather that it promotes the more carnivalesque (fun) aspects of our existence.

7

TELEVISION

In Beverly Hills they don't throw their garbage away. They make it
into TV shows.

Woody Allen (1935–)

Through cinema, pulp fiction magazines, recordings, newspapers, and
radio, pop culture had become, by the 1950s, the default form of culture in America. Starting in the 1950s, pop culture's prominence was further
cemented by the advent of television, the media stage that has remained
dominant for showcasing pop culture and its trends ever since. Like the
other stages, from the outset television has had its critics, who claim (or at
least worry) that the medium has negative effects on people, especially children. As American literacy lobbyist Frederic Glezer phrased it in a *Newsweek*
article in 1986, television is a "four- to five-hour experience with nothing-
ness." Before the advent of video games (discussed in chapter 6), television
was the main scapegoat in the "culture wars" that continue to rage on in
the United States. Ultimately, however, there is no evidence for any of the
alarming claims nor any basis to the fears. The Australian critic Clive James
(1983: vi) has aptly put it as follows: "Anyone afraid of what he thinks television does to the world is probably just afraid of the world."

The purpose of this chapter is to take a look at the television–pop culture partnership that has been in place since the late 1940s. Why do we
continue to love television, even to the point of spending considerable
amounts of money on new television systems, like plasma TV and HDTV?
The writer Barbara Ehrenreich (1991: 12) answers this question cleverly and
insightfully as follows:

> So why do people keep on watching? The answer, by now, should be per-
> fectly obvious: we love TV because TV brings us a world in which TV does

not exist. In fact, deep in their hearts, this is what the spuds crave most: a rich, new, participatory life.

Ehrenreich may have put her finger directly on the reason that we spend, according to some estimates, over fifteen years of our waking lives watching television.

TELEVISION BROADCASTING

The scientific principles underlying the technology leading to the invention of television were established by John Logie Baird (1888–1946), a British electrical engineer. Baird's findings led to a workable television camera that was developed in 1923 by the Russian-born American engineer Vladimir K. Zworykin (1889–1982) and perfected a little later, in 1927, by the American inventor Philo T. Farnsworth (1906–1971). The first television sets for mass utilization were sold in England in 1936 and in the United States in 1938. After World War II, technical improvements and prosperity led to a growing demand for these sets. In America, six television stations were established at first, each one broadcasting for only a few hours per day. By 1948, thirty-four all-day stations were in operation in twenty-one major cities, and about one million television sets had been sold. By the end of the 1950s national television networks had been established in most industrialized countries. Television had replaced radio as the primary source of mass communications virtually across the world. As the twentieth century came to a close, television entered the Internet Galaxy with the advent of digital television and online television formats. Television's total integration with pop culture is evidenced by the current ubiquity of television sets. They are in hotel rooms (largely replacing Bibles), airports, schools, elevators, office waiting rooms, cafeterias, washrooms, and even outer space. The successful U.S.-manned landing on the moon in July 1969 was documented with live broadcasts made from the surface of the moon. The world, it would seem, has morphed into one big television monitor since television came onto the scene. Technology, moreover, has constantly improved this monitor. And television's usefulness seems to know no bounds. Television technology is now applied to other systems, as in medical devices, security systems, and computer-aided manufacturing.

Television has, like all other mass distraction media, been a two-edged sword. On the positive side, it has been instrumental in bringing about significant and important changes in society. For instance, the television images of the Vietnam War broadcast daily in the late 1960s and early 1970s brought about protest and ultimately an end to the war. The constant exposure and treatment of sexual themes on sitcoms has also, through the years, greatly attenuated the widespread puritanical hypocrisy that previously existed with regard to sexual matters in society at large. The Vietnam War protests and the changes in sexual mores were successful because they did not involve just "intellectuals" but also large segments of the populace. On the other hand, whereas reading books requires various degrees of critical reflection, processing television images does not. The ease of watching television may have surreptitiously induced a kind of intellectual lethargy in society at large, as some critics claim.

As mentioned in chapter 4, after World War I the Westinghouse Electric Corporation established the first commercially owned radio station, KDKA, to offer programming to the general public. Early radio broadcasting was dominated by adaptations of pulp fiction, newspaper reports, stage dramas, and vaudevillian variety shows, which were redesigned for radio in the form of weekly action serials, situation comedies, soap operas, and the like. In similar fashion, many of the early television programs came directly from radio. These included westerns such as *Gunsmoke*, soap operas such as *The Guiding Light*, and sitcoms such as *The Jack Benny Show*. The television variety show also evolved in large part from its radio counterpart. It is thus accurate to say that television at first was little more than "visual radio." In the same way that radio brought previous popular print and theatrical genres into the audio domain, television brought radio genres into the visual domain.

The Radio Corporation of America (RCA) showed the American public how effective and appealing television was with its live coverage of the 1939 New York World's Fair. Immediately thereafter, the National Broadcasting Company (NBC), the Columbia Broadcasting System (CBS), the American Broadcasting Company (ABC), and the DuMont Television Network (which went out of business in 1955) became the first television networks in the United States. *Networks* are groups of stations that centralize the production and distribution of programming. By the mid-1950s NBC, CBS, and ABC—collectively known as the Big Three—had successfully secured American television audiences as their exclusive domain. In the mid-1980s the Fox television network went on the air, capturing a segment of that domain. So, before cable television ended channel scarcity in the late

Television Timeline

1880s: The cathode ray tube is invented, making television technology possible.

1884: Paul Nipkow patents the electrical telescope in Germany, which becomes the basis for television technology.

1927: Philo T. Farnsworth transmits the first television picture.

1935: Farnsworth conducts the first public demonstration of television, in Philadelphia.

1936: The first television service debuts, in Britain.

1939: NBC starts regular television broadcasts from New York City.

1941: The FCC sets standards for television broadcasting.

1948: Milton Berle and Ed Sullivan go on air with the first television variety shows, ushering in the golden age of television. The first community antenna television (CAT) is established.

1950: The A. C. Nielsen Market Research Company starts tracking television audience behaviors. The first swear words are heard on *The Arthur Godfrey Show*.

1950s: Television becomes a dominant medium, with previous radio genres and personalities crossing over to television. Programs such as *I Love Lucy* (starting in 1951), *The Today Show* and *The Tonight Show* (1952), and later *The Beverly Hillbillies* (1964) establish the standards for television broadcasting.

1954: Color television technology is introduced but does not become marketable until the 1970s. The U.S. Senate begins hearings on the purported effects of television violence on juveniles.

1958–1959: Quiz show scandals tarnish television's image.

1960: The first satellite system, called Telstar, is established. The Kennedy-Nixon presidential debates show the power of television to influence public opinion.

1961: A second round of Senate hearings on television violence takes place. The first exposure on television of a navel occurs on the *Dr. Kildare* series.

1966: Prime-time programs are broadcast in color.

1967: Congress creates the Corporation for Public Broadcasting, leading to the establishment of public television channels.

1968: *60 Minutes* starts broadcasting. The National Commission on the Causes of Violence concludes that television violence encourages violent behavior. The first interracial kiss on television is seen on a *Star Trek* episode.

1971: *All in the Family* changes the character of sitcoms, introducing controversial social issues into the content of prime-time programming.

1972: The FCC makes cable available to cities. The U.S. Surgeon General releases a report on the relation between television and social behavior.

1975: HBO (Home Box Office) begins broadcasting via satellite. VCRs are introduced. Under FCC pressure, broadcasters adopt a "family hour" format to provide wholesome early evening family programming.

1976: Cable comes onto the scene. Ted Turner's WTBS in Atlanta, which uplinks to satellite technology, becomes the first true "superstation."

1977: The eight-part miniseries *Roots* sets new standards for television broadcasting with its probe of the African-American experience. The miniseries also shows the first bare female breasts on television.

1980s and 1990s: The popularity of sitcoms such as *M*A*S*H* (1983), *The Cosby Show* (1985), *The Simpsons* (1987), *Seinfeld* (1995), and *Friends* (1995) leads some media critics to define these decades as the "era of the sitcom."

1980: CNN premieres as a twenty-four-hour cable news network, owned originally by Ted Turner, revolutionizing newscasting and television formats generally.

1981: MTV is launched.

1987: Rupert Murdoch's Fox Television makes its debut.

1985–1990: New channels and networks start up, such as UPN (United Paramount Network) and the WB (Warner Brothers). Specialty cable channels emerge, from A&E and The Discovery Channel to The Movie Channel and The Disney Channel. Programs such as *The X-Files* and suspenseful series featuring lawyers, doctors, or other professionals become staples of prime time and appeal to large audiences. Quiz shows such as *The Wheel of Fortune, Jeopardy*, and *Who Wants to Be a Millionaire?* are also highly rated.

1990: The Children's Television Act mandates children's programming.

1991: The first homosexual kiss on American television is seen on an episode of *L. A. Law*.

1994: The direct broadcast satellite industry (DBS) debuts.

1996: The Telecommunications Act abolishes most television ownership restrictions.

1997: Parental advisories are mandated for television programs.

1998: The V-chip is introduced. HDTV broadcasting starts.

(continues)

2000s: Narrowcasting becomes a reality, with specialty channels available along with network programming: TBS, Spike, ESPN, The Weather Channel, TLC, USA Network, and so on. Television and the Internet merge to create a co-broadcasting system, whereby television channels and Internet websites deliver the same or complementary content. Sitcoms such as *Everybody Loves Raymond* (2000) and *Will & Grace* (2000) continue to be popular.

2002: The FCC rules to end antenna-based broadcasting by 2007, gradually transforming the television medium into a digital format.

2003: VOD (video on demand) is introduced.

2005 and continuing: Television starts to receive competition from sites such as MySpace and YouTube.

1980s, viewing choices were largely limited to the programming that the major networks provided.

With the widespread growth of cable television in the 1960s, and then of direct-broadcast-satellite (DBS) services in the 1990s, many new channels and types of programming became available to people across the globe. As a consequence, debates about television's impact on children, world culture, global politics, and community life have become common and widespread. On the one side, critics say that television feeds a constant stream of simplified ideas and sensationalistic images to unwitting viewers, that it negatively influences politics and voting patterns, that it destroys local cultures in favor of a bland culture of Hollywood-oriented distraction, and that it encourages passivity. On the other side, defenders say that television provides a great deal of high-quality educational and cultural programming and that it is the major source of local, national, and international news for many modern-day citizens who would otherwise remain uninformed. Whatever the truth, one thing is certain—television has turned out to be the technological invention that has consolidated McLuhan's global village, because it has made the same pattern and kind of programming (the same type of television sitcoms, adventure programs, and variety shows) available across the globe. With online television becoming more and more widespread, it is clear that television may change its physical channel of delivery, but it will continue to constitute a mass communications medium, as it converges more and more with computers and telecommunications technologies.

As in the case of radio, advertising is the fuel that propels television broadcasting. In the United States and Europe, advertising agencies underwrite network programming. Only in the area of public broadcasting is this not the case. Public television services are generally supported by government funding, contributions from viewers, corporate gifts, and foundation grants. Direct broadcast satellite (DBS) now provides viewers with a system capable of capturing satellite signals. However, most channels available from satellites require subscription fees and licenses.

Interactive Television

Online television has become routine. Moreover, services such as TiVo, Replay TV, and America Online television, among others, offer interactive formats that afford viewers more of a choice in what they watch and when they watch it. Interactive television is not new. In the winter of 1953, in the infancy of television broadcasting, a kid's show called *Winky Dink* was the first program to feature an interactive component. To interact with the show, viewers bought a kit that included a piece of plastic to cover the television screen and a "magic" crayon. Kids could then help the hapless Winky character out of jams. Prompted by the show's announcer, they could draw a bridge for him, for example, so that he could cross over a ravine, and then erase the bridge, as instructed by the announcer, so that the bad guys would plunge into the ravine. The show ran for four years and was revived briefly in 1970.

The next step in introducing interactive television was taken on December 1, 1977, in Columbus, Ohio, where cable companies made a "relay box" available to customers so that they could order movies whenever they wished. The system also showed city council meetings during which viewers could express their opinions through the box. There was also a "Your Call Football" service wherein viewers could anticipate the plays in semiprofessional football games. Such "boxes" are still around today, but with many more interactive functions and sophisticated new features added to them. By the early 1990s, interactive television was very much in the air. Some specialty channels provided by cable companies devised schemes that would allow viewers to watch shows whenever they chose to do so. In the mid-1990s, interactivity exploded onto the World Wide Web. Virtually all channels and programs now have websites, which viewers can visit during, before, or after traditional broadcasts of shows, and which include features such as interactive games. With new technologies, moreover, viewers can pause live television and record shows onto low-cost hard drives with the click of a button. Microsoft's WebTV and AOLTV (America Online TV) allow users to pull up detailed information while they are watching a news or documentary broadcast.

Genres

Despite the obvious differences between radio and television, the development of programming genres for both broadcast media constitutes a single history, as mentioned previously. For example, *I Love Lucy* (1951–1957), which starred Lucille Ball, was adapted from her radio show *My Favorite Husband* (1948–1951). It became the first hit program on American television, finishing first in the national ratings for three seasons in a row (1951–1954) and establishing dramatic elements that have been adopted by subsequent sitcoms—such as the battle between the sexes, arguments among neighbors or work colleagues, and other mundane conflicts. Some television sitcoms, such as *Father Knows Best* (1954–1960) and *The Cosby Show* (1984–1992), leaned instead toward the moralistic narrative, often focusing on child rearing. Some sitcoms have also occasionally used fantasy characters as vehicles for comedy—for example, *Bewitched* (1964–1972) and *I Dream of Jeannie* (1965–1969). Others raised the "critical coefficient" of their contents considerably by providing controversial social commentary.

Sitcoms that looked at important social issues include *All in the Family* (1971–1979) and *M*A*S*H* (1972–1983). An interesting early example was a short-lived sitcom called *It's a Man's World*, which premiered on NBC in 1962. It followed the daily lives of four young men: a refugee from a rich Chicago family, a folk singer, and two orphaned brothers. The episodes of the sitcom were truly iconoclastic for the era. They dealt with premarital sex, feminism, and the generation gap much more intelligently and artistically than any of the current sitcoms can claim to do. Mass audiences were not ready for this type of program, however, and after only nineteen episodes, NBC canceled it.

The television *comedy-variety* genre is a hybrid of vaudeville and nightclub entertainment. In the early years of television, many of the medium's first great stars were comedy-variety performers, including Milton Berle, Sid Caesar, Jackie Gleason, Martha Raye, and Red Skelton. A comedy-variety hour typically consisted of short monologues and skits featuring the host, which alternated with various show-business acts, including singers, bands, stand-up comedians, trained animal acts, and other novelties. The variety show—a related genre in which the host served only as master of ceremonies—emerged in the early period of television. For example, *The*

Ed Sullivan Show (1948–1971), hosted by newspaper columnist Ed Sullivan on CBS, featured entertainers as diverse as the Beatles and the Bolshoi Ballet.

The early years of television also offered many highly regarded anthology dramas. Hour-long works by Paddy Chayefsky (1923–1981), Rod Serling (1924–1975), and other television playwrights were presented live on such programs as *Goodyear-Philco Playhouse* (1951–1960) and *Studio One* (1948–1958). As with radio, however, serial dramas proved to be much more popular and, therefore, the anthologies gradually faded from the screen. Filmed series had mass appeal. They included police dramas, such as *Dragnet* (1952–1959, 1967–1970), *The Mod Squad* (1968–1973), and *Hawaii Five-O* (1968–1980); private-eye series, such as *77 Sunset Strip* (1958–1964), *The Rockford Files* (1974–1980), and *Magnum, P.I.* (1980–1988), in which the character of the detective was as important as the criminal investigation; and westerns, such as *Gunsmoke* (1955–1975), *Wagon Train* (1957–1965), and *Bonanza* (1959–1973), which focused on the settling of the west and the human dramas entailed. Other distinct types of television series included war programs, such as *Rat Patrol* (1966–1967); spy series, such as *The Man from U.N.C.L.E.* (1964–1968); and science fiction series, such as *Star Trek* (1966–1969). Many dramatic series have also been based on the exploits of lawyers, doctors, or rich business entrepreneurs. These have included *Perry Mason* (1957–1966), *L.A. Law* (1986–1994), *Ben Casey* (1961–1966), *Marcus Welby, M.D.* (1969–1976), and *Dallas* (1978–1991).

Television soap operas, like their radio counterparts, explored romance, sex, friendship, and familial relations. Among the most popular of the early television era were *The Guiding Light* (which started in 1952) and *The Edge of Night* (1956–1984). The history of the television soap opera is also the history of gender relations in society. At first, the soaps were no more than afternoon interludes of romance for stay-at-home wives; now they appeal to male and female audiences alike and deal with many serious aspects of relations. Clearly, television not only is a main locus for contemporary pop culture but also functions as society's mirror, reflecting its trends and its concerns.

The earliest years of television offered little in the way of news coverage. This changed in 1956, when NBC introduced *The Huntley-Brinkley Report*, a half-hour national telecast presented in the early evening and featuring filmed reports of the day's events. The other networks followed suit shortly thereafter. With the invention of videotape, the cost of such coverage dropped significantly, allowing individual stations to initiate and expand local news coverage. Network and local news have now become an integral part of television programming. In addition to offering daily news coverage, the networks capitalized on the popularity of news reporting by developing weekly prime-time newsmagazine series, such as *60 Minutes* (starting in 1968) and *20/20* (starting in 1978). Such programs consist of a mixture of cultural reporting, investigative reporting, and human-interest stories. They have proliferated, with many adding elements of the crime genre to their text, as in *48 Hours* and *Dateline NBC*. All-news cable channels have become popular since the mid-1980s. The first of these, CNN (Cable News Network), was founded in 1980 by American businessman Ted Turner. CNN was the first twenty-four-hour television network devoted entirely to news broadcasts. In 1991, the network received wide publicity when its reporter Peter Arnett remained in Iraq during the Persian Gulf War to broadcast his reports. Arnett gave a "play-by-play" account of the conflict, not unlike what a television sportscaster does in describing a football or baseball match. A similar approach occurred during the initial phases of the second Iraq war, when "embedded" news reporters actually jumped on army vehicles and took us, the viewers, directly into the action, at least the type of action where victory was imminent or where the gore of war did not come through.

Coverage of 9/11 and the wars in Afghanistan and Iraq has now taken on a subtly different "humane" approach. After 9/11, there was footage of the towers coming down, the rubble in the aftermath, and victims' families dealing with their losses. Also, although the U.S. government actively encouraged and arranged the "embedding" of reporters during the second Iraq war—presumably because these reporters would see and report the "sunnier" sides of the war—some media coverage of the war has included listing the names of casualties. But for the most part, opinion pieces, commentaries, and human stories fill the television screen, with few or no images of actual conflict, death, and tribulation. Clearly, television news reporting has become as much entertainment and "reality drama" as information programming. War is real; television broadcasts, however, transform the events of the war into a daily adventure serial imbued with all the elements of a fictional narrative.

In the United States, news television has had a noticeable effect on electoral politics and public opinion. As mentioned previously, in 1960 presidential candidates Richard M. Nixon and John F. Kennedy agreed to a series of debates, which were broadcast simultaneously on television and radio. According to surveys, most radio listeners felt that Nixon had won the debates, while television viewers picked Kennedy. This event highlighted the power of the visual image over any other type of image in media events.

THE COMEDIC AND THE REAL

The comedic and the grotesque nature of real life constitutes the subtext of most pop culture representations and spectacles, as argued throughout this book. The former is evident in the sitcom genre; the latter has gained more and more airtime through reality shows, as well as through programs specifically dealing with the grotesque aspects of human life, such as obesity, dwarfism, and the like.

Sitcoms

As mentioned in chapter 4, sitcoms trace their ancestry to the improvised theatrical genre known as the commedia dell'arte. In that genre, the same actor always played the same role. Most of the lively, farcical plots dealt with love affairs, family relations, and sex, as in modern-day sitcoms. It is not known how the commedia originated, but by 1575 the companies that performed it had become extremely popular in Italy. Commedia troupes started appearing throughout Europe shortly thereafter.

The six to twelve characters wore half-masks to emphasize the exaggerated features of a character. They did not use a script; rather, they improvised skits both on outdoor, impromptu stages and in conventional staging areas. Each actor played the role of a stereotypical character as, for instance, Harlequin, the clownish valet; the Doctor, who used meaningless Latin phrases and often suggested dangerous remedies for other characters' imagined illnesses; and Pulcinella, who concocted outrageous schemes to satisfy his animal-like cruelty and lust. Unlike in traditional theater, commedia troupes featured skilled actresses rather than males playing the female characters. Therefore, in a sense, commedia troupes prefigured the importance of females in vaudeville and, later, in pop culture more generally. The characters were archetypes, in the Jungian sense. According to the Swiss psychologist Carl Jung (1875–1961), archetypes are universal unconscious figures that enable people to react to situations in ways similar to those of their ancestors. Jung's studies of mythology convinced him that archetypes are deeply rooted and organized into basic patterns, symbols, and character types. Perhaps it is due to the deep imprint of mythological types in our

Sex Highlights from Sitcom History

1952: *I Love Lucy* never uses the word *pregnant* when Lucille Ball is actually pregnant. Lucy and Ricky Ricardo sleep in separate beds.

1961: On *The Dick Van Dyke Show*, Mary Tyler Moore wants to wear capri pants, but CBS allows the tight pants to be worn only on occasion.

1964: On *Bewitched*, married couple Darrin and Samantha Stevens are seen sharing a double bed.

1965: On *I Dream of Jeannie*, Jeannie must hide her belly button, according to the censors.

1971: On *All in the Family*, the Bunkers address taboo subjects such as menopause, homosexuality, and premarital sex for the first time on American television.

1972: On *Maude*, middle-aged Maude decides to have an abortion.

1977: On *Three's Company*, John Ritter's character pretends to be gay to share an apartment with two women.

1987: On *Married with Children*, jokes about vibrators and nymphomania abound.

1989: *Thirtysomething* shows male lovers in bed, although they do not touch or kiss.

1991: On *Murphy Brown*, Candice Bergen's unmarried character decides to have a baby.

1992: On *Seinfeld*, masturbation is described as "[being the] master of your domain."

2000s: Sitcoms generally take an explicit approach to discussing all topics of sexual concern.

minds that comedic personae, such as the ones found in the commedia and on sitcoms, need little explanation. They seem to have their own unconscious logic.

From the cast of stock characters, each troupe was able to put on hundreds of plays. Commedia actors also developed individual comic routines, called *iazzi*, which they could execute on demand, especially when it was felt that a sudden laugh was needed. For instance, a commedia performer might pretend to trip and tumble into a pail of bath water during the exit sequence. Many of the routines and ideas of the commedia are evident in early vaudeville, burlesque, and radio and television sitcoms. Sitcoms entail modern-day iazzi. Traditionally, sitcoms have featured largely self-contained individual episodes, as in commedia performances. Events of previous episodes are rarely mentioned. Incidentally, this very feature of the sitcom has been parodied by a sitcom—*The Simpsons*. For example, the parody can be seen when Mr. Burns, despite repeated close interaction with his employee Homer Simpson, never recalls previous incidents and does not remember who Homer is in subsequent episodes. Sitcoms started introducing ongoing story lines in the late 1990s. *Friends*, for instance, provides an overall story architecture similar to that of soap operas, often with two or three ongoing episodes taking place simultaneously. *Friends* also used end-of-season cliffhanger episodes. Some of these features were, however, already present in *The Beverly Hillbillies*, in the 1960s and early 1970s.

Commedia features are found throughout the spectrum of sitcoms. For instance, the archetype of the sage, who might be someone with a superior intellect, an elderly person, or else an outsider wryly commenting on a situation in which the other characters have put themselves, can be seen in the persona of Wilson on *Home Improvement*. Some characters provide comic relief, like the Pagliaccio of the commedia. Cosmo Kramer on *Seinfeld* was such a character; Ed Norton on *The Honeymooners* was another. The antagonist is yet another archetypal commedia character found in sitcoms. This character functions as a rival of the sitcom's principal character or protagonist. Michael Stivic on *All in the Family* was one such character, opposing the bigotry of the main character, his father-in-law Archie Bunker. On *The Simpsons*, Homer often makes an antagonist of his neighbor, Ned Flanders.

Other archetypal figures in sitcoms include the following:

- The promiscuous character, who is constantly involved in sexual exploits: for example, the Fonz (*Happy Days*), Blanche Devereaux (*The Golden Girls*), Roz Doyle (*Frasier*), Larry Dallas (*Three's Company*), Joey Tribiani (*Friends*), and Glenn Quagmire (*Family Guy*).
- The meddler, who is always curious about others and a spreader of gossip: Ralph Furley (*Three's Company*).
- The complainer or grouch, who is continuously criticizing others and grumbling about life: Archie Bunker (*All in the Family*), Lou Grant (*The Mary Tyler Moore Show*), Ralph (*The Honeymooners*), and Frank Barone (*Everybody Loves Raymond*).
- The lovable loser who cannot do anything right, yet who is amiable and liked by everyone: Cliff Clavin (*Cheers*), Noel Shempsky (*Frasier*), and Gunther (*Friends*).

- The sarcastic servant who, like Leporello in *Don Giovanni*, provides satiric commentary on events in the sitcom: Florence Johnston (*The Jeffersons*), Geoffrey (*The Fresh Prince of Bel-Air*), and Rosario Salazar (*Will & Grace*).
- The overprotective parent, who attempts to save his or her children from socially induced woes: Cliff Huxtable (*The Cosby Show*), Danny Tanner (*Full House*), and Paul Hennessy (*8 Simple Rules for Dating My Teenage Daughter*).

Such stock characters have great popular appeal because they represent archetypal personalities in real life, allowing sitcoms to be perceived as mirrors of real life. Indeed, the comedic has always been a mode for understanding everyday life, exposing the more ridiculous aspects of human behavior. Since comedies have a playful mood and end happily, they contrast markedly with tragedy, which takes the same aspects and gives them a more serious treatment. In a way, comedy is, as British writer Angela Carter (1991: 56) aptly puts it, "tragedy that happens to other people." Through the egregious mistakes, weaknesses, infidelities, betrayals, acts of deception, mischievous actions, and the like of comedic characters we can see the true tragedy of life, as Carter suggests, through the lens of laughter. And as writer Gore Vidal (b. 1925) has aptly written, through the comedic we come to see, and even accept, the absurdity of many of our own systems of belief: "Laughing at someone else is an excellent way of learning how to laugh at oneself; and questioning what seem to be the absurd beliefs of another group is a good way of recognizing the potential absurdities of one's own cherished beliefs" (Vidal 1974: 78).

Reality Television

Sitcoms continue to populate prime time and are now also seen on rerun channels and other specialty sites, including online sites. A recent rival of the sitcom's television hegemony in prime time is the so-called reality program. Police- and rescue-themed programs clutter the prime-time airwaves, as do unscripted programs such as the *Survivor* and *Temptation Island* series of the early 2000s, which thrust real-life people, not actors, into situations involving all the dramatic elements of the soaps—intrigue, danger, betrayal, and sex. The appeal of the unscripted program, which blurs the difference between reality and fiction, lies in its "text-in-the-making" nature. As in the 1921 play *Six Characters in Search of an Author* by Luigi

Pirandello (1867–1936), the audience is presented with real-life characters in search of a script and a narrative. The fun is in figuring out how this will come about.

Consider *Temptation Island* (2001). A group of common people in bathing suits were put on an idyllic island so that their emotional, sexual, and romantic lives could be wrecked on purpose through "temptation" schemes. Who would overcome temptation? Who would yield to it? The reason the couples in the show agreed to be in it was, purportedly, so that they could test their devotion to each other. But, in my view, they were there to become famous. They were victims of Andy Warhol's prophetic "fifteen minutes of fame" syndrome. Because the characters were everyday people, the show provided a voyeuristic template against which viewers could evaluate their own character (Would I react in the same way? Would I become unfaithful under similar circumstances? and so on). Reality television is part of a virtual carnivalesque freak show that serves the same functions as the carnival sideshows in which "freaks" were displayed as objects of derision and as warnings. Shows about extremely obese people on TLC, and programs about dwarfs or deformed people, are the equivalents of those sideshows. All versions of the freak show feature a moral subtext— freakishness is portrayed as the result of immoral, abnormal, or egoistic living.

Unscripted television is not new. It has been a staple of cable networks and public broadcasting outlets for years. The fine series *1900 House* on Britain's Channel 4, for instance, was much more intriguing than *Survivor* or *Temptation Island*, since it followed the misadventures of a family who agreed to live as the Victorians did for three months. The series combined elements of narrative with those of documentary and drama, producing a televised sociology of family life that was truly powerful. Similarly, the 1971 American documentary of the Loud family—involving seven months of uninterrupted shooting and three hundred hours of nonstop broadcasting— created a text-in-the-making that reflected the banality of bourgeois family life. The Loud family fell apart, which begs the question: Did the television cameras cause the rift? Would all families fall apart in the same situation?

When and why did reality television become so popular? Does this popularity result from television's blurring of the lines between the imaginary and the real? I would answer in the affirmative. Such television-induced continuity between the imaginary and the real was the theme of a truly remarkable 1998 movie called *The Truman Show*. Directed by Peter Weir, and written by Andrew Niccol, the film stars Jim Carrey as Truman Burbank, the unsuspecting star of his very own reality television show. Burbank is the first baby to be legally adopted by a corporation, which films every moment of Truman's life for the television world to witness. Burbank goes about his life in the largest studio ever constructed, a world within a world, without knowing that he is in it. His life is captured by over five thousand cameras, all controlled from a room at the top of the domed studio. Truman's friends, family, and wife are carefully selected actors. In the film, *The Truman Show* becomes one of the most popular television shows ever, with a gross national product equivalent to that of a small country. All revenues are generated by product placement. Eventually Truman learns the truth about his life, despite attempts to conceal it from him.

The world manufactured for Truman is a hybrid of the old and the new, blending the society of the 1950s with the technology of the late 1990s. The idea behind recreating the feel of the 1950s was to evoke the optimism and hope associated with the suburban lifestyle of that era. The citizens of Truman's world, which is appropriately called Seahaven, are polite and friendly, biking cheerfully to work and taking strolls down tree-lined boulevards. The setting is nostalgic. However, its integration with new technologies is jarring and conveys the feeling that something is amiss. Truman drives a recent car (a Ford Taurus), uses an ATM card, and works on a computer. Viewers watch him bathe, sleep, and go through the motions of routine living. The show becomes a ritual experience for viewers from all walks of life. The subtext of the movie is obvious—television has eliminated the difference between itself and reality. Significantly, in the film, advertising is at the core of the success of *The Truman Show*, since revenues are generated by product placement. Companies fight each other to have Truman use their particular brand of coffee, eat their particular brand of chicken, and so on. Viewers can flip through the catalogue of *The Truman Show* and place an order, since everything on the show, from the wardrobes to the furniture, is for sale. When Truman and his wife discuss a new kitchen product, their conversation comes off sounding like a commercial. By the end of the movie, we yearn for Truman to escape from his studio prison cell, at the same time that we remain completely obsessed with his life. Ironically, we need Truman both to stay where he is and to escape his artificial reality.

Current reality television employs *The Truman Show*'s principle that contemporary people can no longer distinguish, or no longer want to distinguish, between reality and fantasy. The blurring of the line between real life and the fiction of television shows is a perfect exemplification of the concept of the *simulacrum*, put forward in 1983 by French philosopher Jean

Baudrillard. Baudrillard claims that the borderline between representation and reality has utterly vanished in today's mediated world, resulting in a universal simulacrum, in which the distinction between texts and life has broken down completely.

All this might signal a return to a primordial, mythic state of mind, where the real and the fantastic, consciousness and dream states, are no longer perceived as distinct, but rather as continuous. Maybe the television is finally becoming a "box of dreams," as writer Ursula Le Guin so aptly characterized it a few years back (in the magazine *Horizon*, 1980): "There's a good deal in common between the mind's eye and the television screen, and though the television set has all too often been the boob tube, it could be, it can be, the box of dreams."

TELEVISION AS A SOCIAL TEXT

Television entered the world very hesitatingly in the 1950s. It has morphed, since then, into a powerful *social text* that most people alive today use and consult on a daily basis to evaluate reality and to extract principles of morality. To see what this means, it is useful to step back in time with one's imagination to a village in medieval Europe. What would daily life have been like in that era? How was society organized? What social text would people have been likely to live by?

Social Texts of Religion

As history records, daily life in the medieval era in Europe was informed and guided by a religious social text—the Bible. Residual elements of that period's social patterns inspired by the Bible are still around today. Religious dates such as Christmas and Easter, for instance, are still regularly planned yearly events around which many people in our society organize social activities. In medieval Europe, the religious social text regulated life on a daily basis. In that era, people went to church regularly, lived by strict moral codes derived from the biblical text, and listened conscientiously to the admonitions and dictates of clergymen. Life's underlying subtext was that each day brought one closer and closer to one's true destiny—salvation and an afterlife with God. Living according to the principles contained in the biblical text no doubt imparted a feeling of security, emotional shelter, and spiritual meaning to people's lives.

After the Renaissance, the Enlightenment, and the Industrial Revolution all kinds of religious social texts, Judeo-Christian and otherwise, came gradually to be replaced by a more secular form of textuality. Today, unless someone has joined a religious community or has chosen to live by the dictates of a specific religious text, his or her default social text is hardly a religious one. We organize our day around work commitments, social appointments, and so on that have hardly anything to do with salvation. Only at a few traditional points in the calendar (such as Christmas, Easter, and the like) do we synchronize our secular text with the more traditional religious one. The secular social text necessitates partitioning the day into time slots. Thus we depend heavily upon such devices as clocks, watches, agendas, appointment books, calendars, and so forth. We would be desperately lost without such things. In this regard, it is relevant to note that in his great 1726 novel *Gulliver's Travels*, Jonathan Swift (1667–1745) satirized the tendency of people to rely on the watch to organize their daily routines— the Lilliputians were baffled to note that Gulliver did virtually nothing without consulting his watch! Like Gulliver, we constantly need to know what time it is in order to carry on with the normal conduct of our daily life.

The Social Text of Television

Outside of special cases—such as in cloisters and monasteries—the textual organization of the day is hardly ever conscious. If we started to reflect upon the value of our daily routines, it is likely that we would soon start to question them. Such questioning does indeed happen in the case of those individuals who have decided to "drop out" of society—that is, to live their lives outside of the dictates of social textuality. In the 1950s, when it first entered the pop culture scene, television almost instantly became the overriding social text through which people gleaned (and still glean) information about the world. Even the way network television programming is structured bespeaks social textuality. If we look through the daily television listings and start classifying the programs into morning, noon, and evening slots, we will get an idea of what this means. With cable television and satellite dishes, the range of programming offered would, at first, appear to be broad and random. But network television is still around, and the reason is that it has not yet lost its function of social textuality.

Consider morning programming. Virtually all the networks start off their daily fare of offerings with several stock types of shows. These are, invariably, information programs (news, weather, sports), children's shows, exercise programs, and talk and quiz shows. There is very little digression from this menu. One may, of course, subscribe to a cable movie channel or to a special interest channel to suit one's fancy. But, as ratings research has shown, most people are inclined to watch the regular fare of network-based morning programs (if they watch television). The morning part of the television text changes somewhat on weekends, reflecting the different kinds of social requirements associated with Saturdays and Sundays. But on weekday mornings, "Wake up, people!" is the underlying subtext. "Here's what you need to know!" blurt out the newscasters. "You're sluggish, so get into shape!" exclaim the fitness instructors. "You're bored and need to gossip, so tune in to meet people with bizarre or heart-wrenching stories!" bellow the talk show hosts.

In the afternoon the primary viewing audience is made up of stay-at-home people. The soap opera continues to be the main staple of this time frame. Rather than go out and chitchat or gossip in the village square, as medieval people tended to do, we do virtually the same thing by peering daily into the complicated lives of soap opera personages. The afternoon is also the time for television's version of medieval morality plays. Talk shows and interview programs allow modern-day people to reveal and confess their "sins" or heart-wrenching stories in public. A large viewing audience can thus participate cathartically in other people's acts of self-revelation, repentance, or emotional healing. The afternoon is thus a time slot for moral issues, acted out upon a media stage that has replaced the pulpit as the platform from which these topics are discussed publicly. Television hosts, like medieval priests, comment upon each case, deriving general moral principles from it.

The third part of the television text, called prime time, is the period in the evenings, from about 7 P.M. to 10 P.M., when many people are home and able to watch television. It is significant that the prelude to evening programming is, as it is for the morning time slot, the news hour. After the news, quiz shows and gossip journalism maintain curiosity and interest, until family programming commences for a couple of hours, with sitcoms, adventure programs, documentaries, movies, and the like. Prime-time programming meshes fictional narrative with moral and social messages for the entire family. Documentary programs in particular showcase real-life events, often bolstered by dramatic portrayals of these events, so that appropriate social lessons can be learned.

Prime time is followed by "late night" programming—a kind of coda to the daily text. There was nothing for medieval people to do past the early evening hours. If they did not go to bed early, then they would likely congregate and converse in village squares. But in contemporary consumerist societies, when the kids are safely in bed, television programs allow viewers to indulge their more prurient interests. Under the cloak of darkness and with innocent eyes and ears fast asleep, one can fantasize and talk about virtually anything under the sun on television with social impunity.

Needless to say, there are now many alternatives to this fare of programs, given the huge number of specialty channels that are available. And of course with online programs, one can indulge one's fancies and interests even more. But, as it turns out, this available variety does not impugn the overall communal nature of the television text. Specialty channels provide the same kinds of options as do specialized books in libraries. One can immerse oneself in any hobby or subject area by taking out the appropriate books from a library. But this in no way alters the general reading preferences in the culture. The same applies by analogy to television.

The television text is adapting to new technologies, but we still read it as a socially meaningful text. It is still the primary stage for pop culture to display its new forms, from music to fashion trends. The history of television genres up to the last few years has been shaped by the fact that the audience for television programming was fairly homogeneous in its tastes and expectations. However, the similarity among different stations' programming has been rapidly changing because of the new technologies. Television audiences today are demanding, and getting, programming that is much more tailored to individualized needs and much more based on a diversity of lifestyles. Like modern society, television has become a diverse, eclectic source of news, entertainment, information, and delectation. But its basic structure has remained intact.

Before cable, satellites, and websites, it was syndicated programming that made inroads into the hegemony that the main networks enjoyed. Syndicated programs are those rented or licensed by their producers to other companies for broadcast, distribution, or exhibition. Programs such as *The Wheel of Fortune* (starting in 1983) came forward to challenge the networks' dominion over audiences. This show continues to be a popular prime-time quiz program. Cable television was first developed in the late 1940s to serve shadow areas—that is, areas that are blocked from receiving signals from a station's transmitting antenna. Today, cable and satellite television have become the norm. Techniques of data compression, which convert television signals to digital code in an efficient way, are starting to increase cable's capacity to five hundred or more channels.

Cable television has introduced *narrowcasting* into television. *Narrow-casting* refers to the use of genre channels designed to cater to individual tastes. Currently, such channels feature cultural and educational programming (Knowledge TV, Discovery Channel, Arts & Entertainment Channel, the Learning Channel), movies (Home Box Office, Showtime, the Movie Network), news (CNN, the Weather Channel, Fox News), music (MTV, VH-1), religion (Vision TV, the Christian Network), information about governmental activities (C-Span, S-Span), sports (ESPN, TSN), shopping (Home Shopping Network, QVC), animation (the Cartoon network), and on and on. In addition to basic service channels, most cable systems also offer pay-per-view technology, which allows individuals access to many other kinds of specialized programs, from adult erotic movies to wrestling and boxing tournaments, video games (as on *The Nintendo Channel*), music for highly specialized tastes, and print-based services specializing in news headlines, program listings, weather updates, and the like. Cable companies now also offer computer and Internet services.

Although there appears to be much more choice for viewers in the Digital Galaxy, narrowcasting is in fact producing more of the same thing, as media conglomerates gain control of the channels. With every merger, homogenizing formulas are established. There may be a hundred channels but, as many subscribers quip, "there's nothing on." Indeed, the explosion in the number of channels has simply resulted in a multiplicity of mediocrities that all have the same prepackaged contents. Every new television station looks like every other one.

Nevertheless, one of the consequences of narrowcasting is that television no longer has the same kind of unifying power to influence society as a group. People once watched programs such as *All in the Family* and debated them in other media and in their social milieus. Now, it is unlikely that people will watch the same programs at the same time as a social group. The spreading of television audiences over multiple shows fragments the interpretation of and reaction to programs and, consequently, diminishes the control that television has over social trends. As a consequence, television is starting to lose its hegemony as a social text. However, the impact of television on society cannot be overstated. Since its advent in the 1950s, television has been one of the most powerful stages on which pop culture has been performed. It has had, and continues to have, the ability to unite vast national populations in their viewing of political and cultural events, such as the address of a leader, a singer's performance, a comedian's monologue, a tear-jerking drama, or a sports event.

Will traditional television remain? Yes, in the same way that radio has remained. It is converging with new technologies, but the magic box is an option that people will continue to make use of when they seek entertainment. As a pop culture stage it is still attractive and in tune with people's instinct for the profane. Shows on death (such as *Six Feet Under*), weirdness, and the occult are now common. "Bad guys" such as Tony Soprano (*The Sopranos*), Vic Mackey (*The Shield*), Gregory House (*House*), and Dexter (*Dexter*) rule over prime time. Dexter is especially interesting in this regard. It is worth noting that the antihero as redeemable villain has always been around in narrative traditions, from Robin Hood to Zorro. Even in the 1970s, programs like *The A-Team*, *The Rockford Files*, and *Dallas* had such characters. The difference is that current antiheroes are more brutal.

Television Mythologies

As discussed in previous chapters, mythology theory (introduced in chapter 2) is a particularly useful framework for explaining some (perhaps most) trends in pop culture. Mythology theory can certainly be applied to understand the appeal of particular television genres and the kinds of meanings they encode. The myth of the hero continues on in adventure series such as *24*; the journey myth is recycled in programs that show faraway places to visit; and so on and so forth. In addition, some of the genres employ mythological concepts in ways that reflect social change. Consider, as a case in point, the "mythology of fatherhood" that television has constructed and continually reshaped from the 1950s to the mid-2000s.

Early sitcoms such as *Father Knows Best* and *The Adventures of Ozzie and Harriet* sculpted the father figure to fit the template of the traditional patriarchal family. Therefore, such sitcoms portrayed the family in a rosy fashion. The father was in charge, with his wife working behind the scenes to maintain emotional harmony among the family members. This mythology of fatherhood reflected the social mindset of the 1950s. Television reinforced it and gave it a narrative form on a weekly basis, allowing viewers to evaluate their own family situations in a comparative way. Portrayals of fatherhood in 1950s television offered two notable exceptions: *The Honeymooners* and *I Love Lucy*, both of which revolved around strong-willed wives who were precursors of later feminist characters on television. In general, though, the subtext to the 1950s television sitcom was, indeed, that father knows best.

In the 1960s and early 1970s the mythology changed in response to new social views of the family. On television, the father was portrayed more as a ludicrous character than as a sage. The sitcom that reflected this new subtext perfectly was *All in the Family*. In the early 1970s, the North American continent was divided, ideologically and emotionally, into two camps—those who supported the views and attitudes of the sitcom's father figure, Archie Bunker, a staunch defender of the Vietnam War, and those who despised the war and thus the persona of Archie Bunker. What was happening inside the fictional Bunker family was apparently happening in families across the continent. North American society had entered into a period of emotional turmoil and bitter debate over such controversial issues as war, racism, the role of women in society, and the workability of the patriarchal family. The new subtext that was informing the sitcoms of that era was the notion of the father as an opinionated, bigoted character. Television characters such as Archie Bunker were the symbolic embodiments of this concept. The 1950s mythology of fatherhood were also challenged in the same decade by sitcoms such as *The Mary Tyler Moore Show, Rhoda, Maude, The Days and Nights of Molly Dodd, Cagney and Lacey*, and others that portrayed strong, independent women who lived outside of patriarchal social structures.

The total deconstruction of the 1950s mythology of patriarchal fatherhood took place in sitcoms from the mid-1980s to the late 1990s. A typical example was *Married . . . with Children*, a morbid parody of fatherhood and of the nuclear family. The father on that program, Al Bundy, was little more than a physical brute, a reprehensible character who was hardly deserving of the title of *father*. Indeed, as the name of the sitcom suggested, he was merely married and just happened to have children (who incidentally were just as shallow as he was)—Bud, his boorish, sex-crazed son, and Kelly, his empty-headed, oversexed daughter. There was no sugar coating in that sitcom. *Married . . . with Children* employed a new, parodic subtext: the idea that the father is a moron. The same approach to fatherhood was taken (and continues to be taken) by *The Simpsons*.

Perhaps the reason that *The Simpsons* has remained popular to this day is that it taps into our hidden need for irony. In its seemingly scathing attacks on all things considered sacred, from the family to religion, it engages audiences in a carnivalesque form of theater that is perfect for the times. Watching an episode of *The Simpsons* makes one feel smart and in the know, since it satirizes what is going on in society at that point in time. Basically, though, *The Simpsons* is no different than any other sitcom and, certainly, no more transgressive than commedia dell'arte's spectacles of the past. *The Simpsons* has remained so well-liked because it has played the role of jester brilliantly, mocking all things in the sacred order. Its carnivalesque appeal, however, is perhaps being usurped by the Web, where, rudeness, crudity, and hilarity can be showcased across the world instantaneously at any hour of the day. It is no wonder that clips from *The Simpsons* and from *Comedy Central* are now showcased on various websites. The new "regular" is, in fact, the profane. On websites, one sees vegetables that talk, testicles with eyes, breasts that make comments about foreign policy, and so on and so forth. I will return to this topic in the final chapter.

It is interesting to note that in the midst of the reconfiguration of the fatherhood mythology, *The Cosby Show*—a throwback to the 1950s—achieved unexpected success throughout the 1980s. In hindsight, there were a number of likely reasons for this show's success. First and foremost, Bill Cosby was a great comedian who could easily endear himself to a large audience. Also, *The Cosby Show* reflected an escalating cultural war in America over representations of the family within pop culture generally. Throughout the 1970s, programs such as *All in the Family* and *The Jeffersons* were reflexes of an iconoclastic movement to tear down authority models and figures. However, during the 1980s, with the ascendancy of right-wing moralism (as evidenced by the election of Ronald Reagan in the United States), the mythology of patriarchal authority was starting to make a comeback. Some audiences were searching for father figures on television who were more traditional, albeit gentle and understanding rather than stern. Bill Cosby fit this image perfectly. But there was a difference. Unlike the wife in *Father Knows Best*, Cosby's onscreen wife had a more assertive role to play in the family. The revamped patriarchal family of *The Cosby Show* provided a reassuring dose of traditional values to those who perceived that the world was in moral flux.

In the 2000s, the representation of fatherhood in sitcoms has become highly diversified, with gay fathers, single fathers, and other types emerging on television. This trend shows that television is indeed a social mirror, reflecting what is going on in society and adapting to it textually. Television is fiction; but its representations seem real because of the medium's ability to tap into trends and changing ideologies. The meshing of the imaginary and the real have always been part of television's power. Many of today's sitcoms are designed specifically for audiences with diverse views of traditional symbols and mores. And, like the makeover shows, sitcoms now reflect society's need to cover up blemishes through cosmetic and fashion-based solutions. Paradoxically, the same audiences also see "ugliness" as unimportant. This ambiguity is evidenced by the popularity of a sitcom called *Ugly Betty* (starting in 2006), which plays on the theme that beauty is not skin-deep but rather a character trait, tapping again into an emerging mythology of womanhood as boasting more than the just the assets of the traditional beauty queen.

EFFECTS

Most people today cannot remember a time when there was no television set in their home. There are now more than 2 billion television sets around the globe. As the automobile did at the turn of the century, television has changed the general shape of world culture. Demographic surveys show consistently that people spend more time in front of television sets than they do working. As a consequence, it is claimed that watching television is bringing about a gradual decline in reading, which is leading to the demise of the concept of the nation-state, as ideas and images cross national boundaries daily through the same television programs. Critics also argue that television is responsible for inducing an insatiable appetite for entertainment. The basic premise in this view of television, as mentioned in chapter 2, is that people imitate television. So, it is claimed, violence on television breeds real violence; vulgarity on television brings about an increase in vulgarity in society; and so on.

Marshall McLuhan was among the first to decry that television had an impact far greater than that of the material it communicated. Television is a representational system that blends the imaginary and the real, as have many media, from the ancient myths to gory crime stories in pulp fiction novels. But television is no more responsible for society's problems than are any other contemporary social texts, including religious ones. The effects produced by television are the same as those produced by pop culture generally. That is, television influences how we see people and how we respond to events—just as newspapers and radio did in the past and, before them, village gossip and other modes of communication. Television has become a target for the simple reason that it has become so much a part of the social landscape. Its total integration into modern society can be seen in the fact that television sets are everywhere. The world, it would seem, has become one big version of *The Truman Show.* The reason is simply that we like television. Or, as Orson Welles so aptly put it, we hate to love it, in the same way that we hate to love fattening foods: "I hate TV. I hate it as much as peanuts. But I can't stop eating peanuts" (Welles 1956: 12).

Mythologization

There are several effects, however, that television has undeniably produced. I will refer to one of these as the *celebrity-making effect*, or as the *mythologizing effect*, because the celebrities that television creates are perceived as mythic figures, larger than life. Like any type of privileged space designed to impart focus and significance to someone (for example, a platform or a pulpit), television creates mythic personages simply by containing them in a box-like space, where they are seen as suspended in real time and space, in a mythic world of their own. The box is psychologically similar to the magic speaking box of many childhood fantasies.

Television personages are infused with godlike qualities by virtue of the fact that they are seen inside the magic box. It is because of the "magic" of pop culture that meeting television actors, sitcom stars, and the like causes great enthusiasm and excitement in many people. These stars are perceived as otherworldly figures who have stepped out of the box to take on human proportions, in the same way that a mythic hero comes into our human world to live among us. Television personages become household names, looming larger than life. Actors and announcers become lifestyle trendsetters. Television celebrities are the contemporary equivalents of the graven images of the Bible. The same effect is produced by other media. An author of best-selling books, a radio personality, a recording artist, a movie actor, and so on are all perceived mythologically. However, since television reaches more people, the mythologizing effect is more widespread. Moreover, it is significant to note that for an author to become truly popular and successful, he or she would probably have to be interviewed on television, by Oprah or another television celebrity. The importance of television even in the creation of celebrities from other media indicates that it is still the dominant stage for constructing the *popular* in pop culture.

In the golden age of television, television celebrities were known throughout the society, for the simple reason that the whole nation watched the same programs at the same time. Clayton Moore (the actor who portrayed the Lone Ranger) and Fess Parker (who played Davy Crockett) became nationwide heroes to children and their parents alike. Spin-offs ensued, with Lone Ranger and Davy Crockett toys, costumes, comics, pop songs, and so on. These characters became true icons, idolized by children and easily able to influence children in various subtle ways. In 1977, after the Fonz (the main character on *Happy Days*) got a library card in one of the sitcom's episodes, nearly five hundred thousand young viewers apparently did so as well.

As the 1970s rolled in, with programs like *The Smothers Brothers, All in the Family,* and *M*A*S*H* gaining popularity, the new celebrities reflected counterculture values that were taking root. As such, however, television icons had lost their value of representing fantasy. The character of the Lone Ranger had been part of a fantasy world and thus akin to ancient mythic heroes. The Smothers brothers, on the other hand, were part of a real world that was too controversial for true mythologization to crystallize. The new celebrities were fighters against bigotry, sexism, war, and racism. The tube had truly become a social text. Its heroes were voices for social change, not for adventure or mythic heroics. But that trend did not last. Indeed, television started losing its function of mythologization in the 1980s for a different reason, as it became more and more a fetishistic medium, catering to specific recreational or even intellectual and aesthetic desires.

All this means, perhaps, that television has lost its status as a social text, although not its traditional structure, since the most popular shows are still crime procedurals (such as *CSI*), soaps (such as *Grey's Anatomy*), and sitcoms. Reality shows, when considered closely, are really about nothing more than contemporary voyeurism. *American Idol* and *Dancing with the Stars* are not much more than sophisticated, nostalgic revisitations of shows like *The Lawrence Welk Show* of the 1950s and 1960s. When cleverly designed programs such as *24* attempt to highlight the absurdity of war, they do so in a fashion that leaves audiences thrilled but not necessarily socially motivated. Unlike James Bond, the protagonist in the series, Jack Bauer, appears tired of war, which has cost him not only physically but also psychologically. He keeps fighting, but for people, rather than for political ideologies. In typical postmodern fashion, the series has a few good guys, a few bad guys, and in between a lot of question marks. The audience is suspended in the simulacrum. There are no James Bond–style victories over evil, just those nagging questions. The television text has indeed developed into a simulacrum itself, which indicates that it may have lost its cultural hegemony as a social text.

Fabrication

I will use the term *history fabrication effect* to refer to the fact that television, in its fifty-year hegemony, has often been the maker of history. Events that are showcased on television are felt as being more significant and historically meaningful to society than those that are not. A riot that gets airtime becomes a historical event; one that does not is ignored. For this reason terrorists are seemingly more interested in simply getting on the air than in

American Idol *and* Dancing with the Stars *are sophisticated, nostalgic revisitations of programs like* The Lawrence Welk Show *of the 1950s and 1960s.*

[American Idol Prod./19 Television/Fox TV Network/Fremantle Media North America/
The Kobal Collection/Mickshaw, Ray]

having their demands satisfied. Television imbues their cause with significance. Political and social protesters frequently inform the news media of their intentions and then dramatically stage their demonstrations for the cameras. Sports events such as the World Series, the Super Bowl, the Stanley Cup Playoffs or the World Cup of soccer are transformed by television coverage into battles of Herculean proportion. Events such as the John Kennedy and Lee Harvey Oswald assassinations, the Vietnam War, the Watergate hearings, the Rodney King beating, the O. J. Simpson trial, the death of Lady Diana, the Bill Clinton sex scandal, the 9/11 attack, the Iraq war, and so on are perceived as portentous and prophetic historical events through the filter of television coverage. People make up their minds about the guilt or innocence of others by watching news and interview programs; they come to see certain behaviors as laudable or damnable by tuning into talk shows or docudramas; and the list could go on and on.

Television has become simultaneously the maker of history and its documenter. People experience history through television rather than just reading about it in a book or studying it at school. Edward R. Murrow

(1908–1965) of *CBS News* became a society-wide hero when, on his *See It Now* documentary in 1954, he fought back against the fanatical senator Joseph McCarthy (1908–1957), who at the time was leading a campaign against a purported Communist subversion of the media program. Murrow used footage of McCarthy's own press conferences to expose the excesses of his anti-Communist campaign. Murrow's rebuke led to the Senate's reprimand of McCarthy, which paralyzed him from taking further political action. The horrific images of the Vietnam War that were transmitted into people's homes daily in the late 1960s and early 1970s brought about an end to the war by mobilizing social protest. Significantly, an MTV flag was hoisted by East German youths over the Berlin Wall as they tore it down in 1989. More people watched the wedding of England's Prince Charles and Princess Diana, and later Diana's funeral, than had ever before in human history observed such events communally. The Bill Clinton–Monica Lewinsky sex scandal allowed common people to become privy to the sexual flaws of a powerful political figure. The images of the two planes smashing into the World Trade Center buildings on September 11, 2001, brought about an international reaction, the consequences of which are still being felt.

Television's role in influencing social mores also cannot be overstated. As Elana Levine (2007) has written, in the 1970s television was awash with representations and references of a sexual nature, which mirrored the aftereffects of the women's liberation movement and the gay rights movement. Television thus became the forum through which society debated and related to shifts in sexual mores. Through such female icons as the characters in *Charlie's Angels* and *Wonder Woman*, and such sitcoms as *Laugh-In* and *Three's Company*, sexuality was legitimized, for the first time in American history, in a public medium.

As mentioned previously, the history-making power of television has led many to stage events for the cameras. The social critic W. T. Anderson (1992: 125–130) appropriately calls these "pseudoevents," since they are not spontaneous but rather planned for the sole purpose of playing to television's huge audiences. Most pseudoevents are intended to be self-fulfilling prophecies. The American invasion of Grenada on October 25, 1983, the Gulf War in 1991, the attack on Afghanistan in 2001, and the war in Iraq starting in 2003 were concomitantly real events and pseudoevents. The actual military operations and conflicts were real events. But the reporting of those wars was orchestrated by a massive public-relations operation. Reporters were censored and kept away from the more brutal action so that the news coverage could be stylized and managed more effectively. The idea was to fabricate a military and moral victory for the viewing public. Pseudo-events constitute unscripted reality television at its best, because they mesh reality (the real killing and terrorizing of people) with news commentary and docudrama representations. As Anderson (1992: 126–127) aptly puts it, the "media take the raw material of experience and fashion it into stories; they retell the stories to us, and we call them reality."

Of course, other media fabricate (or have fabricated) history as well. Books written about wars, historical eras, and the like have always shaped how we perceive certain events of the past. However, since the rise of television in the 1950s, most people have been perceiving history through the tube, so to speak, rather than through print or another medium. The history-making power of television has changed the way we perceive history itself. Now we see history not as a story with a long arc but rather as a kaleidoscopic pastiche of narrative, bits of information, and images compacted for time-constrained transmission. Channels such as CNN's Headline News are formatted in precisely this kind of pastiche, with side-bars and captions giving information on sports, the weather, and subsidiary news items as announcers recite the news. Such a format affords viewers little time to reflect on the topics, implications, and meanings contained in televised information. Just like any variety act, news has become part of the overall entertainment spectacle, stylized for an entertaining effect. The camera moves in to show selected aspects of a situation, such as a face that cares, that is suffering, that is happy, that is angry, and then shifts to the cool, handsome face of an anchorman or to the attractive face of an anchorwoman, who will tell us what it's all about. The news items, the film footage, and the commentaries are all fast-paced and brief. They are designed to present dramatic snippets of easily digestible information in spectacular form. "Within such a stylistic environment," remarks Stuart Ewen (1988: 265), "the news is beyond comprehension." Thus it is that as "nations and people are daily sorted out into boxes marked 'good guys,' 'villains,' 'victims,' and 'lucky ones,' style becomes the essence, reality becomes the appearance" (Ewen 1988: 265–66).

The above discussion is not meant to imply that television has never been used as a powerful medium of social protest or as an agent for social change. Indeed, because television has showcased racial protests, riots, and other significant social events, it has forced the hand of change several times. Without it, there probably would have been no civil rights legislation, no Vietnam War protests, and no politics of accountability after Watergate.

Moreover, many television programs were pivotal in bringing about a change in certain social mores. With the advent of satellite transmission, television has also become a powerful medium for inducing political changes in cultures across the world. When asked about the stunning defeat of Communism in Eastern Europe in the late 1980s, the Polish leader Lech Walesa was reported by the newspapers as having said that it "all came from the TV set," implying that television had undermined the stability of the Communist world's relatively poor and largely sheltered lifestyle through images of consumer delights seen on Western programs and commercials. As McLuhan has often commented, television has indeed shrunk the world into a global village. This is perhaps the reason for the great culture wars that we see in the world today. Having viewed images that contrast sharply with traditional ways of life, many denizens of Planet Earth are rejecting these scenes and are fighting to preserve their localized cultures.

8

ADVERTISING, BRANDING, AND FADS

It is useless to invent something that can't be sold.

Thomas Edison (1847–1931)

Pop culture could not have become a default form of culture in a non-capitalist society. To gain and maintain a foothold in the social main-stream, it needs (and has always needed) the support of business. In the decade following World War I, the American economy embarked on a period of spectacular growth. Spurred on by the good times and a desire to be modern, large numbers of Americans adopted new lifestyles. The booming economy and fast-paced life of the decade gave it the nickname of the Roaring Twenties (as mentioned several times previously). It was during the Roaring Twenties that pop culture became a society-wide reality. Shopping for the fun of it became a ritual in the same decade, as department stores started spreading all over the United States. People continue to perceive shopping as a form of recreation and buy things that they may not need, finding the act pleasurable in itself. Shopping, advertising, and pop culture have developed such an intrinsic partnership that we no longer are able to separate them in our minds. This continuum between pop culture and the market is perhaps the reason that, as the Frankfurt School philosopher Herbert Marcuse (1964: 18) suggested, culture, art, religion, and philosophy are now "sold" and "packaged" in the same way as commercial products.

> If mass communications blend together harmoniously, and often unnotice-ably, art, politics, religion, and philosophy with commercials, they bring these realms of culture to their common denominator—the commodity

217

form. The music of the soul is also the music of salesmanship. Exchange value, not truth value, counts.

The purpose of this chapter is to look at the partnership between consumerism and pop culture in light of the themes that have guided our trek through pop culture history so far. As noted, advertising has become broadly integrated with pop culture. Many children's cartoons, for example, are little more than program-length commercials that promote action figures, dolls, and other figures of the same name as the programs.

ADVERTISING

The contemporary advertising industry was founded at the threshold of the twentieth century on the premise that sales of a product would increase if the product could be linked to lifestyle trends and other socially significant patterns. Indirect proof that product advertising has achieved its goal of blurring the line between the product and culture can be seen in the fact that advertising is now used as a technique of persuasion by anyone in society who wants to influence people to do something—to endorse a political candidate, to support a cause, and so on and so forth. Business firms, political parties, candidates, social organizations, special-interest groups, and governments alike routinely use advertising to create favorable images of themselves. Since the 1960s, advertising campaigns have been routinely mounted not only to promote products but also to publicize issues of social concern (such as cancer, AIDS, human rights, or poverty).

The messages of product advertising are everywhere. They are on billboards, on the radio, on television, on buses and subway cars, in magazines and newspapers, on posters, and on clothes, shoes, hats, pens—and the list could go on and on. To say that advertising has become a ubiquitous form of communication is an understatement. It is estimated that the average American is exposed to over three thousand advertisements each day and watches three years' worth of television commercials over the course of a lifetime. Advertising is designed to influence attitudes and lifestyle behaviors by covertly suggesting how we can best satisfy our innermost urges and aspirations. Using both verbal and nonverbal techniques to make its messages as persuasive as possible, advertising has become an integral category of modern-day pop culture. Indeed, ads and commercials are often more entertaining than are the programs sponsored.

Historical Sketch

The term *advertising* derives from the medieval Latin verb *advertere*, meaning *to direct one's attention to. Advertising* designates any type or form of public announcement intended to promote the sale of specific commodities or services, or to spread a social or political message. The first advertising materials of human civilization were the many outdoor signs displayed above the shop doors of ancient cities of the Middle East. As early as 3000 BCE, the Babylonians used such signs to advertise what was in the stores. The ancient Greeks and Romans also hung signs outside their shops. Since few people could read, the merchants of the era used recognizable visual symbols carved in stone, clay, or wood for their signs. Throughout history, poster and picture signs in marketplaces and temples have constituted popular media for disseminating information and for promoting the barter and sale of goods and services. With the invention of the printing press in the fifteenth century, fliers and posters could be printed quickly and cheaply, and posted in public places or inserted into books, pamphlets, newspapers, and the like. The printing press also spawned a new form of advertising, known as the *handbill*. The handbill was more effective than posters or signs because it could be reproduced and distributed to many people in diverse areas.

The increasing use of advertising and its growing influence on people's perception of products led to the establishment of the first advertising agency by Philadelphia entrepreneur Volney B. Palmer in 1842. By 1849, Palmer had offices in New York, Boston, and Baltimore in addition to his Philadelphia office. In 1865, George P. Rowell began contracting with local newspapers as a go-between with clients. Ten years later, in 1875, N. W. Ayer and Son, another Philadelphia advertising agency, became a rival of Rowell and Palmer. In time, N. W. Ayer and Son hired writers and artists to create print ads and to carry out complete advertising campaigns for clients. It thus became the first ad agency in the modern sense of the word. By 1900, various agencies in the United States were writing ads for all kinds of clients and were starting to assume responsibility for full campaigns. By the 1920s, such agencies had themselves become large business enterprises. The agencies were constantly developing new techniques and methods to influence the so-called typical consumer to buy products. At this point in time, corporate executives came to truly understand advertising as an instrument of persuasion. Business and psychology had joined forces, which helped companies build better conceptual bridges between their products

An Advertising Timeline

1625: The first ad appears in an English newspaper.

1735: Benjamin Franklin sells ad space in the *Pennsylvania Gazette*.

1792: The first propaganda ministry is established in France.

1804: The first classified ads in colonial America run in the *Boston News-Letter*, featuring land deals and ship cargoes.

1830s: The penny press becomes the first advertising-supported media outlet.

1841: The first ad agency is established in Boston by Volney Palmer.

1860s: Advertising is incorporated into magazines.

1871: P. T. Barnum establishes his Greatest Show on Earth, creating a wave of publicity stunts, posters, and the like, which brings about the modern advertising age.

1875: The first modern ad agency working for advertisers and companies is established by N. W. Ayer in Philadelphia.

1880s: Brands (products with names) appear.

1887: *Ladies' Home Journal* is designed for consumer advertising.

1914: The Federal Trade Commission is established to help monitor advertising practices.

1920s: Newspapers and magazines start depending heavily on advertising revenues for their survival.

and the consumers' desires and aspirations. Advertisers started to pay close attention to trends in the ever-expanding pop culture world and often used, in their jingles and slogans, the same kinds of musical and linguistic styles that were found in pop culture. In the 1920s, people listened to radio as much for the commercials as for the programs.

In the same era, the increased use of electricity led to the possibility of further entrenching advertising in the social landscape through the use of new technologies. For example, electricity made possible the illuminated outdoor poster. At around the same time, photoengraving and other printing inventions helped both the editorial and advertising departments of magazines create truly effective illustrative material. The radio commercial—a mini-narrative or musical jingle revolving around a product or service—became a highly popular form of advertising, since it could reach masses of potential customers, print-literate or not, instantaneously, providing a minute or so of pleasing music or catchy verbal play. The commercial

1922: Newspaper columnist Walter Lippmann publishes a controversial book, *Public Opinion*, in which he illustrates how slogans and other such devices shape public perception. The first radio commercial is aired.

1942: The systematic study of propaganda and advertising is started by the U.S. military.

1950s–1960s: Thirty-second and sixty-second television commercials become routine.

1957: Vance Packard's *The Hidden Persuaders* is published, warning people of the dangers of advertising.

1971: Tobacco ads are banned from television.

1984: Apple's Macintosh commercial at the halftime of the Super Bowl shows that advertising has become an art form in itself.

Mid-1980s: Brand placement and a general partnership between advertising and pop culture solidifies.

1994: Internet banner advertising begins.

1995: The Internet advertising agency DoubleClick is founded.

1998: Tobacco ads are banned from billboards.

2000s: The Internet and the World Wide Web become increasingly attractive as sites for advertising. New forms of advertising, such as pop-ups, appear.

became even more influential as a vehicle for disseminating advertising messages with the advent of television in the early 1950s. Television commercials of the day were familiar across society. Recently, the Internet has come forward to complement and supplement both the print and commercial (radio and television) forms of advertising. As in television commercials, Internet advertisers use graphics, audio, and various visual techniques to enhance the effectiveness of their messages.

Today, we assimilate and react to advertising texts unwittingly and in ways that parallel how we respond to artistic texts. Ads thus mirror and shape cultural trends in a synergistic fashion. There are now even websites, such as www.AdCritic.com, that feature ads for their own sake, so that people can view them for their aesthetic qualities alone, enjoying them as they would any other type of modern performance or spectacle. Among the most popular entries on YouTube are ads, such as those shown during the Super Bowl or those that have social value, including Dove's "real beauty" ads.

The two techniques that are intended to merge advertising into the social substratum are called *positioning* and *image creation*. *Positioning* is the placing or targeting of a product for a specific group, known as a market segment. For example, Budweiser beer is normally positioned for a male audience, whereas Chanel perfume is positioned for a female audience. Ads for these products will be found in magazines or on television programs that cater to the interests of the appropriate gender. The Mercedes Benz is aimed at well-to-do car buyers; Dodge vans, on the other hand, are targeted at middle-class suburban dwellers. In these cases, the vehicles' respective ads and commercials will be associated with magazines, programs, and other forms that cater to the interests of the appropriate economic class.

Creating an *image* for a product inheres in fashioning a "personality" for it so that it can be positioned for specific market populations. The image is an amalgam of the product's name, packaging, logo, price, and overall presentation that creates a recognizable identity for it. Take beer as an example. What kinds of people drink Budweiser? And what kinds drink Stella Artois instead? Answers to these questions would typically include remarks about the educational level, economic class, and social attitudes of the consumer. The person who drinks Budweiser is perceived as socially different from the one who drinks Stella Artois. The former is imagined to be a down-to-earth (male) character who simply wants to hang out with the guys; the latter is envisioned as a smooth, sophisticated type (male or female) who aspires to climb the ladder of social success. Budweiser commercials are thus run on sports programs, whereas Stella Artois ads are run on current affairs programs. The idea behind creating an image for the product is to speak directly to particular types of individuals, not to everyone, so that the targeted individuals can see their own personalities represented in the lifestyle images created by the relevant advertisements.

Product image is further entrenched by the use of myth. For instance, the quest for beauty and the pursuit of eternal youth, among other mythic themes, are constantly being worked into the specific images that advertisers create for beauty products. The models who appear in beauty ads and commercials tend to be attractive people with an unreal, almost deified, quality of appearance. The modern advertiser stresses not the product but rather the social or mythic effects that consumers are led to expect from its purchase. The advertiser is clearly quite adept at treading the same subconscious regions of psychic experience as are explored by philosophers, artists, and religious thinkers.

Advertisers are also among the most creative users of new technologies. On the Barbie dolls website, for instance, visitors are invited to design their own doll and then buy it. At the Hot Wheels website, visitors are invited to play games and then to buy the toy cars.

Advertising has certainly become a powerful form of message-making that both mirrors and shapes trends. It is no wonder, then, that advertising has become an issue of debate and a target of legislation across the world. Some countries have laws prohibiting or restricting the use of women in advertisements unless the product is specifically aimed at female consumers. Other countries forbid the advertisement of certain hygiene-related products, including toilet paper, for reasons of modesty. Clearly, in the global village some societies are scrambling to protect themselves from advertising's images, many of which emphasize sex, attractiveness, youth, and pop culture trends.

Advertising is, fundamentally, a form of theater. It employs techniques of narrative, myth, and art in several basic formats. In some ads, the product exists on its own, as the center of focus, much like the main actor in a play. In other ads, the product is associated with images that are not directly attributable to it. For instance, an ad may show a watch associated with a cool mountain stream. As in surrealist drama, the connection is symbolic and imaginary, rather than realistic, turning the ad into a symbolic text. The product may also be associated with human personality, becoming the subject of character study.

Integrating with Pop Culture

We rarely reflect upon the degree to which pop culture celebrities, spectacles, and events have become integrated with sponsors. Whereas once the boards of hockey rinks were white, today they display all kinds of brand names, logos, and other advertising material. The branding of hockey can be seen even more dramatically in European hockey leagues, where even players' jerseys feature ads. The case of hockey is repeating itself throughout the social sphere.

The line between ad culture and pop culture is now virtually non-existent. The same styles and trends characterize both. For instance, naming practices in the advertising-marketing world are constantly attempting to keep in step with the times. In early 2000 some automobile makers started considering newer naming trends that were designed to appeal to a new generation of customers accustomed to an Internet-influenced style of communication. Cadillac, for example, announced a new model with the monogram name CTS in 2001. Acura also transformed its line of models with new names such as TL, RL, MDX, and RSX. The use of such names has since proliferated, with Saab's Aero X as one recent 2006 example. Mobile phones, predictably, are also named in a similar way, with alphanumeric forms such as Sony's W810i and Motorola's RZAR V3T; so too are video games, with names such as XBox, PS3, and Wii. This naming strategy also taps into a hip-hop style of writing words as they sound, not as they would traditionally be spelled. Products named with trendy spelling styles, with combinations of words and parts of words, or with uppercase letters in the middle of compound words now abound. Here is an illustrative list (Frankel 2004: 106–7):

GoVantage
PlainSight
Revelist
Solutionary
WorldWise
AvantGuide
Oriens
Mentium
FedEx
Verizon
Vonage

The integration of advertising and pop culture involves not only products but also entire corporations. Often the connecting link between the two is a logo or fictitious character. Take, for example, the cartoon character Mickey Mouse. In 1929, Disney allowed Mickey Mouse to be reproduced on school slates, effectively transforming Mickey into a company logo. A year later Mickey Mouse dolls went into production. Throughout the 1930s the Mickey Mouse brand name and logo were licensed with huge success. In 1955 *The Mickey Mouse Club* premiered on U.S. network television, further entrenching the corporate brand and image—and by association all Disney products—in the cultural mainstream. The Mickey Mouse case has repeated itself throughout modern pop culture. The idea is to get the brand or corporation to become intertwined with cultural spectacles (for example, movies or television programs) and social trends generally. In the case of the Disney Corporation, toys, television programs, films, videos, DVDs, theme parks, and the like have become part of the mythology of childhood.

The integration of advertising and pop culture can also be seen in such trends as Dove's recent "real beauty" campaign. Women with curvaceous figures ("real women" with "real curves") were enlisted as the models in Dove's print ads and in television and Internet commercials. In these ads, convergence with the culture of reality television is unmistakable. Real people are more interesting than actors because they are perceived to represent commonality. The Dove models hit closer to home with female consumers than models who were attractive, sexy, and ultra-thin would have. The literal text of the campaign blurts out, "Real women have real curves," implying that Dove wants to celebrate those curves. However, as in reality television, the ploy is transparent. After all, the manufacturer wants women to "improve themselves" by buying Dove products. In the "Dove Evolution" commercial for the Dove Self Esteem Fund, which was found in 2006 on websites, television, and other media, an average-looking woman gets a makeover analogous to the kind showcased on television programs such as TLC's *What Not to Wear.* Like the ordinary-looking women on that show, the actor in the Dove commercial is magically transformed into a beautiful princess. TLC and Dove thus employ what can be called a *Cinderella subtext.* Like Cinderella, these companies assure us, common women can be transformed into beautiful princesses with the right clothes or the right soap and cosmetics.

Another commercial for the Dove Self Esteem Fund targets younger girls. In it, we see a redhead who hates her freckles, an ordinary girl who thinks she's ugly, an Asian girl who wishes she were blonde, and a thin girl who thinks she's fat. In the background we hear the song *True Colors* playing. This commercial connects with the viewers in the same way that reality television does. It warns females that they need not feel pressured to look perfect at a young age. Dove is telling them that they are already beautiful, with a dab of its soap, of course.

AD CULTURE

As the foregoing discussion implies, advertising has become an intrinsic part of modern society. Like many elements of pop culture, it has also developed into a sui generis art form. Advertising even has its own prize category at the annual Cannes Film Festival and at other such festivals. Advertising is adaptive, constantly seeking out new forms of representation that reflect fluctuations in social trends and values. Although we may be inclined to condemn its objectives, as an aesthetic experience we invariably enjoy advertising, in the same way that we enjoy pop culture texts. Advertisements sway, please, and seduce.

Because of advertising's powers, restrictive legislative measures to constrain advertisers are now common. Such restrictions mirror prohibitionists' efforts to ban the use of alcohol and and its attendant lifestyle during the Roaring Twenties. Campaigns against advertising often backfire, as did Prohibition. In early 1998, the U.S. Congress was mulling over banning the Joe Camel and Marlboro Man figures from cigarette advertising. In response, the ad creators came up with ingenious alternatives. For instance, an ad for Salem cigarettes featured a pair of peppers curled together to look like a pair of lips, with a cigarette dangling from them. Benson and Hedges ads in the same year portrayed cigarettes acting like people—floating in swimming pools, lounging in armchairs, and so on. Ironically, such government-permissible advertising was a huge success, and cigarette smoking among young people rose dramatically. The new ads were even more effective in communicating the glamour of smoking than was the Joe Camel figure.

The Ad Campaign

The integration of advertising into the social mainstream is perpetrated and reinforced by *advertising campaigns*, which can be defined simply as the use of a series of slightly different ads and commercials based on the same theme, characters, jingles, and messages over a specified time period. An ad campaign is comparable to a musical piece consisting of one theme with many variations. One of the primary functions of ad campaigns is to guarantee that the product's image is in step with the times. The Budweiser ad campaigns of the 1980s and early 1990s emphasized rural ruggedness and female sexuality from a male viewpoint. The actors in the commercials were untamed, handsome men and the women their prey. In the early 2000s, Budweiser changed its image to keep up with the changing sociopolitical climate. Its new ad campaign showed young urban males who hung around in groups, loved sports, and did whatever such males tend to do together. So appealing was the *Whassup!* campaign that its signature catch phrase was joked about on talk shows, parodied on websites, mimicked in other media, and used by people commonly in conversations. The makers of Budweiser had clearly adapted their advertising style to social changes and trends.

The campaign showed how integrated advertising and pop culture had become. The *Whassup!* campaign did not begin in an ad agency, but rather as a short film by Charles Tone. The film caught the attention of an ad agency that worked for Anheuser-Busch, the manufacturer of Budweiser, who saw in the film the potential for Budweiser's new image. The ad agency was prophetic. The phrase *Whassup!* was taken from hip-hop culture. It caught on with young people everywhere, who in jest started greeting one another as do the characters in the ads. As mentioned, the phrase *Whassup!* also found its way also into late-night talk shows and into imitation ads, especially on the Internet. As Frankel (2004: 165) recounts it, rather than sue other advertisers for breach of copyright, Anheuser-Busch welcomed the imitations. The brand manager for the company put it as follows: "But we said, Stop? What, are you crazy? This is great, this idea is cool, and Bud is an integral part of it."

The campaign won numerous industry awards, highlighting the degree to which advertising, pop culture, and society had become integrated facets of the modern world. By becoming part of pop culture lingo, Budweiser increased recognition of its brand name. *Whassup!* became (and probably still is) a trademark of Budweiser. The ads were hilarious, the humor was perfect for the times, and the whole experience of greeting someone in imitation of the campaign was fun. Everyone did it, from television actors to office coworkers.

Co-optation

As the Budweiser case illustrates, the most effective advertising strategy is not only to keep up with the times but also to co-opt trends. In the 1960s, for example, advertisers co-opted the lifestyle images and imitated the language of the hippies to promote their products. The strategy worked brilliantly, especially since the images and language were counterculture ones. Advertising models wore counterculture clothing fashion to promote all kinds of products, counterculture music style was used as background in television commercials, and so on. In this way, people in the broader society could feel that they were ersatz participants in the ongoing youth revolution.

Campaigns such as "the Pepsi Generation" and Coke's message of universal brotherhood (*I'd like to teach the world to sing in perfect harmony . . .*) directly incorporated the rhetoric and symbolism of counterculture youths, thus creating the illusion that the goals of the hippies and of the soft drink manufacturers were one and the same. Rebellion through purchasing became the subliminal thread woven into the ad campaigns. The campaigns for the Dodge Rebellion and the Oldsmobile Youngmobile followed the soft drink ones, etching into the nomenclature of the cars themselves the powerful connotations of rebellion and defiance. Even a sewing company came forward to urge people to join its own type of surrogate revolution, hence its slogan *You don't let the establishment make your world; don't let it make your clothes.* In effect, by claiming to "join the revolution," advertising created its own real revolution. Because of the advertisers' efforts, since the late 1960s the worlds of advertising, marketing, youth trends, and entertainment have become synergistically intertwined.

Today, the integration of ad campaigns into social discourse has become so versatile and ubiquitous that we hardly realize how pervasive it is. As Canadian social activist Naomi Klein (2000) has emphasized, modern-day consumerist economic systems depend almost entirely on the partnership that has been conveniently forged among the previously autonomous worlds of business, media, and entertainment. It is no exaggeration to say that the history of pop culture is intrinsically interwoven with the history of advertising. In looking back over the last century, it is clear that the messages of advertisers, the methods of their ad campaigns, and their peculiar uses of language have become the norm in other creative domains, from cinematography to pop music. As McLuhan (1964: 24) aptly put it, advertising has become the "art of the modern world."

BRANDING

The technique of integrating products with pop culture is called *branding.* The intent of the technique is to tap into cultural tendencies that govern lifestyle, values, and beliefs, turning the product into a symbolic means for becoming part of those tendencies. As Alex Frankel (2004: 81) aptly puts it: "The most common marketing definition of a brand is that it is a *promise*—an unspoken pact between a company and a consumer to deliver a particular experience." The first act in the branding process is the naming of the product. It is impossible to advertise nameless products with any degree of persuasion or to integrate them into the larger pop culture domain. Brand names imbue products with identities in the same way that names given to human beings impart a distinct identity, allowing the bearer entry into a social reality.

Brands and Pop Culture

There is today an implicit law of the marketplace that can be articulated as follows: Trends in pop culture cross over to advertising and advertising styles mirror what is emerging in pop culture. It is for this reason that pop culture celebrities, from movie actors to sports figures, are often advertising celebrities as well. As P. T. Barnum had cleverly anticipated, consumerism can be fun, especially if advertised to be so.

Consider the case of McDonald's. The hamburger sandwich was introduced to America at the St. Louis Fair in 1904 (incidentally, hot dogs were popularized by the same fair). The first hamburger stand was opened up in 1940, in a drive-in near Pasadena, California, by movie theater co-owners Richard and Maurice McDonald. The McDonalds then opened up the first burger joint in 1948. (The McDonalds had started out with a hot dog drive-in restaurant in 1937.) The modern-day restaurant chain was founded in 1955 by Raymond A. Kroc, a distributor of machines for making milkshakes. Kroc learned of a hamburger stand that had eight of the machines, which of course was the one opened by Richard and Maurice. Kroc visited this early McDonald's and was impressed with how quickly customers were served. Kroc persuaded the stand's owners to let him start a chain of fast-service restaurants with the same name. Kroc opened the first McDonald's restaurant in Des Plaines, Illinois, in 1955. It is significant to note that this event coincided with the rise of youth culture in the 1950s. The number of McDonald's eateries began to proliferate, as young people flocked to it. By 1961 Kroc had established more than two hundred restaurants and had built McDonald's into a powerful business.

The astute Kroc realized that in order to survive in the long run, he needed to attract adults as well. Aware that fewer and fewer families had the time to prepare meals within the household, he wisely decided to change the image of McDonald's and began promoting it as a place where the family could eat together. His plan worked beyond expectations. En masse, families started to eat at McDonald's more and more often. The golden arches logo reflected the chain's new image perfectly. Arches reverberate with mythic symbolism—they beckon good people to march through them in anticipation of reaching a world of cleanliness, friendliness, hospitality, and family values. Kroc made sure that McDonald's was run like a religion—that is, from the menu to the uniforms, he exacted and imposed standardization.

Kroc's advertising campaigns effectively reinforced this new image and entrenched it throughout society. McDonald's was a place that would "do it all for you," as an early slogan phrased it, keeping family members united at meal times. Many outlets even installed miniature amusement parks for children. Kids' meals were introduced throughout the restaurant chain. As a family-oriented company, McDonald's started sponsoring Ronald McDonald House Charities, which operates hundreds of Ronald McDonald Houses worldwide, in which the families of critically ill children may stay when the young patients undergo medical treatment away from their homes. Within a few decades, McDonald's had turned fast food into family food.

The origin of the Ronald McDonald clown figure is informative. The McDonald's Corporation's first mascot was a winking little chef named Speedee, who had a head in the shape of a hamburger. This character was later renamed Archie McDonald. In 1960 Oscar Goldstein, a franchisee in Washington, D.C., decided to sponsor *Bozo's Circus*, a local children's television show. Bozo's appearance at the Washington restaurant drew a large crowd. When the local NBC station canceled the show, the franchisee hired its star to invent a new clown who would make restaurant appearances. An ad agency designed the clown's outfit and designated the rhyming name of Ronald McDonald.

Placement

Today, the branding of society entails placing products into pop culture spectacles as props within them. Thus, one sees brand-name computers displayed visibly in movies, designer clothes shown prominently in sitcoms, and so on and so forth. Placement is the natural outgrowth of the partnership that started decades ago between advertising and pop culture. Psychologically and socially, branding has had concrete consequences. Being a part of an in-crowd today entails sensitivity to the right brand of shoes, T-shirt, jeans, and so forth. Through the brand we can symbolize our own "brand" of lifestyle. Brand names are so powerful because they provide a coded membership or entry card to a specific lifestyle sector. In the 2000s, iPods were such entry cards, designed to be tucked away but also displayed as accessories.

Brand placement has become the most effective of any of the advertising strategies devised. In the 1940s and 1950s brand placement was a simple matter. In radio and television programs such as Texaco Theater, General

Electric Theater, or Kraft Theater, the program itself was associated exclusively with one sponsor. Children's programming, like *The Mickey Mouse Club*, was similarly sponsored. The show employed young actors hired by Disney who became icons of child culture, promoting the whole Disney brand of products. However, this form of sponsorship was not applicable to all kinds of programs and formats. Therefore, other placing strategies crystallized and spread across media. Often, a brand would be included as part of an entertainment script. The movies entered the placement fray in 1982 when the extraterrestrial creature in Stephen Spielberg's *E.T.* was seen snacking on Reese's Pieces—which increased sales for the product enormously. That event started a trend in Hollywood. In 1983, for example, after movie actor Tom Cruise donned a pair of Wayfarers in *Risky Business*, sales for the product shot up, as did generally the wearing of sunglasses.

The placement of brands in the scripts of television programs and movies is now so common that it goes largely unnoticed. Its main objective is to amalgamate brand identity with pop culture celebrities and spectacles. A good example of this amalgamation was the launch of the teenage-targeted television sitcom *Dawson's Creek* in January of 1998. All of the characters in the program were outfitted in clothing and accessories made by J. Crew. They looked like models who had stepped out of the J. Crew catalogue—and the actors were featured in the catalogue that very same month. Two seasons later, as the cool look changed in society, the characters got a makeover and a new wardrobe from American Eagle Outfitters. Once again, the company used the actors as models for their own purposes, featuring them on their website and on materials for in-store promotions.

Celebrity endorsement of brands has become commonplace. It is an effective strategy because it transfers what people perceive in the celebrity to the product. Also prevalent is the creation of fictitious characters to promote specific brands. Many of these have become pop culture celebrities themselves, independently of the products they represent. Mr. Clean, Uncle Ben, Charlie the Tuna, and Hostess's Twinkie the Kid have become such an intrinsic part of cultural lore that they were even featured in cameo roles in a 2001 animated film called *Food Fight*. In the same year, Barbie became a ballerina in the movie *Barbie in the Nutcracker*.

Sometimes, the product itself becomes a fad. In the 1950s, Silly Putty, Slinkies, and Hula Hoops became so popular that they were the inspiration of songs and jokes. Silly Putty was introduced in 1949 by advertising marketer Peter C. L. Hodgson, who discovered a substance developed by General Electric researchers who had been looking for a viable synthetic rubber.

The useless silicone substance could be molded like soft clay, stretched like taffy, and bounced like a rubber ball. Slinky was a coil toy that could be made to "walk" down a staircase by itself when one placed it on a higher step in a specific way. The Hula Hoop was a light plastic hoop that could be whirled around the body for play or exercise by the movement of the hips. These products became icons of pop culture and remain so to this day.

With new media, placement is becoming easier and easier to realize. For instance, in the early 2000s the toymaker Mattel started a Planet Hot Wheels website, from which one can download a game. Hot Wheels are small toy cars made to resemble real cars. They are inexpensive and highly popular with young boys. The website offered upgrades for "virtual vehicles" as a means of imparting a cool image to the brand so as to attract teenagers, whom little children look up to. The Mattel case is part of a new and growing form of branding that can be called *embedding*. Embedding can involve cooperation among brands. The site www.neopet.com is a case in point. Offering a host of recreational and educational activities to children, in 2004 it created a virtual McDonald's site, a Lucky Charms game, and other brand embedments.

Examples of embedding abound. The Pillsbury Doughboy was used by the Sprint Corporation in 2004 and 2005 to promote their own product in a campaign in which he paired up with the Sprint Guy. Similarly, the Maytag repairman has occasionally turned up in ads for the Chevrolet Impala and the Taco Bell chihuahua in ads for Geico. Co-branding, as it is called, is another form of embedding. The merging of bookstore chains with coffee giants such as Starbucks is a case in point. Sipping coffee in the atmosphere of a bookstore reverberates with images of intellectuals discussing life, art, culture, science, and the like at chic cafés. This *blended signification system* is actually in line with the history of coffee, which was originally viewed as an exotic substance.

The subtext of branding is often that the products being promoted are meant for individuals who are well-rounded and cultured, who enjoy the finer things in life. The association of brands with intellectualism and the arts is long-standing. Those with political, religious, or economic power have always attempted to promote themselves as cultured by becoming patrons of the arts. Sponsoring arts events is a way to gain respect and authority and to reveal concern for one's society. In the past, artists (such as composers of classical music) would dedicate their works to a benefactor or sponsor, thus acknowledging the benefactor's help and support. Strangely, such dedications have not yet occurred in instances in which the sponsor is a brand. To the best of my knowledge, there has never been the case of an artist dedicating a work to a cigarette brand, a beer manufacturer, or the like.

Another way that brands blur the lines between themselves and the general culture is by creating ads and commercials that simply are enjoyable to masses of people in and of themselves. As mentioned previously, some ads are so ingenious that they are no longer distinguishable from works of art.

Finally, some brands attempt to mesh with the outside world by showing themselves to be involved in, or sensitive to, social issues. For example, Natural American Spirit Cigarettes (Santa Fe Natural Tobacco Co.) put the following "politically correct" acknowledgment on its packages in the early 2000s: "We make no representation, either expressed or implied, that these cigarettes are any less hazardous than any other cigarettes." The cigarette packs also contained fliers featuring endangered species and expressing support for small-scale farmers. In all, this marketing was a transparent ploy to convey the image of an environmentally concerned and socially responsible brand.

FADS

The crystallization of fads and crazes not only is connected to strategies such as those mentioned above but also is the result of a more general partnership between pop culture and advertising. A *fad* is an object, a fashion style, or an event that becomes very popular relatively quickly but loses popularity just as quickly. Some fads may come back if a subsequent generation finds out about them through media retrospectives.

Fads and movies often go hand in hand. There is little doubt that the fad of practicing karate is due to the popularity of the Bruce Lee movies and, later, of the series of *Karate Kid* movies. Fashion and hairstyle fads also generally come from the movies. The frizzy male hairstyle that is seen everywhere today no doubt came from the way Brad Pitt wore his hair in several major movies, including *Seven*. The list of such synergies is a long one indeed.

Toys

Perhaps in no domain of consumerist culture can the emergence of fads be seen to occur as readily as in the "toy culture" set aside for children.

An Illustrative Selection of Fads

1820s–1830s: beetle collecting
1879s: the fifteen puzzle
1920s: doughboy lamps, flagpole sitting, crossword puzzles
1930s: goldfish swallowing
1940s: poodle skirts, bobby socks
1950s: Hula Hoops, beanies, coonskin caps, droodles, phonebooth stuffing
1960s: Dalekmania, drive-in theaters, lava lamps, troll dolls
1970s: bell-bottom pants, pet rocks
1980s: Cabbage Patch dolls, video game consoles, Rubik's Cubes, Smurf toys, Teenage Mutant Ninja Turtles
1990s: cell phones, PDAs, Barney dolls, Mighty Morphin Power Rangers
2000s: iPods, digital mobile devices, sudoku, Rolie Polie Olie

---

A look at any listing of fads and crazes since the 1920s will invariably show the presence of toys. Toy fads and pop culture go hand in hand.

Some fads are so intertwined with society that they have the capacity to generate mass hysteria. A case in point is the Cabbage Patch doll craze of 1983. Children have always played with objects—broom handles can be imagined to be swords, rocks can be imagined to be baseballs, and so on. But a commercial toy is different. It is an adult-made object that is given to children in accordance with social traditions. Dolls are particularly interesting in this regard because they are icons of the human figure. As early as 600 BCE dolls were made with movable limbs and removable garments, so as to reinforce the resemblance to human anatomy. Dolls have been found in the tombs of ancient Egyptian, Greek, and Roman children. Evidently the objective was to provide the children with a lifelike human form so that they could play with someone in the afterlife.

Perhaps the metaphysical function of ancient dolls can be enlisted to explain why hordes of parents were prepared to pay almost anything to get one of the Cabbage Patch dolls for their daughters during Christmas of 1983. Scalpers offered the suddenly and unexplainably out-of-stock dolls (a marketing ploy?) for hundreds of dollars through the classified ads. Grown adults fought each other in lines to get one of the few remaining dolls left in stock at a mall toy outlet. A *Newsweek* article of that year, titled "Oh, You Beautiful Dolls," offered the following depiction (cited in Berger 2005: 82):

> It was as if an army had been turned loose on the nation's shopping malls, braving the *Ficus* trees, sloshing through the fountains, searching for the legendary stockrooms said to be filled with thousands of the dough-faced, chinless, engagingly homely dolls that have become the Holy Grail of the 1983 Christmas shopping season: the Cabbage Patch Kids. Clerks were helpless before the onslaught.

How could a simple doll have caused such mass hysteria? As previously suggested, only something imbued with the power of mythology could do so. It is instructive to note that the Cabbage Patch dolls came with "adoption papers." Each doll was given a name—taken at random from the 1938 state of Georgia birth records—which, like any act of naming, conferred upon the doll a human-like personality. Also, owing to computerized manufacturing, no two dolls were alike. Each doll was an ersatz child who was adopted into the family as a sibling. It is no wonder, then, that the Cabbage Patch episode was fraught with so much hysteria. Parents did not buy a simple doll; they bought their child another member of the family, in much the same way that Egyptian parents gave their child a doll for companionship. Toys, as the name of a major toy chain overtly puts it, are indeed us.

In many societies dolls have mythological meanings or functions. In the aboriginal Hopi culture of the United States, for instance, *kachina* dolls are given as sacred objects to children as part of fertility rites. In many Christian traditions, dolls have been used since the Middle Ages to represent the Holy Family in the Nativity scene, as part of the celebration of Christmas. In Mexico, dolls representing Our Lady of Guadeloupe are ceremonially paraded every year. And in some cultures of the Caribbean, it is believed that one can cause physical or psychological damage to another person by doing something injurious to a doll constructed to resemble that person.

The commercialization of dolls as both fashion models and playthings for children can be traced to Germany in the early fifteenth century. Fashion dolls were created to model clothing for aristocratic German women. Shortly thereafter, manufacturers in England, France, Holland, and Italy also began to manufacture dolls dressed in fashions typical of their respective locales. The more ornate dolls were often used by rulers and courtiers as gifts. By the seventeenth century, however, simpler dolls, made of cloth or leather, were being used primarily as playthings by children.

During the eighteenth century, doll manufacturing became more sophisticated. The fashion dolls looked so lifelike that they were often used to illustrate clothing styles and were sent from one country to another to display the latest fashions in miniature form. After the Industrial Revolution, fashion dolls became commonplace toys of little girls. By the early part of the twentieth century, it was assumed that all female children would want to play with dolls. Noteworthy design innovations in dolls manufactured between 1925 and World War II included eyes with lids and lashes, dimples, open mouths with tiny teeth, and fingers with nails. Also, some dolls made of latex rubber could drink water and wet themselves. Since the 1950s, the association of lifelike dolls with female childhood has been entrenched further both by the quantity of doll types produced and by their promotion in the media. Since their launch in 1959, the Barbie dolls, for instance, have become part of the experience of growing up for many little girls in North America. Incidentally, the Barbie dolls also started the trend of fashionable clothing and accessories for American dolls. Their stylishness functions to enhance their humanoid nature even more. In the course of her history, Barbie has also been designed to reflect many varied occupations— astronaut, athlete, ballerina, businesswoman, dancer, dentist, doctor, fire-fighter, paleontologist, police officer, lead singer of a rock band (Barbie and the Rockets), and even UNICEF volunteer. Each of her occupational phases reflected a changing perception of American womanhood. Barbie continues to be faddish because she keeps in step with the times.

Interestingly, Barbie's faddishness started sagging in 2001 with the debut of the Bratz dolls, which have a new and brassy feminine look, with bare midriffs, sequins, fur, and eye shadow. The sexual suggestiveness of the Bratz dolls is transparent, emphasized especially by "trashy" clothing (such as halter tops, faux-fur armlets, and ankle-laced stiletto sandals) and cosmetics (such as eyeshadow and dark lipliner). Bratz dolls have become a fad because they are perfect for the times. They have tapped into the knack of young girls to assume a sassy, "Lolita-like" look, in sync with the look of current female celebrities. School boards across America have prohibited the Bratz dolls. Simply put, they do not meet the dress code.

Fetishism

Dolls (and toys generally) are fetishes, objects perceived to possess a life force. In traditional tribal cultures, the fetish is typically a figure modeled or carved from clay, stone, wood, or another material, resembling a deified

Dolls have been a part of popular culture in many societies for hundreds of years.
©iStockphoto.com/Luis Sierra

animal or another sacred thing. Sometimes the fetish is the animal itself, or a tree, river, rock, or place associated with it. In some societies belief in the powers of the fetish is so strong that it becomes an idol. The strong hold that a fetish has may explain why the term *fetishism* is often applied in our society to describe sexual fantasies that involve the use of objects (for example, shoes or stockings) that stand erotically for a part of the human body.

Fads are evidence that fetishism is not limited to tribal or pre-modern cultures. On the contrary, it is alive and well in consumerist cultures. In the 1970s, for example, American society went mad for "pet rocks." Many considered the fad a ploy foisted upon a gullible, consumerism-spoiled public by a crafty manufacturer—that is, they thought it was simply a quick way for that manufacturer to make money. However, the fad could not have been perpetrated in the first place unless a psychic force was at work—and that force was fetishism. The same tendencies can be seen in the common view held by people that some objects are inexplicably magical. If such an object is lost, then impending danger is feared. On the other hand, if such an object is serendipitously found (as when one finds a "lucky penny"), then it is believed that the gods or Fortune will look auspiciously upon the finder.

Games

Any listing of fads will show not only toys but also games of various kinds, from crossword puzzles to the Rubik's Cube and, more recently, sudoku books. The first such fad was the jigsaw puzzle, which British map-maker John Spilsbury invented around 1760 as a toy to educate children about geography. Eventually the jigsaw puzzle had become so popular among both children and adults that in 1909 the company Parker Brothers devoted an entire part of their factory to its production. The crossword puzzle became a runaway craze in the United States in the 1920s and millions of Rubik's Cubes were sold around the world in the early 1980s. Why do such crazes occur? Puzzles and other games are as much a part of recreational culture as are spectacles, toys, music, and all the other things that link pop culture to leisure time and affluence. The satisfaction (not to mention the effort) that comes from solving a puzzle seems to provide relief from life's routines. The integration of games with pop culture became evident in the Roaring Twenties. In 1925, the Broadway play *Puzzles of 1925* hilariously satirized the crossword craze. The heart of the play featured a scene in a "crossword sanitarium," where people driven insane by their obsession over crossword puzzles were confined.

The crossword puzzle was created by Englishman Arthur Wynne, who immigrated to the United States in 1905. As editor of the "fun page" of the *New York World*, Wynne introduced what he had intended to call a *word cross* on December 21, 1913, after he had seen something similar to it in England. Because of an error in typesetting, the puzzle appeared with the title *cross-word* instead—a name that has stuck ever since. Wynne's first puzzle (reproduced as figure 8.1) caught on instantly.

Readers inundated Wynne with requests for more puzzles. Overnight, the crossword had become a veritable craze in the city of New York. By 1924, crosswords had grown into a national pastime. In that year the American publishing company Simon and Schuster printed the first compilation books of such puzzles. Each book came equipped with a pencil and eraser and a penny postcard, which buyers could mail to the publisher to request the answers. The first book alone sold nearly half a million copies. To take advantage of the spreading crossword mania, manufacturers soon began making jewelry, dresses, ties, and so forth with crossword designs on them. A song called "Crossword Mama, You Puzzle Me, but Papa's Gonna Figure You Out," hit the top of the charts in 1924. To this day, crossword magazines, books, and electronic games based on crosswords are a part of pop (recreational) culture, just as are newspapers, fashion magazines, and the like.

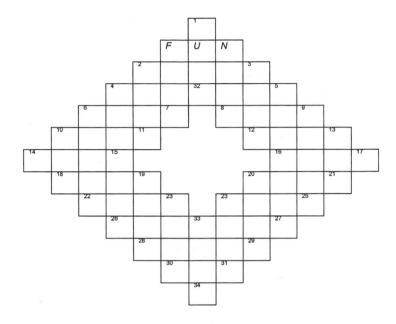

Clues

2–3	What bargain hunters enjoy	10–18	The fiber of the gomuti palm
4–5	A written acknowledgment	6–22	What we all should be
6–7	Such and nothing more	4–26	A daydream
10–11	A bird	2–11	A talon
14–15	Opposed to less	19–28	A pigeon
18–19	What this puzzle is	F–7	Part of your head
22–23	An animal of prey	22–30	A river in Russia
26–27	The close of a day	1–32	To govern
28–29	To elude	33–34	An aromatic plant
30–31	The plural of is	N–8	A fist
8–9	To cultivate	24–31	To agree with
12–13	A bar of wood or iron	3–12	Part of a ship
16–17	What artists learn to do	20–29	One
20–21	Fastened	5–27	Exchanging
24–25	Found on the seashore	9–25	To sink in mud
		31–21	A boy

Figure 8.1.   The Original Crossword Puzzle

1		7	4		3		6	5
				6				9
	5				7		2	1
7	1			3	8	2		
	3	6						8
8				4			1	
		2	3		4		5	7
3	7		2				8	4
	8				1			2

Figure 8.2.   A Typical Sudoku Puzzle

The same type of hysteria was generated by the Rubik's Cube in the 1980s and, more recently, by sudoku. Once they understand its simple principle of construction, sudoku seems to entice countless people to get lost in its symmetrical layout, defying them to complete the missing parts—much as the crossword entices people to fill in every single cell in its grid. The sudoku puzzle shown in figure 8.2 is a typical example. Various number clues are given. The remaining digits from 1 to 9 have to be placed just once (that is, without repetition) in each row and each column of the large 9 × 9 grid and in each of the smaller 3 × 3 boxes. There is only one solution.

To paraphrase a well-known saying, an hour of sudoku a day keeps the doctor (and everyone else for that matter) away. Despite its Japanese name, sudoku was invented in the United States in 1979 under the name *number place*. It appeared in Dell's *Pencil Puzzles and Crossword Games* magazine in May of that year. It is not clear who invented the game. The generally accepted story is that someone at the magazine came up with the idea. In 1984, an editor for *Nikoli* magazine in Japan came across a number place puzzle, changed its name to *sudoku* (meaning *single number*), and included it in his magazines. Within a year every major daily Japanese newspaper was carrying the puzzle. In 1997 Wayne Gould, a retired judge from New

Zealand, saw a sudoku puzzle and started making his own, eventually convincing the *Times of London* to print them. The newspaper did so for the first time in November of 2004. By early 2005, sudoku had become a craze in Britain. It quickly spread throughout the globe and has now become an enduring feature of puzzle pages in newspapers alongside the ever-popular crossword puzzle.

There are now hordes of websites that contain new sudoku puzzles daily, information on how to solve them, general information on sudoku championships, descriptions of different kinds and styles of sudoku puzzles (there are board and three-dimensional versions, for example), and so on and so forth. Sudoku is, clearly, a craze! Its emergence bears witness to the fact that in pop culture games, toys, and various other kinds of mass-produced objects can easily become as popular as celebrities and pop icons.

9

LANGUAGE

> Slang is a language that rolls up its sleeves, spits on its hands and goes
> to work.
>
> Carl Sandburg (1878–1967)

In the 1950s a term emerged among youths that became a shibboleth for the lifestyle that the golden era of rock entailed. That term was *cool*. Simply put, it meant (and continues to mean) knowing how to look, walk, and talk in socially attractive ways. Cool male teens modeled themselves after Elvis Presley; cool female teens wore bobby socks and put their hair in a ponytail. To this day, coolness means dressing, looking, and behaving in ways that are fashionable, trendy, hip.

How can a simple word stand for so much? Words are powerful symbols that document social trends and movements. Language has always played, and continues to play, a key role in the constitution and evolution of pop culture. Pop language, as it may be called, is as much a part of the whole carnivalesque spectacle as is dance and music, manifesting itself in trendy words that are spread by the media. The purpose of this chapter is to look at the forms and functions of pop language. Although this topic rarely finds its way into pop culture texts, I believe that it is as crucial in theme as any other. Pop culture is not only performed; it is also spoken. Many of its tendencies are imprinted in the various forms and modalities of pop language.

WHAT IS POP LANGUAGE?

The word *cool* is a perfect example of what pop language is all about and what kinds of images and meanings it encodes. As the history of the word shows, these meanings are hardly literal. They are mainly metaphorical and suggestive. The word *cool* has been used by young people to describe attractive lifestyle images since at least the 1920s. The choices people have today for looking cool are much more eclectic than in the past, but the underlying rhetorical meaning of the word is the same—it refers to a stylish and smart mode of dressing, acting, and talking that is in sync with the times. Flappers were cool; rock stars were cool; rappers are cool; celebrities are cool; and so on. Synonyms for *cool* have cropped up throughout pop culture history. These include *hip* and *groovy*, of which the former is still around today, while the latter is now considered to be a part of the hippie era. Incidentally, it is not a coincidence that the counterculture youths of the Vietnam War era were called *hippies*. They were indeed *hip*, rejecting the customs, traditions, and lifestyles of mainstream society. The same kind of meaning, indicating transgressive yet highly appealing behavior, is imprinted in the descriptor *hip-hop*, which emerged in the 1980s to describe the lifestyle associated with rap music.

Words like these have crystallized constantly throughout pop culture's history, as have certain phrases and various mannerisms that became popular through hit songs, movies, jingles, and the like. The complex of these words, phrases, and mannerisms constitute *pop language*. Pop language allows people to "talk the talk," as the expression goes. It is part of the fun of the whole spectacle. One of the shrewdest showmen of all time, P. T. Barnum (1810–1891), clearly understood the power of pop language. To promote his attractions, Barnum relied on colorful language, using exaggeration and deception to create interest in his shows and exhibits. Barnum introduced expressions such as the following:

> Don't miss this once-in-a-lifetime opportunity!
> Limited edition at an unbelievably low price!
> All items must go!
> Not to be missed!

Barnum realized that language can be used to create a mood of fanfare. The same types of linguistic mannerisms used by Barnum are found today in pop culture areas and spectacles such as advertising, sportscasting, movie trailers, and news headlines.

What's Hip?

In an interesting book titled *Hip: The History* (2004), John Leland has dated the origin of the word *hip* to 1619, when the first blacks arrived off the coast of Virginia. Without black culture, Leland maintains, there would be no trends of hip in American pop culture. Being hip is all about having a smooth and subtly transgressive attitude, similar to the one exemplified by current rap artists in their videos. It is something that one feels, rather than understands, and that is why it has always been associated with musical styles—the blues, jazz, swing, hip-hop, and so on. In 1973, the funk group Tower of Power defined *hip* as follows: "Hipness is—What it is! And sometimes hipness is, what it ain't." Hip is about a distinct identity that people wish to convey through both vocal and body language. The blues were hip. Jazz was hip. Hip-hop is hip. Hip is about a flight from mainstream conformity, a way to put oneself in contrast to it, to stand out, to look and be different. Leland writes that Bugs Bunny—the loveable cartoon character—exemplified hip, with a kind of sassy attitude that always got the better of Elmer Fudd, the ultimate square. Bugs's verbal protocol, *What's up, Doc?* is pure hip talk. It is little coincidence that the same verbal protocol became an intrinsic expression of hip-hop talk (*Whassup?*) in the 1990s.

The term *hip* describes an unconscious pattern of general lifestyle, perpetrated and reinforced by media images. The intent of purveyors of hip is really no different from that of carnival performers and burlesque actors of previous eras. Like the iazzi of the commedia dell'arte (discussed in chapter 7), the qualities of being hip are intended both to entertain audiences and to imbue the performer with an inner strength and finesse.

Most people would categorize word coinages such as *cool* and *hip* as slang. But the term *slang* gives the wrong impression. Such coinages are, more accurately, verbal forms created to refer effectively to things that matter in lifestyle. Incredibly, such forms have been making their way more and more into the linguistic mainstream. Words and expressions such as *chick, dude, chill out,* and *24/7,* among many others, have become so much a part of our everyday vocabulary that we no longer remember that they originated in hip talk. We hardly perceive these phrases as slang and instead see them as elements in contemporary modes of colloquial talk. Young people—the main users of hip talk—were once expected to learn and use adult forms of grammar and vocabulary. Today, however, proper usage seems to have gone out the window with the fashions of the old. Like never before, language is being shaped by the ever-changing categories of pop language, not because the latter is better than the standard language, but because it is everywhere.

Defining Pop Language

Pop language is the language of pop culture. The writing style and vocabulary used in early pulp fiction magazines and novels were in sync with the language of common folk, who understood its tones, rhythms, and colloquialisms perfectly. The term *pop language* was introduced by linguist Leslie Savan in her entertaining and controversial book *Slam Dunks and No-Brainers: Language in Your Life, the Media, Business, Politics, and, Like, What-ever* (2005). Throughout contemporary society, Savan notes, people are using a sitcom-inspired conversational style, which seems to carry with it a built-in applause sign or laugh track. She writes that phrases such as *That is so last year, Don't go there, Get a life, I hate it when that happens, It doesn't get any better than this*, and the sneering *I don't think so* are everywhere, always seeming to convey a theatrical mode that is waiting for an audience reaction. Pop language is used by ordinary people, Savan claims, to portray themselves as hip. It is light, self-conscious, and highly ironic, replete with put-downs and exaggerated inflections. It constitutes a pastiche of catchy phrases acquired from the pop culture media stage. Savan compares the 1953 Disney cartoon *Peter Pan* with the 2002 sequel *Return to Never Land*, pointing out how remarkably free the former one was of packaged phrases and trendy verbal mannerisms. The sequel, on the other hand, is replete with such phenomena, including such phrases as *In your dreams, Hook, Put a cork in it, Tell me about it, You've got that right*, and *Don't even think about it*.

Pop language is a boldly bland language that revels in its ironic and parodic style. It is equivalent to the language of carnivalesque performances such as those of the commedia dell'arte, in which actors used the language of the street to captivate and entertain audiences and to get them to pay attention. Most of the time pop language is meant to showcase the boredom of serious talk. In the 1920s, jazz introduced into discourse a whole series of mannerisms, including words such as *hip, stylin', cool*, and *groovy*. The words *pot* and *marijuana*, which were part of a secret criminal jargon in the 1940s, became common everyday words in the 1960s when the hippies adopted them and spread them through recordings and other media. In the 1990s hip-hop culture supplanted jazz and hippie culture as a source for new vocabulary. Expressions such as *bad, chill*, and *nasty* come from that culture. The words that make it into the mainstream today tend to have a pop culture history behind them. Take *bad* as an example. The trend today of using this word in a nonliteral antonymic way (meaning *attractive*) was initiated by Michael Jackson with his album titled *Bad* in 1987. Then, in 1989, hip-hop artist LL Cool J introduced the phrase *not bad* "meaning bad, but bad meaning good," as he defined it in his song "I'm Bad." Today, when people say that something is *bad*, the pop culture semantics built into that word are typically evoked.

Pop language has so many sides to it that a full treatment is well beyond the scope of the present chapter. Suffice it to say that it is a profane theatrical language that allows people to imprint lifestyle savvy directly into its structure through such devices as mode of delivery and catchy phraseology. Savan decries the abuse of pop language in common conversation. Her point seems to be that, in the past, the primary conduits of slang vocabulary were writers. Shakespeare, for instance, brought into acceptable usage such slang terms as *hubbub*, *to bump*, and *to dwindle*. But not before the second half of the twentieth century did it become routine for the media to act as a conduit. The number of pop words that have entered the communal lexicon since the 1960s is truly mind-boggling, constituting strong evidence that pop culture has become a major social force in all domains of modern-day life.

The way actors speak on the silver screen, for instance, has always served as a model of how to speak on the streets. *Animal House* (1978) introduced slang terms still used today, such as *wimp*, which is a commonly used term for someone who is scared or has no courage, and *a brew*, which means *a beer*. *Clueless* (1995) introduced pop language mannerisms such as *as if*, an exclamation of disbelief, and *whatever*, used to convey disinterest in what another person is saying. In 2004, the film *Mean Girls* helped spread a new form of pop speech now used by young females across North America, with words such as *plastic*, describing fake girls who look like Barbie dolls, and *fetch* (an abbreviation of *fetching*), used to describe something cool and trendy.

FEATURES

As mentioned above, pop language is not equivalent to slang. However, it easily and willingly absorbs real slang features into its constitution. Pop language is thus highly "slangy." Slang originates typically in youth culture. The relation between pop language and slang, therefore, is a close one. The use of slang items helps to create or reinforce group identity. However, when they reach the mainstream, many people use such items because it might make them seem fashionable and modern. Others use them because they convey a frank and friendly attitude. Others still use slang to insult. Words such as *creep*, *dork*, *geek*, and *loser* originated as insults.

Slang expressions, incidentally, arise in the same ways that all words come into being, namely through the use of old words in new ways, the shortening of existing words, figurative coinages, and various blending techniques. Especially prominent is the shortening of words by dropping one or more syllables. Technically, this is called *clipping*. Clipping has produced such common contemporary slang terms as *demo* (meaning *demonstration*), *psycho* (meaning *psychopath*), and *wacko* (meaning *wacky person*). Acronymy is another common shortening technique. Acronyms are words formed from the first letters or syllables of the words in a phrase. Common examples include *DJ* (for *disc jockey*) and *kidvid* (for *kid's video*). Blending is another shortening strategy. Blends are new words created by joining the first part of one word to the second part of another. Examples include *sexploitation* (from *sex* + *exploitation*) and *megaplex* (from *mega* + *cinemaplex*).

Devices

Words such as *duh*, *like*, and *man* that gain popularity are communicative devices that have a theatrical effect, as Savan correctly points out. *Duh* first surfaced in the late 1990s and was, at first, much satirized by language purists. However, like the hedging devices in adult language—*yeah*, *uh-huh*, *well*, and so on—*duh* is really no more than a conversational gambit. The difference is that, as mentioned, it is highly theatrical, like all other aspects of pop language. With its perfectly paired linguistic partner, *yeah*, *right*, it functions, above all else, as a means for conveying savvy and sarcasm. It is the equivalent of *Tell me something I don't know*. *Duh* is assertive, a perfect tool for undercutting mindless chatter or insulting repetition.

Like surfaced in the 1980s at first as a simple device used during hesitation, giving speakers time to put words to ideas without losing input in a communicative situation: *I, like, wanna come but, like, I'm a little busy now*. But it subsequently took on other functions, through constant usage on sitcoms and by celebrities in other contexts. One of these is the function of softening the negative impact of a statement. Saying that a "song is, like, bad," as a celebrity once put it on an MTV program, is much less harsh and confrontational than saying flatly that the "song stinks." Another function of *like* is indirect citation—that is, it is used in place of expressions such as *she said* or *he repeated*, followed by a quotation. For example, in place of *Sherry said: "What are you doing?"* pop language style dictates *Sherry was like:*

"What are you doing?" A third common function of *like* is as a quantifier, replacing words such as *nearly, approximately, very,* and so forth: *The CD's, like, twenty dollars; It's, like, late, ya know;* and so on. A fourth function of the term is exemplification: *They're comin' back with like, baseball bats, hammers; so get ready like for a fight.*

Incidentally, some of these functions predate current pop language. A 1954 *Time* magazine article—"You Wanna Hear Some Jazz, Like?"— decried it as a mannerism of the teenagers of that era, acknowledging that it had been used previously by jazz musicians and beat poets as a hedge in place of *uh* and *um*. Also, incredibly, *The Oxford English Dictionary* reports that the use of *like* meaning *in a way* or *so to speak,* as in "I'm, like, so in the mood," goes back to 1778! The use of *like* as a device for quotation was satirized in 1982 by the late Frank Zappa in his song "Valley Girl," in which he parodied a form of slang that was in vogue at the time among female teens with the lyrics: "Your toenails are like so grody" and "She's like, 'Oh, my God.'" Pop words, like pop fashions, are part of a profane theatrical script. Recently, I discovered the use of *like* as a hesitancy device in the *Scooby-Doo* comics and cartoons of the late 1960s. The story of *like* is a perfect case in point of how media and pop culture have formed a dynamic bond in the promulgation and dissemination of features from that culture. Linguistic particles such as *like* would have remained part of true slang—the language of restricted groups—if it were not for the media's appropriation of youth forms of behavior, which often results in their spread beyond the perimeter of youth culture.

The interjection of *man* in various kinds of utterances—*That guy's a loser, man; I'm so hammered, man, I think I'm going to heave*—is also part of pop language, albeit to a more limited extent. Its use in phrases such as *He's seriously wasted, man* surfaced in the hippie era. In this context, *man* functions as a code word through which male teens express camaraderie—similar in purpose to the *Whassup* protocol used by males in the Budweiser commercials discussed in chapter 8. Today, *man* has gained currency with both genders and, significantly, with speakers of various ages. A comparable history can be charted for the word *guys,* which is now used by both males and females to refer to peers. For example, *Hey, guys, let's get going,* can refer to males, females, or both. The spread of this word too is due to the media. It is worth mentioning here the Cheech and Chong movies of the 1980s in which the word *man* was used by both actors virtually in every one of their sentences as a code word. The word comes out of black culture, in which it was previously a code word for camaraderie among male black slaves, who excluded white males from their concept of true manhood.

A contemporary counterpart to this word is *dude*, a descriptive term referring to inarticulate personages such as surfers, skaters, and slackers (Kiesling 2004). It is also used in greetings (*What's up, dude?*); as an exclamation (*Whoa, dude!*); to convey commiseration (*Dude, I'm so sorry.*); to one-up someone (*That's so lame, dude.*); and to convey agreement, surprise and disgust (*Dude!*). In all these uses it is suffused with the same sitcom-inspired irony found in other items of pop language. *Dude* is the contemporary version of *man*, but having a tinge of irony, rather than being a direct acknowledgment of masculinity. It is relevant to note that, originally, *dude* meant *old rags*. In rural parlance, a *dudesman* was a scarecrow. In the late 1800s, the word *dude* was used as a synonym for *dandy*, a meticulously dressed man with an eye for feminine beauty. *Dude* began its foray into the pop language lexicon with the 1981 movie *Fast Times at Ridgemont High*.

Profanity

Predictably, a characteristic feature of pop language is profanity. Like some clothing styles (such as those of punks and goths) the profanities used constantly by youths among themselves bespeak a ritualistic engagement in the profane—no more, no less. Glorified by movies and music videos, profane language affords many young people the opportunity to talk tough, just for the sake of it. In such use, however, profane language becomes neutralized or at least diminished in its impact. The four-letter "F-word" is a case-in-point. It is used with regularity in movies, in a matter-of-fact manner that hardly captures people's attention any longer. It has also developed a noun form on the pop culture stage: *What are you doing, you f***!* Originally, however, the word had a more subversive function in pop culture performances. For instance, the influential and controversial comedian Lenny Bruce used it as a key component of his act. Unlike many other comedians, Bruce did not tell jokes. Instead, he attacked hypocritical attitudes toward sex, politics, and religion, speaking in a conversational manner and injecting frequent Yiddish words and profanities into his material, especially the F-word. Many were offended by his use of that word, and he was frequently arrested on obscenity charges. His use of the F-word clearly had a subversive impact; its use today in movies and television programs, on the other hand, has no such impact. If the word is offensive today, then it is so in a mildly theatrical way. In a recent study, Robert Wachal (2002) found that swear words are now common in all types of theatrical media. In a single two-hour episode of the HBO series *The Sopranos* alone, Wachal recorded one hundred uses of the F-word. Profanities are now also part and parcel of a new form of pop language that is evolving on cyberspace hangout sites such as MySpace and YouTube, which suggests that they are starting to lose their transgressive qualities.

The loss of profanity's content can be seen in the use of many words today, such as *slut*, which have had their meanings enucleated. Along with *ho* and *pimp* to describe a fiancée and fiancé respectively, *slut* can be used in a complimentary rather than derogatory way, designating an attractive female. The word *slut*, which actually originated in the Middle Ages, has now been appropriated by pop culture to make fun of its previous meaning. In a duet with Eminem, Nate Dogg describes his search for a "big old slut" in the single "Shake That"; in the Broadway musical *Avenue Q*, an ample-bosomed puppet is named Lucy the Slut; shops and websites now promote a brand of cosmetics called *Slut*; and so on. It seems that in pop culture, subversion quickly becomes conversion.

Words such as *slut* and *ho* (the latter from *whore*) are now used by women themselves as symbols of empowerment, implying that women can put on a "slutty" appearance without reprobation, donning all the trappings of promiscuity without actually being promiscuous. The raunch on the burlesque stage of pop culture has become a pattern of lifestyle and fashion. Despite all the warnings of experts and moral guardians that such profanity sends the wrong message—similar warnings to those expressed against the flappers in the Roaring Twenties—no one is listening, outside of the pulpit and academia. For the lack of a better term, the moralists' perception of womanhood can be said to derive from the *chastity belt syndrome*, whereby the only type of woman that a segment of society seems to find acceptable is a chaste one. It is interesting to note that those who are under the influence of this syndrome are those on the religious right and a number of academics. The double standard comes not from the streets but from the lectern.

VERBAL THEATER

Discussion of profanities in pop language brings us to the use of language to mock the mainstream social order, either directly or by implication. Such mockery can be seen, for instance, in how hip-hop artists spell their names.

The phonetic style adopted by such artists bespeaks an attitude that says, "I'll do it my way, not the way of the mainstream American speakers of English." Here is a small sampling of rap artists' names:

Snoop Dogg
Ja Rule
Eazy-E
Lil Jon
LL Cool J
Timbaland
Busta Rhymes
Coolio
Jay-Z
Mystikal
The Notorious B.I.G.
Bubba Sparxxx
Ol' Dirty Bastard

These are not simple black phonetic adaptations of mainstream American English. They are identity-forging symbols. Snoop Dogg is known not only for his music but also for his use of the suffix *-izzle*, which he employs in phrases such as *fo shizzle my nizzle*, which is his version of *For sure, my black brother* or *I concur with you, my African brother*. The N-word is now a taboo word for referring to African Americans, because it bespeaks a history of slavery and victimization. So, in mocking style, Snoop Dog rewrites this word with his suffix (resulting in *nizzle*) both to refer to that history and to show brotherhood with his fellow blacks. *Fo shizzle my nizzle* is a perfect example of subversive language.

It is interesting to note that the Internet is also a source for validating and spreading trends in pop language, even those that are perceived to be subversive. Interestingly, in early 2005, www.Gizoogle.com was founded by web designer John Beatty to promote "izzle-speak." Emulating Snoop Dogg's MTV comedy talk show, *Doggy Fizzle Televizzle*, which started in 2003, the website began more or less in jest of and in homage to Snoop Dogg's role in the empowerment of African American identity. Unexpectedly, the site became very popular, indicating that izzle-speak may have lost its subversive potency. It should also be noted that the roots of izzle-speak may go back to a 1981 song titled "Double Dutch Bus" by Frankie Smith in which the first two words of the title (*Double Dutch*) are transformed at the end into *Dilzzouble Dizzutch*.

Hip-Hop Style

Subversive spelling style is symbolically powerful. By flying in the face of orthographic and grammatical traditions, which bespeak "whiteness," rap artists are declaring a kind of sui generis sociopolitical autonomy from the hegemony of white culture. Correct spelling, like correct speaking, is more than a sign of education. In the case of hip-hop talk, rebellion against correct spelling reveals how young blacks feel about traditions that have historically excluded them from the mainstream. Here are some examples of such language (taken mainly from rap lyrics):

i dont know why
you da right person
how ya doin
wanna know why
i got enuf
it wuz lotsa fun
i fine
me is 31
you feeling better npw?
Supadupa fly
Tupac is da gangsta of da sky

The attitude of noncompliance built into such constructions is instantly transparent. As such artists know, to speak the language of a culture correctly is to validate that culture. Hip-hop talk symbolizes a rejection of the mainstream culture, with an emphasis instead on camaraderie and solidarity among blacks. It exudes linguistic empowerment, giving African Americans control over an alien tongue—English—that was forced upon them during their days of slavery. The driving force that attracted hundreds of inner-city-ghetto African American and Hispanic youths to rap music was its anti-hegemonic attitude and its ability to give expression to socially powerless voices. Rapper Chuck D boldly and clearly articulated rap's anti-hegemonic stance in a 1992 interview with *XXL* (a popular rap magazine): "This is our voice, this is the voice of our lifestyle, this is the voice of our people. We're not going to take the cookie cutter they give us [or] let them mold us." However, as rap continued to grow and influence the lifestyle of many city youths in the late 1990s, its audience became broader. As a consequence, rap's original subversive subtext started to evanesce. Today, mainstream rap culture is inundated with rappers who mimic the once-despised white upper-class lifestyle. These changes do not mean that rap's original anti-hegemonic subtext has been completely obliterated. Like other trends in pop culture, present and past (for example, the punk and goth movements), rap can and often does serve as a subversive voice for dispossessed people. However, it no longer has the broad impact in this regard that it once had.

The spelling style used by rap artists has made its way across the pop culture landscape. It is now the main technique for naming pop musicians and groups or artists. However, it should be mentioned that long before hip-hop talk, similar tendencies could be found in naming practices. For example, a number of 1970s and 1980s rock groups spelled their names phonetically rather than traditionally: Guns N' Roses, Led Zeppelin, The Monkees, and so forth. Current spelling oddities in pop music naming practices are really no more than modern-day manifestations of a tendency that seems to have always existed within pop culture. Here are some examples (Cook 2004: 22–23):

Letters for syllables: x-wife, ofx, v-male, l8r, Salt-N-Pepa
Number names for words: 2 sweet, 2Pac, 6teens, 2gether
The letter *k* for *c*: Outkast, kontakt, kurupt, Boomkat
The letter *z* for *s*: jaz-z, 4 girlz, airheadz, rascalz, outlawz, beginerz, kartoonz, playaz
The letter *x* for *-ex*, *-cs*, or *-cks*: xploding, rednex, xscape, xtraordinary
Odd punctuation: @junkmail, d!:-nation, b'z4
The use of *da* for *the*: da mob, da muttz
The use of *ph* for *f*: phixx, Phish, phuture
Elimination of word spaces: Americathebeautiful, Amillionsons

It is relevant to note that the use of spaces between words was introduced as a writing practice in European languages in the eighth century, as people discovered how useful they could be. The space, like the zero in mathematics, allows us to detect boundaries, thus facilitating the reading process. The elimination of word spaces today is more for special effects than anything else. The poet e. e. cummings (1894–1962), who wrote only in lowercase letters, and who used distortions of syntax, unusual punctuation, new words, and elements of slang, also eliminated spaces in many of his works. Similarly, James Joyce (1882–1941) did away with spaces in many parts of his novel *Ulysses* (1922).

Often, the spelling pattern is constructed deliberately by a pop musician to simulate his or her vocal accent. For example, 2Pac's song titles include "Letter 2 My Unborn" and "2Pacalypse." This technique had previously been used by Prince in the 1980s, as can be seen by the titles of some of his songs:

"If Eye Was the Man in Ur Life"
"What Do U Want Me 2 Do"
"Lovesexy"
"Live 4 Love"
"Emale"

Perhaps the greatest sign that hip-hop style has lost its subversive power is the fact that is has been adopted by advertising, stores, and various institutions. It has become a veritable fad. Here are the names of a selection of businesses, products, services, and so forth that have co-opted this style (Cook 2004: 44, 48):

Alphanumeric spelling: 4 Ever Nails, 4 Runners Only, Cabs 4 Kids
Letter-name spelling: Xpert Stationers, Fax-U-Back Services, E Z
   Taxi, Xpressair, Spic N Span
Letter substitutions: Hotpak, Kidz Karz, Krispy Kreme, Bratz dolls,
   Playskool

In a way, such trends are not particularly innovative. The history of English shows a constant attempt to make the spelling reflect the pronunciation. All one has to do is look at the writings of authors such as Chaucer and even Shakespeare to realize the extent to which spelling has changed over the years. Many of the trends in hip-hop and pop language spelling today were also proposed by many in the past. In 1828, Noah Webster proposed the elimination of *u* in words such as *colour, favour, harbour,* and *odour.* His proposal was accepted, and the resulting spelling difference is a feature that distinguishes American from British English—and that, by extension, divides America from its British past. Changes of this kind have always come about to symbolize a break with tradition. American English itself was once considered by the British to be subversive (since it was not the king's or queen's English). So, although hip-hop style implies a break with white culture, it is also, paradoxically, a contemporary symptom of a broad tendency in America to constantly break from the past. As Vivian Cook (2004: viii) has perceptively remarked:

> Our discussions of spelling often suggest that there is an ideal of perfect spelling that people should strive for. Correct spelling and punctuation are seen as injunctions carved on tablets of stone; to break them is to transgress the tacit commandments for civilized behavior. Spelling and punctuation can become an emotional rather than rational area of dispute.

The writer George Bernard Shaw often made fun of English spelling, pointing out, for example, that the word *fish* could be legitimately spelled *ghoti* given that *gh* is used in place of *f* in a word such as *enough*, *o* for *i* in a word such as *women*, and *ti* for *sh* in a word such as *nation*.

Sexuality

Hip-hop talk is not just about forging black identity. It is also part of the sexual carnivalesque. Thus, it it no surprise that hip-hop talk ventures constantly into explicit sexuality. Critics of hip-hop claim that through video and language, rap often presents a degrading and socially harmful picture of women. However, at least to my mind, a more critical look at rap style tells a different story.

2 Live Crew, for example, is a rap group that has developed a reputation of being "too nasty," because of the blatantly sexual nature of their lyrics. In their song "M & S," one finds phrases such as "So I pulled a little girlie, this is what I did, jumped in the ride, took her to the crib." Their phraseology is typical of many (if not most) rap artists. In rap lyrics, words such as *slut*, *ho*, and *bitch* are used constantly to refer to women. Even though they have an antonymic intent, as mentioned above, these words still reverberate with a double meaning, suggesting ultimately that females exist to be of service to males as sexual entertainers and pleasers. Slang words like *hump*, *trunk*, and *lumps* for the female buttocks are also found throughout rap lyrics. Black men, on the other hand, are typically depicted as endowed with unique sexual prowess—an image satirized, by the way, by Beyoncé in "Me, Myself, and I," a song about how disappointing her black boyfriend turned out to be.

Beyoncé and many other women have answered the men lyrically, indicating that the image of sexual relations implicit in rap lyrics is nothing more than a carnivalesque form of male sexual fantasizing. As an example, consider the 2005 song by pop artist Gwen Stefani, "Hollaback Girl." The term *Hollaback* is not defined anywhere by Stefani. It could mean *hollering back*, suggesting that females should take a stand against male attitudes regarding female sexuality. In contrast, it could also indicate a desire to play along with the male game, since the word is used in cheerleading. Both meanings seem plausible, as Stefani portrays herself as aggressive ("So I'm ready to attack"), physical ("Gonna get a touchdown, gonna take you out"), and decisive ("Both of us want to be the winner, but there can be only one"). Stefani has articulated a very clever response to the perpetuation of male sexual fantasies in pop music.

Stefani's response, however, is not unique. Throughout the history of pop music, female voices have always been prominent in emphasizing the power of their own sexual identity, along with their ownership of it. From the Shangri-Las to Madonna, the Spice Girls, and Avril Lavigne, pop music has consistently served as a vehicle for female voices to articulate their slant on sex, romance, and relations. In a basically patriarchal world, only on the stage of profane theater—pop culture—could this have occurred without any serious consequences. The lyrical and video content of female artists' pop music performances today are all about the construction of female sexuality—a construction often fraught with contradictions that call into question what it means to be both female and sexual in the modern world. But stereotypical views of what constitutes female sexuality have been most powerfully challenged by the very variety of female performers' messages.

The musical approach of both Madonna and Britney Spears perfectly shows the contradiction inherent in women's harnessing and flaunting of their own sexuality. Aware of the view that females are objects of male voyeurism, both Madonna and Spears have assumed a "peep show" style of performance in their videos, complete with breathy voices and orgasmic groans. As Spears's 2004 song "Toxic" highlighted, this perception of women is indeed toxic, especially for men. In other words, while on the textual surface such a performance seems to be catering to a male-centered understanding of women, a song like this actually offers a subversive depiction of the male-focused view by showing the power of women themselves when they take over agency in sexual representations. In her 2002 video "Dirrty," Christina Aguilera shows the force of this agency even more dramatically. Aguilera is seen in a boxing ring, where she has just defeated her opponent. She fights "like a man," with hooks and jabs rather than in a stereotypical "catfight" manner. She is the embodiment of "dirty-ness," with the double "r" simultaneously mocking the catfight stereotype and emphasizing female power. Aguilera also satirizes male sexuality by saying "I need that shit [to get off]," speaking of sweating and clothes coming off, while simultaneously mock-grabbing her crotch to suggest both what males do and what they want. The whole video is yet another clever representation of what females can do to claim agency over their own bodies.

ONLINE COMMUNICATION

Young people are the main users of new communicative technologies. Chat rooms and websites such as MySpace, Facebook, YouTube, and the like are now the venues through which social communication is unfolding among the young. Not surprisingly, a cottage industry of consultants, ad executives, and marketing researchers has sprung up to help corporations find a way to access the increasingly lucrative, and conveniently unstable, online market.

More specifically relevant to the theme of this chapter, that online communities have arisen bears far-reaching implications for the future of verbal communication. For one thing, many of the features of hip-hop style, and of pop language generally, have become routine in such communities. In an age where miniaturization reigns supreme in both technology and lifestyle, it is little wonder that the language used online, known as *net lingo*, is also undergoing its own form of miniaturization. Since there are few, if any, corrective forces at work in cyberspace, two relevant questions emerge: Is the process of miniaturization a contemporary phenomenon or has it always existed as a general tendency within language? Is net lingo spreading and thus changing how people will communicate?

At one level, the trend toward miniaturization is nothing new. Scholars and scientists have always used abbreviations and acronyms of various kinds to facilitate technical communications among themselves, making delivery of such communications swift and precise. Abbreviations such as *etc.*, *et al.*, *op. cit.*, and *N.B.* are still part and parcel of "scholarspeak," as it may be called. But what sets the reductive tendencies in net lingo apart from all economizing tendencies of the past is the speed and extent to which miniaturized forms are spreading and becoming part of communicative behavior throughout the online world and, seemingly, spreading to offline language.

Net Lingo

As the stage for pop culture shifts to cyberspace, or at least converges with it, online trends will both mirror and dictate the future course of pop culture and, perhaps, even transform it radically. It is thus of enormous importance for pop culture studies to grasp what online culture is all about, starting with the nature of its language. What is net lingo? The linguist David Crystal (2006) defines it simply as a language designed for efficiency of communication so that a message can be sent in the shortest time possible. Hence, sentences showing abbreviations and simplified spelling patterns, such as the ones listed in table 9.1, now abound in the English version of net lingo. Similar patterns are observable for most other languages of the world. As can be seen, these expressions have many of the characteristics of hip-hop style. The convergence of the two styles is not surprising, given the great influence of hip-hop on current pop culture in general.

There are five types of forces of miniaturization that are generally at work in net lingo: abbreviation, acronymy, phonetic replacement, compounding, and symbol replacement. Abbreviations are shortened words: *ppl* for *people*, *b/c* for *because*. Acronyms are forms composed of the first letter of every word within a phrase: *OMG* for *oh my God*, *LOL* for *laugh out loud*.

Table 9.1.   Net Lingo Shorthand

Shorthand	Translation
:-P	You're being sassy; I'm sticking out my tongue at you.
8-)	I'm wearing glasses; I'm acting smart.
afk	away from keyboard
brb	I'll be right back.
btw	by the way
g2g	Got to go.
hhok	Ha ha; I'm only kidding.
how ya doin	How are you doing?
i dont know why	I don't know why.
i fine	I am fine.
i got enuf	I've got enough.
imho	in my humble opinion
it wuz lotsa fun	It was lots of fun.
pos	parents on site/parents over shoulder
tttt	to tell the truth
u feeling better now?	Are you feeling better now?
wanna know why	Do you want to know why?
you da right person	You're the right person.

Phonetic replacement occurs when certain letters and numbers replace entire words or parts of words because they represent the pronunciation more compactly: for example, *cu* for *see you* and *18r* for *later*. Compounding consists of a combination of separate words, or of their parts, to make a new word that is shorter than the forms it compounds taken separately: *mousepad, webonomics, netlag, netizen, hackitude, geekitude*. Symbol replacement, as its name implies, is the use of symbols, or letters with the value of symbols (such as *e-*), in place of letters or words: *e-zine, e-commerce*, and so forth.

Are such trends radical? Do they spell out (literally) the end of language as we have known it for millennia? Actually, such trends are nothing new to many linguists, since they fall under the rubric of the Principle of Least Effort (PLE). That such a principle was operative in the constitution and evolution of linguistic systems was first discovered in the 1930s by the Harvard linguist George Kingsley Zipf (1902–1950). Zipf claimed that many phenomena in language could be explained as the result of an inborn tendency in the human species to make the most of its communicative resources with the least expenditure of effort (physical, cognitive, and social). This tendency was found to be independent of specific individuals and cultures. The PLE, Zipf argued, explains why speakers minimize articulatory effort by shortening the length of words and utterances. At the same time, people want to be able to interpret the meaning of words and utterances unambiguously and with the least effort.

In one of his most famous studies Zipf demonstrated that there exists an intrinsic interdependence between the length of a specific word (in number of phonemes) and its rank order in the language (its position in order of its frequency of occurrence in texts of all kinds). The higher the rank order of a word (the more prevalent it is in actual usage), the shorter it tends to be (that is, the fewer phonemes it tends to include). For example, articles (*a, the*), conjunctions (*and, or*), and other function words (*to, it*), which have a high rank order in English (and in any other language for that matter), are typically monosyllabic, consisting of one to three phonemes. Even more intriguing is that this force of compression does not stop at the level of function words, as Zipf and others subsequently found. This phenomenon manifests itself, above all else, in the tendency of phrases that come into popular use to become abbreviated (*FYI, UNESCO, Hi, 'Bye, ad, photo, Mr., Mrs., Dr., 24/7*, and so forth) or to be converted into acronyms (*aka, VCR, DNA, laser, GNP, IQ, VIP*, and so forth). This pattern can also be seen in the creation of tables, technical and scientific notation systems, indexes, footnotes, bibliographic traditions, and so on and so forth. The general version of Zipf's Law, as it is now commonly called, proclaims that the more frequent or necessary a form is for communicative purposes, the more likely it is to be rendered in compressed or economical physical structure. The reason seems to be an inherent psychobiological tendency in the human species to expend the least effort possible in representation and communication.

Nowhere is the operation of Zipf's Law as apparent today as in the forms that are created online, as discussed previously. For increasing the speed at which messages can be inputted and received, shortened structures are now commonplace. Many of these seem to be spreading to pop language generally (online and offline). The ones listed in table 9.2 are found virtually everywhere, joining the previous *ASAP* for *as soon as possible* and *TGIF* for *thank God it's Friday*, which were used long before the Internet.

Writing takes time and effort. In today's cyber universe, both come at a premium. Not answering the barrage of e-mails or text messages that one receives on a daily basis is perceived negatively. Slowness in response is, at times, even penalized by social ostracism or various other forms of reprobation. Logically, reduction of forms helps counteract this situation by making it possible to respond to messages more quickly.

Abbreviations and other shortened forms of words are staples of text messaging.
©iStockphoto.com/Izabela Habur

Table 9.2.   Widespread Net Lingo Shorthand

Shorthand	Translation
AFK	away from the keyboard
B4	before
BFN	'Bye for now.
C2C	cheek to cheek
CUS	See you soon.
F2F	face to face
GAL	Get a life.
Gr8	great
H&K	hugs and kisses
IC	I see.
KISS	Keep it simple, stupid.
L8R	later
LOL	laughing out loud
PLZ	please
P2P	person to person
RUOK	Are you OK?
SWIM	See what I mean?
TY	Thank you.
WB	Welcome back.
YW	You're welcome.

It is interesting to note, parenthetically, that cyberspace encourages self-styled constructions of identity. The coinage of *handles*—the names that users create for themselves in order to interact in chat room situations and in cyber communications generally—is a case in point. Handles such as *@lessi@* for *Alessia* are found commonly in chat rooms. These are essentially nicknames; and, of course, nicknames have been around since time immemorial. However, while in the past nicknames were given to people by others, in cyberspace people christen themselves. Remarkably, such handles are being used increasingly as offline names, becoming personal brands that seemingly empower individuals to construct their own persona.

Another way in which online identity construction occurs is through the technique of mismatching letters: for example, *Ashley* might be written as a mixture of upper- and lowercase letters, as in *AsHLeY*. The Internet is not only changing language itself in specific ways but also assigning linguistic authority to people in truly radical ways that have obvious implications beyond language, reaching into the very structure of social interaction and ritual.

Implications

Pop language has always been an intrinsic part of pop culture, from the slang of the Roaring Twenties (including words such as *jazz*) to the slang of hippies in the 1960s (including words such as *pot*) to today's hip-hop spelling patterns. The online context has simply increased the power of common people to become directly involved in the construction of new pop language trends.

Dramatic language has always been required by circus announcers, burlesque emcees, television newscasters, and the like. On the stage of profane theater, language is effective as part of the act. There is nothing particularly surprising about the presence of such dramaturgy in discourse. It is an option for every speaker of a language. What is surprising is the degree to which pop language characterizes the speech of individuals today. Also noteworthy is the current tendency of trendy slang coinages and verbal mannerisms to make their way into the mainstream language almost as soon as they are invented. As mentioned, the style of these mannerisms resembles that used on television programs dealing with ordinary life—sitcoms, serials, and so forth. Research on slang discourse throughout the world shows that many such coinages have a very short lifespan. However, the same domain of research also shows that there are many terms that gain general currency, cutting across age, class, and gender boundaries. Whereas the main source of lexical innovation was once the literary domain, such innovation now tends to come from the language of television and the language of the chat room.

The influence of pop language on social groupthink is unquestionable. Television, pop music, and the like (whether they are delivered in traditional electronic form or online) inform people what to say and, more significantly, *how* to say it. The reason that pop language has become so dominant is that people gain insights into the events of the world through the medium of television or through online navigation. The high incidence of dramaturgy as a delivery style, of slang coinages as part of a general lexical style, and of the compression of sentence structure are consequences of living in an age of digital media. Whereas once it took decades for a change to penetrate the language, now it seems to take only days. The reason is that electronic media are accessible to one and all. The greatest influence on the development of language today comes not from the pen but from the computer screen.

As a final word on pop language, I cannot help but comment on the role of American English on the new online stage for pop culture. Known as *weblish* (English on the Web) or *globish* (global English), the English language is clearly the default language of global communications. Enchanted by the lure of American pop culture, increasing numbers of young people throughout the world are embracing English, not because it is any better than their own languages, but because it is there—everywhere.

10

FOREVER POP

Man consists of two parts, his mind and his body, only the body has more fun.

Woody Allen (b. 1935)

Pop culture is everywhere today. And where it is not, more than likely the reason is that a particular society has taken steps to keep it away, fearing that this new form of culture might radically alter its existing (more traditional) one. Pop culture is both appealing and controversial (and has always been so). Thus in America—where it is the default form of culture—the debate on what constitutes legitimate or acceptable culture seems to be always ongoing. One of the themes of this book has been that despite pop culture's controversial nature it has nevertheless survived and spread. The main reason appears to be that it provides an outlet for an engagement in the profane—an engagement that is clearly as crucial for maintaining a psychic balance as is engagement in the sacred.

The purpose of this brief concluding chapter is to go over the main themes that I have attempted to interweave throughout this book and to tie some loose ends together. One recurring theme has been that trends in youth culture subsequently become the basis for trends in pop culture. The importance of youth culture in pop culture has promoted an emphasis in America on all things "young," leading to a radical reevaluation of traditional notions such as the role of older people in society. Another theme offered in this book, as just mentioned, is that there is an unconscious need within us to balance the forces of the sacred and the profane. Modern society does not any longer need ritualistic enactments of the profane such as carnivals. It has pop culture in their place. Like carnivals, pop culture is all about spectacle, pastiche, and a polyphonic dialogue among common people. However, pop culture is also a locus where artistic creativity and innovation now take place. Although many popular expressive products are ephemeral and fall by the wayside, others become part of larger artistic traditions throughout the world. In my view, the problem with pop culture today is not its crassness. Rather, the problem stems from an imbalance that occurs from time to time in communal life in the dichotomy of the sacred versus the profane. Such an imbalance occurs when a society places too much emphasis on either pole of the dichotomy.

THE SHOW MUST GO ON

The 2002 movie *Chicago* has been cited throughout this book. The reason is that the film showcases many of the main ideas expressed in this book in a truly effective pop culture way, through movie imagery and great, catchy music. The movie is about fame-hungry Roxie Hart, who hopes to flee from her boring husband Amos and who dreams of a successful life on the vaudeville stage, in the bright lights of Roaring Twenties Chicago. Roxie is in awe of club singer Velma Kelly (who has been arrested after murdering her husband and her sister, on discovering their affair). Roxie meets Fred Cassely, a man who convinces her that he can make her show biz career take off. However, after catering to his sexual gratifications, Roxie discovers that he has no more connections in show business than she herself does. She thus shoots and kills Fred. Upon discovering her infidelity, Roxie's husband refuses to take the blame for the murder and Roxie is sent to jail to hang. In jail she finally meets Velma Kelly, who is receiving media attention for the double murder she committed. She also meets other females awaiting trial for the murders of their own partners.

The subtext of the movie (which was based on a 1976 musical play) is clear—the vaudevillian stage has empowered females to metaphorically kill their controlling men. They can now control their own destiny. When Roxie hires slick Chicago lawyer Billy Flynn, he convinces her to get the media to think of her as an innocent victim. The tabloids react positively to the new girl on the cell block, and Roxie finally becomes a star.

The Role of Women in that Show

Pop culture, as the makers of *Chicago* clearly understood, is all about the emotional power of the show. The expression *The show must go on* emerged early on in pop culture, indicating that regardless of what happens, the show must be put on for the waiting audience. The expression can be applied to pop culture generally—it must go on, or else we risk resorting back to an era of Prohibition and fanatical right-wing authoritarianism. The importance of the show in human life is a basic theme in many narratives and dramatic works. For example, it is the central theme in the opera *Pagliacci* (1892) by Ruggero Leoncavallo (1858–1919). The opera is about a commedia dell'arte troupe in which the person who plays the clown forces himself to go onstage, even though he is breaking up emotionally over the infidelity of his wife. Ironically, his skit onstage is all about that very infidelity and the actors in it are his real wife and her lover. In a bizarre twist of fate, the clown must act out in the form of *iazzi* (comic routines) what he knows to be true. The show must go on, he cries out in his marvelous aria *Vesti la giubba* (meaning *Put on your costume*).

Profane theater, with its sexual subtext, can beguile with its hidden pathos, lure with its sexually charged pyrotechnics, and inspire with its energy. The sensuality of women's bodies on the stage of that theater is intoxicating. And as *Chicago* suggests, the power of female sexuality works even better when society attempts to prohibit it. *Chicago* takes place in the era of Prohibition, when such clubs as speakeasies, with booze and sex available "after midnight," became the rage.

In some ways the movie, like the commedia dell'arte, is really all about the role of women in popular forms of culture. There simply would be no pop culture, with its erotic subtext, without women. That is why representations of the feminine form permeate pop culture, from stripteases to dances (such as the Charleston and booty-dancing) and fashion shows. As Linda Scott (2005: 167) has acutely observed, awareness of the power of feminine sexuality emerged in the Roaring Twenties. In that era, women's sexuality found its symbolic embodiment in the *flappers*, who dressed, smoked, drove, danced, and lived in a new form of sexual freedom based on jazz, breaking away dramatically from Victorian strictures. They terrified society's puritanical moral guardians:

> The flapper's dress was particularly well-suited to her nightlife. Going without a corset left the girl free to move—and all the fringe, beads, and spangles shimmied with her. Just as has happened with every other musical sensation coming from the African American community in the twentieth century— ragtime, swing, rock, blues, rap—the conservatives charged that jazz would corrupt the morals of white youth. (Scott 2005: 167)

The feminine form is powerful onstage because it simultaneously stands for an unconscious, earthy spiritual wisdom and a sexual force. It is an intoxicating blend of Eve and Lilith. As such, it is particularly menacing to the stability of patriarchal systems. Thus portrayals of "loose women" have always caused great consternation and reprobation in such systems, as *Chicago* portrays. In this sense, pop culture is feminine; it is "goddess culture." To my mind, that is what gives pop culture a large part of its unconscious power. Without women, not only would the show not go on, it wouldn't make sense in the first place.

In a fascinating recent study, Maria Elena Buszek (2006) has shown how the so-called subverting images of women in erotic movies, pin-ups, and the like are actually empowering of femininity. Starting with burlesque and later *Playboy*, Buszek argues that the story of erotic, or at least of sexually tinged, pop culture is a story of true feminism. In a similar vein, Linda Scott (2005) has argued that the type of early feminism that reduced women's representations in erotic spectacles, advertising, and the like to sexual objectification was an attempt by puritan-minded, middle-class, white, American female intellectuals to control all women, not free them. The power of pop culture to liberate women from any form of oppressive ideology, including (and ironically) the feminist one, is what makes it attractive. As Scott (2005: 9) writes, the women involved in pop culture, from burlesque to the production of beauty magazines, have been "social activists, who argued passionately for the rights of women to have beauty and pleasure, especially in sexual expression." Similarly, Lynn Peril (2006) points out that the freedom that pop culture has ascribed to women has been met, generally speaking, with hypocrisy or suspicion. But the fact remains that sexual culture has been good for women.

However, all this does not mean that women have not been victimized. The line between sexism and sexuality has always been a thin one in pop culture. Perhaps no one has understood this better than Eve Ensler, creator of *The Vagina Monologues*, which have been translated and performed throughout the world. Ensler's objective is to stop violence against women, physical and psychological. She has also created V-Day, a global movement to stop such violence. The *Monologues* are the result of interviews with more than two hundred women. With humor and grace, they celebrate women's sexuality and emotional strength. The subtext of the *Monologues* is that violence can be stopped if women's sexuality is understood, openly and frankly, and not shrouded in myth and misunderstanding. Indeed, as I read it, Ensler's main subtext is that women can now take full charge of their sexuality, becoming the "goddesses" of pop culture that they always have been, but on their own terms. Clarissa Smith (2007) has also argued this very point in a truly insightful study showing that women should not consider themselves to be enslaved by the sexuality of the images coming out of popular media. Smith debunks the myth that women are objects of the male gaze. She argues that the goddess has finally started to take command of her image, rather than letting the looker do so.

The power of goddess culture was cleverly tapped by Dan Brown in his runaway bestseller *The Da Vinci Code* (2003), which revolves around the notion of the "sacred feminine," or the view that women play a harmonizing role in the world by balancing the masculine traits of societies. In ancient cultures, the masculine and feminine roles were regularly celebrated as equal partners in the divine scheme of things—Isis and Osiris, Aphrodite and Adonis, and other such pairs populate ancient mythologies. This partnership was eliminated by Christianity, claims Brown. The theme of its recovery transforms Brown's fictional novel into a theological and social treatise. Brown, though, ignores history conveniently. Womanhood has always been considered an integral part of Christianity, as can be seen in the pivotal role the Madonna has always played in Christianity. Worshipped by Christians since apostolic times in the first century, Mary is the object of shrines and places of pilgrimage throughout the world. The early Christians also venerated Mary by calling her Mother of God, a title affirmed in 431 at the Council of Ephesus. Brown's novel became an overnight success, not because it assessed history accurately but because it articulated in narrative form what pop culture has always assumed implicitly—that goddess culture needs to be legitimized, not marginalized.

The Instinct of the Profane

Of all the theoretical frameworks proposed for explaining pop culture (elaborated in chapter 2), the one that seems most capable of providing a truly meaningful understanding of the phenomenon is carnival theory. It simply makes sense psychologically, since carnivals and spectacles have historically functioned as vehicles for expressing the instinct of the profane. Simply put, pop culture, like traditional carnivals, circuses, and fairs, constitutes a release valve for the instinct of the profane buried within human nature, giving it a communal expressive form and thus rendering it harmless. Pop culture is *cathartic*, as philosopher Walter Benjamin has argued (discussed in chapter 2).

Benjamin was part of the Frankfurt School, albeit a sidelined member because of his anti-Marxist stance. Jurgen Habermas (b. 1929), a late member of the School, also broke somewhat with its rigid Marxist philosophy, seeing in pop culture spectacles the power of individual human agency. If there is to be progress, he claimed, then it must come from the people, not from intellectuals. The Marxist members of the School seem to have been oblivious to the psychological reasons that pop culture appealed so broadly to people of all economic classes. As John Lough (2002: 219) has aptly phrased it, the Frankfurt model "presupposes an audience of powerless dupes, with all constituents making the same reading." The basic assumption of the Marxist hegemonic model of Antonio Gramsci (mentioned briefly in chapter 2) is that the people in power (corporations, governments, and the like) are able to rule by cultural influence, rather than by force, indoctrinating and manipulating the powerless dupes, generating in them a false consciousness that is immune against its own falsehood.

Such ideological discourse completely misses the whole point of pop culture. Pop culture is really nothing more than a contemporary descendant of such ancient ritualized forms of profane theater as carnivals and circuses. Carnival theory would thus explain why sexuality, occultism, and the like are so intrinsic to pop culture, and why their attempted eradication by fanatic religious elements in America has never succeeded. The Dracula legend, for instance, is not only the stuff of occult narrative traditions; it is now as intrinsic to pop culture as are sitcoms. It was introduced to the modern world through the pen of Bram Stoker (1847–1912), whose novel *Dracula* was first published in 1897 and has remained in print ever since. His treatment became the yardstick by which all future vampires in pop literature and film would be measured. The figure of Dracula challenges religious authority and simultaneously resuscitates the mythical search for eternal youth and immortality. Stoker's Dracula was the embodiment of evil, but the Dracula that finds its way into modern-day pop culture is a much more ambivalent creature. His offspring range from goths to modern-day ersatz vampires who base their lifestyle on drinking blood and dressing up as Dracula look-alikes (McLelland 2006). Such is carnival.

Frankfurt theory is completely incapable of explaining such phenomena, because they are generated by common people themselves in defiance of the mainstream culture, and often in resistance to hegemonic powers (such as radical right-wing governments). Pop culture itself acts as a safeguard against the spread of dangerous forms of sexism and occultism, since it is always prepared to satirize deeply rooted notions. Horror themes are both glorified and satirized by pop culture. Alongside a Dracula movie is the television series *The Addams Family*, which is a parody of the horror genre.

As Bakhtin emphasized, the only way to understand the appeal of pop culture is to look at the rituals of carnivals—from the phallophors of the Saturnalia, whose role was to joke and cavort obscenely, to the rogue comedians at turn-of-the-century country fairs. From ancient times, ritualistic tears and laughter have balanced the psychic tension between the sacred and the profane present within us. The laughter induced by carnival performances is festive laughter and, thus, the laughter of all people, not just intellectuals and cognoscenti. Because it mocks and derides the sacred order it is also emotionally powerful. The instinct of the profane has always manifested itself in a pastiche of forms that are meant to evoke laughter. It brings the sacred (politics, religion, business) under the microscope of comedy, where it can be examined harmlessly and cathartically. As Beatrice Otto (2007) has carefully documented, fools and jesters are found across time and cultures, from the courts of ancient China and India to the courts of medieval Europe, Africa, the Middle East, and the Americas. Not surprisingly, they have had the same function everywhere—to simultaneously mock and entertain, fulfilling a deep human need to understand oneself through the comedic. As Swiss psychologist Carl Jung (1875–1961) claimed, all these personae are really narrative, ritualistic, or symbolic manifestations of the archetype that he called the Trickster. An archetype, in Jungian theory, is a primordial image buried in the collective unconscious of humanity that gains physical expressive or symbolic form differentially in cultures across the world. The surface details vary, but the underlying archetype is the same. In every person there exists a predilection for puerile mischief. So, at the personal level, the Trickster archetype may manifest itself in a desire for frivolity, in playing devil's advocate in a discussion, in a sly craving to mock someone's success, in an urge to steal something for the sheer thrill of it, and so on. At a cultural level, it may manifest itself in myths, legends, poetry, paintings, stories, and the like. In Western culture, for instance, the trickster surfaces in Dickens's Artful Dodger, in the fabled character known as Rumpelstiltsken, in Shakespeare's Puck in *A Midsummer Night's Dream*, in the character assumed by many modern-day comedians, and so on and so forth.

Especially troubling to both intellectuals and religious fanatics is the role of sexuality in pop culture. However, as argued in this book, sex is nothing more than part of the show. The Canadian director Atom Egoyan (b. 1960) clearly shows the role of sex in pop culture in his brilliant 1994 movie *Exotica*. Using a blend of styles—police story, tabloid, fantasy, melo-drama, erotica, and journalism—Egoyan projects the movie around a strip-per whose salacious performances constitute a metaphor for who we are. In the strip joint the real voyeur is the camera—hence the audience. The presence of strip joints, populated by common people, from lawyers and judges to factory workers and housewives, threatens false standards of morality. The people are there for the pure enjoyment of it. Striptease is profane theater and, thus, highly appealing.

A similar understanding of sexuality's threat to artificial standards of morality is evident in *The Rocky Horror Picture Show*, mentioned briefly in chapter 1. It is a collage of vampirism, rock culture, transvestitism, pornography, and all the other aspects that make up the allure of pop culture carnival. The show debuted in 1975 and, remarkably, is still being put on in some cities. Its appeal is due, in large part, to its overtly porn-style showmanship, which is blatantly critical of bourgeois and fanatical religious values. It has become a tradition in many areas of the United States for the film to be shown at midnight on Halloween, when audiences can show up dressed in drag and lingerie. The film, the accompanying theatrical performance, and the audience are part of this ersatz carnival, where the occult and the sexual are intertwined in true pastiche style. The movie explores such forbidden topics as transvestitism, homosexuality, cannibalism, voyeurism, adultery, and even incest. The master of ceremonies, Dr. Frank-N-Furter (an obvious satirical pun on the word *frankfurter*) instructs his audience at the outset with the following Dionysian advice: "Give yourself over to absolute pleasure. Swim the warm waters of sins of the flesh—erotic nightmares beyond any measure, and sensual daydreams to treasure forever. Can't you just see it? Don't dream it, be it." With that signal, the audience indulges itself in drinking, smoking marijuana, and various forms of sexual debauchery without interruption by the theater staff.

The Rocky Horror Picture Show is modern-day carnival at its transgressive best. Men attending the show often wear corsets and fishnet stockings, while the women display themselves in revealing costumes and act in an overtly porn-like fashion. The film itself is replete with sexual acts and references, from Dr. Frank-N-Furter's animated corpse sex-toy to the liberalization of the uptight, morally hypocritical couple Brad and Janet. As in traditional carnivals, the audience dances and sings along, shouting lewd comments at the screen, and throwing objects at certain points in the film. The group experience and feeling of community that is achieved through such fantasy-based, transgressive behavior creates a cathartic effect. Such spectacles have emancipatory power, allowing people to engage in imagined anarchy through a ritualistic ridiculing of the artificial norms that society imposes. As Danny Fingeroth (2004: 178) has aptly put it, in pop culture "reality informs fantasy, fantasy informs reality."

In sum, the dichotomy of the sacred versus the profane is critical for understanding the constitution and spread of pop culture over the last 150 years. The profane is traditionally associated with the body (and its "desecration") and the sacred with the spirit (and its "exaltation"). Both require vehicles for expression, not repression. There is no awareness of the sacred without the profane. The two balance each other out, as can be seen by the traits associated with them.

The sacred was mythologized in Greek culture as the realm of Apollo (the god of beauty and of the fine arts) and the profane as the realm of Dionysus (the god of wine, who represented the irrational, undisciplined, and orgiastic side of the psyche). Pop culture is Dionysian, revolving around all that is carnal and orgiastic; the sacred world is Apollonian, encompassing all that is mental and rational. Pop culture forces us to come to grips with the carnality of the human condition before tackling its divinity. Such a tendency is found in narrative traditions throughout the world, from the story of Siddhartha to that of the prodigal son. Siddhartha was the Buddha (c. 563–483 BCE), an Indian philosopher and the founder of Buddhism. He married at an early age and participated in the worldly life of the court, but he found his self-indulgent existence dull. He left home and began wandering in search of enlightenment. The lesson to be learned from such traditions is that passage from the world of the profane (the courtly life) to the world of the sacred (enlightenment) involves living and aging.

The importance of the sacred versus profane dichotomy as an Apollonian versus Dionysian form of symbolism was captured eloquently by the Jungian scholar Joseph L. Henderson (1964: 146) in his classic study of initiation rites and other crucial social rituals. He puts it as follows:

Table 10.1. Characteristics of the Sacred and of the Profane

Sacred	Profane
tragedy	comedy
grief	pleasure
pathos	laughter
seriousness	humor
respect	mockery

The symbols that influence many vary in their purpose. Some men need to be aroused, and experience their initiation in the violence of a Dionysiac "thunder rite." Others need to be subdued, and they are brought to submission in the ordered design of temple precinct or sacred cave, suggestive of the Apollonian religion of later Greece. A full initiation embraces both themes, as we can see when we look either at the material drawn from ancient texts or at living subjects. But it is quite certain that the fundamental goal of initiation lies in taming the original Trickster-like wildness of the juvenile nature. It therefore has a civilizing or spiritualizing purpose, in spite of the violence of the rites that are required to set this process in motion.

The Pop Culture Memorate

Pop culture is, in summary, a means through which the profane is expressed in contemporary capitalist societies. This does not mean that each person in such societies wishes to be a participant in the theater of the profane, but rather that it is an unconscious pattern in social behavior. Its manifestations are everywhere. It is now part of our social memorate. *Memorate* is the term used by anthropologists to refer to an unconscious pattern of thought that has become so common that it is no longer recognized as originating in a specific idea, trend, or event. Sexuality, occultism, and the like are now part of that memorate. They are controversial because they are felt to be part of a decaying social system, rather than connected with healthy themes.

Even the simple act of smoking is (and always has been) controversial, not only because of its negative health implications but also because it is linked to sexuality. In *Casablanca*, for instance, cigarettes are conspicuous sexual props in Rick's café. Swaggering imperiously in his realm, Rick (Humphrey Bogart) is rarely seen without a cigarette in his mouth or in his hand. This image of sexual cool was so captivating to cinema-goers that it became a paradigm imitated by hordes of young males in the 1940s and 1950s. Incidentally, that very paradigm was satirized by Jean Luc Godard in his 1959 film *Breathless*. In one scene, Jean-Paul Belmondo stares at a poster of Bogart in a cinema window. He takes out a cigarette and starts smoking it, imitating Bogart in *Casablanca*. With the cigarette dangling from the side of his mouth, the sexually conversant Belmondo approaches his female mate and bluntly inquires, "Sleep with me tonight?" The parodic intent is obvious. In Nicholas Ray's 1955 movie *Rebel without a Cause*, the sexual cool associated with smoking comes out forcefully in the "car chicken" scene, in which teen idol James Dean can be seen dangling a cigarette from the side of his mouth as he gets ready to duel his opponent to the death with his car.

It is true that we see less smoking in movies now—a fact reflecting the change in social opinions on smoking. There are even movies that parody the association between smoking and sex. As a case in point, consider the 1980 movie *Caddyshack*, which contains a scene satirizing smoking as a come-on, with actor Chevy Chase smiling at a woman as smoke comes out of his mouth in a ludicrous, farcical way. Nevertheless, the sexual allure of the cigarette is alive and well even in such a prohibitive environment, and this will remain so until the cigarette is replaced by another sexually suggestive prop. As Margaret Leroy (1997) has suggested, smoking is attractive because it is taboo. The history of smoking in Western society shows that tobacco has been perceived at times as a desirable thing and at others as a forbidden fruit. But in almost every era, as Richard Klein (1993) has eloquently argued, cigarettes have had some connection to sex, or to something that is erotically, socially, or intellectually appealing. As Michael Starr (1984) puts it, "smoking is, in many situations, a species of rhetoric signifying certain qualities of the smoker." The 2006 movie *Thank You for Smoking*, directed by Jason Reitman, showed the absurdity of the prohibitionist mentality against smoking. Today, it would seem, smoking is a much more subversive act than it has ever been at any time in its history. The trangressive symbolism of the cigarette has not as yet been erased from the communal memorate.

THE SPREAD OF POP CULTURE

In Marxist theories, pop culture is seen as one huge ploy revealing capitalism's ability to create, shape, and profit from our base instincts. As mentioned in chapter 2, Matthew Arnold began the critical onslaught against capitalism by depicting it as a corrupting force in cultural evolution. Like that of the Marxist critics who came after him and who took up his rally against pop culture, Arnold's stance was, to my mind, really an expression of anti-Americanism. The same implicit stance is latent in most critiques of pop culture. The Frankfurt and British Marxist intellectuals saw American pop culture as vulgar and threatening of world order, because it had mass appeal.

In some ways, however, the Marxist view is correct. There would be no pop culture without American capitalism to promote it. And pop culture may even be the cause of world conflicts today, as people in vastly different cultures attempt to rebuff its influence in any way they can. But the Arnold-Frankfurt view is ultimately simplistic. It assumes that all participants in pop culture are passive and that economics motivates everything within human life. As mentioned throughout this book, such an argument is highly elitist, assuming that only intellectuals know what is appropriate culture and what is not. Pop culture existed before the capitalist industries realized its power and helped to make it lucrative. Arnold and Marx put the cart before the horse. The horse is the appeal of pop culture itself. It provides the fun, the thrills, the nostalgic memories, and all the other things that make human life bearable; capitalism is a cart (among others) that provides the means to deliver it. Like pop culture itself, capitalism is really a collage of economic, social, and political ideas and forms that involve consumption, art, and life-style coming together into one huge bricolage that we call modern life. It is the gaining of pleasure through consumption that sets the capitalist agenda apart from all other previous systems of politics. Therefore the distinction between capitalist economics and pop culture is now barely discernible.

"Joining the Revolution"

As mentioned briefly in chapter 8, in the era of counterculture dissidence the business world co-opted the pop lifestyles and ideologies of youth as part of its overall marketing philosophy. The rock-and-roll culture of the 1950s had proven to be a profitable one indeed, no matter how iconoclastic it had appeared to the self-appointed moral guardians of society in that decade. So, by the time of the hippie movement of the 1960s, the business world was inclined to pay very close attention to youth trends, realizing that it was in its own best interest not to fight the new images of youth insurgency but rather to embrace them outright, and thus to change with the times. One highly effective early strategy of this "if-you-can't-beat-them-join-them" approach was the development of an advertising style that mocked consumerism and advertising itself!

The strategy worked beyond expectations. Through the matter-of-fact use of hippie lifestyle images and symbolism in advertising and marketing, business itself gave an appearance of being anti-establishment and subversive. The image masters had cleverly "joined the revolution" by deploying the language and aesthetics of hippie rebellion to market their goods and services. The underlying subtext of this clever approach allowed common folk to believe (in a bizarre way) that the clothing they bought and the records they listened to ipso facto transformed them into revolutionaries, regardless that they did not pay the social price of true nonconformity and dissent. This strategy continues to be used to this day. Its effects are everywhere in the marketplace. Never before in the history of humanity have so many spectacles (such as movies and television programs) and products (such as CDs and cell phones) been created with an eye on trends within youth culture.

The business world discovered fortuitously in the counterculture era how to incorporate the emotional power of adolescent rebellion into the grammar of everyday life. Advertising campaigns of the late counterculture era—such as "the Pepsi Generation" and Coke's message of universal brotherhood—can be fruitfully recalled here again. These campaigns directly incorporated the images, rhetoric, and symbolism of the hippie movement, thus creating the illusion that the goals of the hippies and of the soft drink manufacturers were one and the same. Rebellion through purchasing became the subliminal thread woven into many other ad campaigns. As also mentioned previously, Dodge and Oldsmobile, respectively, followed the lead of the soft-drink companies with the Rebellion campaign and the Youngmobile campaign, etching into the names of the cars themselves the powerful connotations of youth rebellion. In effect, it was the marketing world that brought about the real revolution—that of marketing to the young and old through the power of youth symbolism. Thus, since the 1960s, the worlds of advertising, marketing, entertainment, and youth culture have become totally intertwined. The counterculture threat passed because in the end the hippies joined the Pepsi Revolution. According to many, the only authentic rebel was Abby Hoffman, whose *Steal This Book*—a handbook of how to survive by stealing that Hoffman wanted readers to shoplift from stores—offered the only kind of subversive gesture that was truly hostile and menacing to the corporate world order.

The signs of the amalgamation of the media, the business world, and pop culture are unmistakable. Nowadays, the fashion trends of celebrities, pop musicians, movie stars, and the like are recycled and marketed shortly after their invention as the fashion styles of all; pop music trends quickly become part of the music tastes of society at large; pop slang surfaces in the everyday discourse of adults and is even given official status by reputable dictionaries; and the list could go on and on. Being hip and cool, no matter what the age, has become the norm. Transgressive music has moved from the margins of American popular culture to the center of a multi-billion-dollar global industry. Previously feared lifestyles associated with the likes of punks, goths, and rappers now influence fashions, language, attitudes, and political views. The popular culture of the United States—and, increasingly, of the world—is fast becoming the only kind of culture. Without the capitalist economic system behind it, and the marketplace model of success that it engenders, there simply would be no spread of pop culture. The rejection of such culture by some countries of the world today, and the indirect culture wars that it generates, do not necessarily constitute a rejection of capitalism. To my mind, rather, these show a rejection of the strategy of co-optation.

Controlling Pop Culture's Spread

The spread of American pop culture started with recordings, long before the era of satellite television. Music needs no linguistic translation. So, records were bought in other countries because, as in America, the music held great appeal. With the advent of television in the 1950s, the spread gained momentum, reaching truly international proportions with satellite television in the 1990s. As a consequence, debates about the quality of pop culture and the impact it purportedly has on world culture and politics have become common and widespread. On the one side, critics say that such culture feeds a constant stream of simplified ideas and sensationalistic images to unwitting viewers, that it negatively influences politics and voting patterns, that it destroys local cultures in favor of a bland Hollywood-based culture of distraction, and that it encourages passivity. On the other side, defenders say that it provides a great deal of high-quality spectacles, that it is the major source of recreation for many people, if not most, and that it is a stimulus for making changes in politics that would otherwise never cross people's minds. Whatever the truth, one thing is for certain—the media–technology–pop culture partnership has turned out to be *the* vehicle that has consolidated what the great Canadian communications theorist Marshall McLuhan (1911–1980) called the "global village." The global village has arisen because the same pattern and kind of culture (including the same television sitcoms, adventure programs, and variety shows) is available across the globe.

As mentioned in chapter 2, the theory that the mass media and mass culture can directly influence behavior negatively is called hypodermic needle theory. This theory claims that media are capable of directly conditioning people to act in specific ways. The phenomenon of "junk food" is often cited in support of this theory. When fast food eateries first appeared in the 1950s—then called burger and milkshake "joints"—they were designed to be socializing sites for adolescents. The food served at such places was viewed, correctly, to be "junk," injurious to one's health and only to be consumed by young people, since their metabolism could ostensibly break it down more quickly and since they could purportedly recover from its negative health effects more easily than older people. However, very soon junk food, promoted by effective advertising campaigns, became an indulgence sought by anyone of any age, from very young children to seniors. The compulsion to consume junk food has, consequently, become a fact of contemporary life, inducing dangerous eating habits. The inordinate consumption of junk food is one of the main factors contributing to the rise in obesity.

In this world of imagistic collage, obesity is at odds with the ultra-slim body images that the media perpetuate as the norm for attractiveness. This disjunction of images is sometimes thought to be one of the sources of culture-based diseases, previously unknown, such as anorexia nervosa and bulimia. Studies, though, have shown no causal relation. The hypodermic

The compulsion to consume junk food has become a fact of contemporary life,
aided by successful advertising.
©iStockphoto.com/Bonnie Schupp

needle view of media-induced eating disorders simplistically ignores history. The ravages of overeating or undereating are not just contemporary maladies. They have always been part of lifestyles, rituals, and traditions across the world. Undereating is known as fasting. The ancient Assyrians and Babylonians observed fasts as a form of penance. Among Jews, too, fasting as a form of penitence and purification is observed annually on the Day of Atonement, Yom Kippur. The fast observed by Muslims during the month of Ramadan is an expression of atonement. The early Christians associated fasting with penitence and purification. Native North Americans hold tribal fasts to avert impending disasters. The counterpart to fasting is indulging in food. Traditionally, this has been the prerogative of the aristocracy. But feasts and festivals including overeating for common folk reach back into human history, from the Roman Saturnalia to contemporary carnivals such as the Mardi Gras.

The view that mass culture (especially of the American variety) is detrimental to human beings ignores not only history but also the fact that people can discriminate between levels of culture. The negative understanding of mass culture has a hidden interventionist agenda behind it. But intervention, history also teaches us, has never worked. Prohibition didn't work. Censorship doesn't work and can even backfire. As Peter Blecha (2004) has documented, some of the most famous songs of Billie Holiday, Elvis Presley, Woody Guthrie, the Beatles, the Rolling Stones, Jimi Hendrix, Frank Zappa, the Sex Pistols, Patti Smith, Public Enemy, Ice-T, 2 Live Crew, Nirvana, Bruce Springsteen, Eminem, the Dixie Chicks, and many more were either censored or stifled in some way at the start. All this did was make the songs even more popular than they otherwise would have been. Prohibition seems to do more to pique interest in the prohibited item than does any intrinsic merit it might have. Moreover, the imposition of censorious strictures in a democratic society raises the question of *what* content is appropriate and *who* has the right to decide so. The danger in pinpointing certain representations as "harmful" and others as "acceptable" is that this practice might lead to oppression and even tyranny, as has been evidenced by such movements as the Inquisition in Europe and McCarthyism in the United States. The former was a judicial institution, established by the papacy in the Middle Ages, charged with seeking out, trying, and sentencing persons guilty of heresy. The latter was a public investigation over which the infamous U.S. senator Joseph McCarthy presided, in which he accused army officials, members of the media, and public figures of being Communists.

Most people can easily distinguish between what is art and what is not.

Great works of art foster engagement; many popular media artifacts, on the other hand, simply provide distraction, even though often the dividing line between engagement and distraction is blurry indeed. Many of the forms intended originally for easy leisure have themselves evolved into works of highly engaging art, as mentioned throughout this book. Some pieces of jazz and rock music produced in the last one hundred years are worthy of being listed alongside the works of the great classical composers; many movies are among the best works of visual art ever created; and even some television sitcoms, past and present, have significant artistic merit.

It is useless, in my view, to propose drastic measures to censor or repress popular expressions of any kind, in order to counteract any purported hypodermic needle effect. For one thing, media messages produce such an effect only if individuals are already predisposed toward their content; and for another, media moguls will find ways around such measures. Nonetheless, more and more right-wing groups in America have started to suggest censorship as a means of gaining control over the levers of the media and cultural content. However, the answer to the dilemma of the media is not to be found in censorship or in any form of state control. Even if it were possible in a consumerist culture to control the contents of the media, doing so would invariably prove counterproductive. In my view, the answer is to become aware of the meanings that are generated by pop culture representations. When the human mind understands these, it will be better able to fend off any undesirable effects that they may cause.

This is in fact what some groups are now suggesting. For instance, in *Culture Jam* (2000), the Canadian activist Kalle Lasn makes a case for "jamming" the messages found in advertising. Lasn has founded *Adbusters* magazine to do exactly that. He believes that corporate America is no longer a country but rather one overarching brand shaped by the cult of celebrity and the spectacles that generate it. Culture and marketing are, according to Lasn, one and the same. What is of interest here is not Lasn's political take on capitalist culture but rather how he and his followers approach the problem of meaning. As a simple example of what jamming implies, take a slogan such as McDonald's *I'm lovin' it!* As it stands, this catchy phrase means nothing and yet everything, since it can allude to almost anything (the food fare, the lifestyle associated with it, and so on). It has rhetorical force. This message can be "jammed" by adding a simple phrase to it that will alert people to what the product is really all about. One such phrase is the following: *I'm lovin' it, as my arteries clog up with cholesterol!* In a nutshell, this example shows what culture jamming is all about.

WILL POP CULTURE SURVIVE?

Economic prosperity and the obliteration of the authoritative structures of the past are, of course, good things. Because of social movements spearheaded by young people, starting in the Roaring Twenties, tolerant attitudes are common today. The Charleston led to an acceptance of female sexuality as a fact of life, not something to be hidden behind hypocritical traditions. As Scott (2005: 166) has aptly observed: "This era [the Roaring Twenties] brought a wave of sensualism, in which legions of young women—particularly though not exclusively those of modest means—asserted themselves by their dress, their dancing, and their romances." Since then society has changed drastically in its view of women, making possible the women's liberation movement. On the other hand, entertainment for its own sake, sexual or otherwise, seems to have become a primary (if not singular) goal of many people today.

There seems, in other words, to be an imbalance between the sacred and the profane in contemporary society—an imbalance probably brought about by the partnership between business and pop culture. It is in the obvious interest of business to ensure that trends come and go quickly, for this guarantees an attractive bottom line. However, sooner or later the balance will have to be restored if American society is to thrive psychically. More correctly, the balance will have to reestablish itself, as it has across time in cultures that have experienced a similar form of disequilibrium. There seems to be a corrective mechanism in the human species that is constantly seeking to ensure a perfect balance between the sacred and the profane. Without the restoration of this balance, there is a serious danger that pop culture will not survive but will be replaced by a more authoritarian form of culture, controlled by extremists (to the left or the right of the political spectrum).

Internet Mayhem

One social locus where the imbalance is clearly obvious is the Internet, the stage on which pop culture is currently unfolding (Montgomery 2007). Enormously popular social networking sites such as MySpace and YouTube offer many examples. These function very much like the malls and burger joints of previous eras. As videos launched on these sites by indie amateurs remake the entertainment landscape, common folk are being catapulted into the limelight of pop culture trends like never before. Andy Warhol's prediction of fifteen minutes of fame for everyone has become true. Do-it-your-self music and art may be reshaping pop culture on the Internet stage, but this medium is also bringing about an unprecedented threat to pop culture's survival. As in previous eras of pop culture history, the indie trend is not unexpected, and it highlights once again the role of common people in the constitution of pop culture. However, unlike the popular art trends of the past, the new stage allows for absolutely anything to be showcased. It takes great effort and much patience to produce art. But patience is at a premium in cyberspace.

The Internet is blurring the lines between performer and audience, giving free reign to self-expression like never before. The tendency for ordinary people to produce artistic expressions is not without precedent, of course. *America's Funniest Home Videos*, letters to the editor, and graffiti on city walls are all examples of previous self-expressive forms. The difference is that, because of technology, the self-expression factor in pop culture has become more and more random and meaningless. The new pattern of countless individuals posting art on the Internet is creating cultural mayhem and may even be damaging the integrity of the 150-year-old pop culture experiment itself—an experiment designed, ironically, to empower common people to express themselves. My guess is that this pattern will correct itself as the Internet takes on more and more of the traditional functions associated with popular performances and representations. That is my hope. The alternative is a likely demise of the pop culture experiment.

The signs of the demise of the experiment are on the Internet for all to see. Subversiveness and transgression, for example, are now merely fashionable Internet styles, not effective modes of carnival. Moral panic theory (elaborated in chapter 2) seems to be no longer applicable to the Internet. Nothing shocks us. Therein lies the rub—as Shakespeare aptly put it. The power of pop culture is, and has always been, its ability to turn out low-level products such as the *Scream* movies alongside high-level ones such as *Mystic River*. In this factory, entertainers and artists, performers and audiences, have always been partners. In offline culture, this continues to be the case. The vocalizations of Paris Hilton or the pompous musings of Donald Trump are promoted alongside the music of Philip Glass and Nino Rota (the composer of the soundtrack to the *Godfather* and of the scores to several of the Fellini movies). This balance is being jeopardized, though, by the mayhem of indie culture that is populating cyberspace. Only by restoring that balance will the Internet allow the pop culture experiment to live on.

So, What Is Pop Culture?

Pop culture has had an effect on all of us alive today. It continues to be appealing because, as discussed throughout this book, it taps into our instinct of the profane. Pop culture has opened up the aesthetic channels to one and all, not just the elite or the cognoscenti. It has made personal choice a reality. However, it has also created the conditions whereby people tend to hang on to their youthful lifestyles well beyond their adolescent years. It is noteworthy that in 2002 the remix of Elvis's minor 1968 song "A Little Less Conversation," spliced with techno sounds and electronic warps and woofs and used on the soundtrack for the even more minor film *Live a Little, Love a Little*, made its way to the top of the charts. All that can be said in explanation is that Elvis has become a pop culture myth—a poor country boy who made good and became an international symbol. His memory continues to fuel a passionate denial of aging and extinction. His home, Graceland, has become a pilgrimage site for the forever-young people to whom he remains an ageless hero.

As I see it, whatever the effects, pop culture will survive. The indie orientation that it now has will eventually settle down, turning the new stage into a more traditional-looking one. Pop culture is culture by the people for the people. That is why it will continue to hold sway over us. However, the make-up of pop culture is no longer homogeneously American. People of various ethnicities and backgrounds, from diverse societies, are now playing an increasingly prominent role in the global village. For years, Japanese *manga* (comic books) and *anime* (animated features), along with characters such as Pokémon and Hello Kitty, have been the rage of youths throughout America. In 2006, Virgin Comics introduced *Devi*, a comic book based on Indian mythology and traditional legends. The comic book experience is clearly proliferating across media and genres.

POP CULTURE FOREVER

Efforts are being made today to broaden the stage on which pop culture is enacted, to take into account the newly globalized audience, and to connect trends to larger psychosocial forces in human civilization. The latter point is highlighted in M. Night Shyamalan's brilliant movie *Unbreakable* (2002), which was inspired by the mythological nature of comic books. Comic books, we are told in the movie, are modern manifestations of something universal, constituting a mode of pictorial mythic history mirroring that of the stories imprinted in the Egyptian hieroglyphs. Both the camera work and the dialogue in the film are suggestive of comic books. The camera shots are long, with infrequent changes and very little action during shots. Movements by the actors are static, suggesting the static illustrations of comic books. Dialogue between characters never overlaps, as in comic book sequences. And as in many comic books, the name of the hero, David Dunn, is alliterative (similar examples in comic book history include Bruce Banner, Scott Summers, Peter Parker, Matt Murdock, Reed Richards, Wally West, and Susan Storm). Shyamalan shows that comic books can offer a modern-day exemplar of ancient mythic picture-based fantasy.

The movie implies, moreover, that pop culture now has its own true theorists among the makers of pop culture themselves—namely, the filmmakers, the television programmers, and the like. Such creators of pop culture highlight and sometimes even directly discuss pop culture themes in their spectacles and texts. In effect, pop culture is itself becoming a meta-theory of who we are. The best theory of the cinema can be found in the movie *Cinema Paradiso* (1988), and the best theory of rock music in Bob Seger's signature tune "Old Time Rock and Roll." To paraphrase a well-known slogan (that of Toys "R" Us), there is little doubt that pop culture is us. Marshall Fishwick (2002: 24) has commented appropriately on this aspect of modern life as follows:

> Popular culture has many facets, like a diamond, and can be subversive and explosive. Scorn may be mixed with the fun, venom with laughter; it can be wildly comical and deadly serious. Popular culture is at the heart of revolutions that slip in on little cat feet. Those most affected by them—the elite and the mighty—seldom see them coming. Popular culture sees and hears, being close to the people. If the medium is the message, then the reaction might be revolution.

There is little doubt in my mind that, with a few touches to restore the imbalance between the sacred and the profane here and there, the pop culture experiment will continue. In fact, it is probably more accurate to say that it is no more an experiment but, as mentioned throughout, the default form of culture today—a form of culture that has become largely unconscious. The invisibility of its ubiquity is due in large part to its democratic nature—it is culture by the people and for the people. Democracy seems to be the only way that cultures evolve dynamically. However, the context of evolution is changing because of the global village. In the future, the forms of pop culture will be determined not only by those living in America, but more and more by people in diverse places, as they search for new ways to interact in the global village and seek to understand who they are.

GLOSSARY

The following glossary contains many of the terms introduced in this book that might require a formal definition. Terms that are used in a descriptive manner (such as *carnivalesque*) are not included here. Also excluded are terms for technological devices such as *iPods* and *cell phones* and terms that are generally well-known (for example, *broadcasting*).

acronym   a word formed from the initial letters of a series of words. WAC = *W*omen's *A*rmy *C*orps; radar = *r*adio *d*etecting *a*nd *r*anging; laser = *l*ight *a*mplification by *s*timulated *e*mission of *r*adiation; UNESCO = *U*nited *N*ations *E*ducational, *S*cientific, and *C*ultural *O*rganization. Acronymy is a major feature of the language used in chatrooms, text messages, and other types of digital forms of communication: *cm* = *call me*; *ruok?* = *Are you o.k.?*

addressee   the receiver of a message; the individual(s) to whom a message is directed

addresser   the sender of a message; the creator of a message

advertising   any type or form of public announcement designed to promote the sale of specific commodities or services (primarily through persuasion)

aesthesia   the experience of sensation. In art appreciation this term refers to holistic stimulation of our senses and feelings by art works.

alliteration   the repetition of the initial consonant sounds of words: *super sounds*; *pitter patter*

anagram   a word or phrase made from another word or phrase by rearranging its letters: *won* = *now*; *dread* = *adder*; *drop* = *prod*; *stop* = *pots*

archetype   an original model or type after which other similar things are patterned

audience   the specified group of individuals toward whom media products are directed or who attend or engage in specific kinds of pop culture spectacles

baby boomer   the age category of people born after World War II from 1947 through 1961. This term is used often in the media and in pop culture literature.

binary opposition   refers to people's perception of many aspects of meaning in terms of opposites, such as *good* vs. *evil*, *night* vs. *day*, and so on. An opposition often leads to a connected set of derived oppositions. So, for example, in a narrative the *good* characters are opposed to the *evil* ones in terms of derived oppositions such as *us* vs. *them*, *right* vs. *wrong*, *truth* vs. *falsity*, and so on. These categories are manifested in actions, statements, plot twists, and the like. In cultural theory, some binary oppositions—such as *self* vs. *other*, *us* vs. *them*, *man* vs. *woman*, and *young* vs. *old*—are seen as potentially dangerous because of people's tendency to identify with one of the two elements in the opposition and to consider the other element negatively or as a derivative.

blockbuster   a film or book that gains widespread popularity and achieves enormous sales

brand image   the recognizable traits or "personality" of a product created through its name, packaging, price, and style of advertisement

brand name   the name given to a product

branding   the integration of products with media and pop culture events, programs, celebrities, and so forth

bricolage   the technique of putting together different elements to create something new. This term has been used in particular to refer to subcultures' appropriation of elements from the mainstream culture in order to transform or subvert their meanings (as in punk fashion).

bull's-eye model   a model that depicts communication as a process consisting of a sender aiming a message at a receiver as if aiming at a bull's-eye target

burlesque   a comic performance characterized by ridiculous exaggeration. Burlesque first appeared in the plays of the Greek dramatists Aristophanes (448?–388? BCE) and Euripides (480?–406 BCE) and the Roman playwright Plautus (254?–184 BCE). The seventeenth-century French playwright Molière (1622–1673) made dramatic burlesque a high art form. In the United States, the word *burlesque* was applied to a form of theatrical production, especially popular in the 1920s and 1930s, characterized by ribald comedy and scantily clad women, and often including stripteases.

cabaret   live entertainment in a locale such as a club or restaurant consisting of singing, dancing, and comedy

carnival   a traditional form of outdoor amusement that consists of exhibits, games, rides, shows, feasting, and merrymaking. The carnival event has been used to explain the appeal of pop culture spectacles.

cartoon   a drawing, often with a caption, caricaturing or symbolizing an event, situation, or person of topical interest; a strip of drawings that tell a story; an animated humorous film intended primarily for children (also called *toon*)

catharsis hypothesis   the claim that the representation of sex, violence, and aggression in media and pop culture spectacles has a preventive purging effect, since an involvement in fantasy aggression may provide a release from hostile impulses that otherwise might be acted out in real life

celebrity   a person in the public eye primarily because of media exposure. A celebrity is usually an actor, a television personality, a pop musician, or the like.

censorship   control of what people may say, hear, write, or read

channel   the physical means by which a signal or message is transmitted

character   a person portrayed in an artistic piece, such as a drama or novel

Charleston   a dance style characterized by kicking out the feet sideways while the knees are kept together. The dance popularized the image of stylish young women of the 1920s called *flappers*.

chick flick   a film that is intended or perceived to appeal primarily to women, given its romantic, sentimental, or human relations plots, or else its focus on the changing role of women in society

closed text   a text that elicits a singular interpretation or a very limited range of interpretations

codex   a proto-book used in the Middle Ages, especially to write about classic works or the Scriptures

collage   an artistic arrangement of materials and objects pasted on a surface or computer screen, often with unifying lines and color

comic book   a magazine using cartoon characters. Most comic books tell stories, although they have also been used for education, artistic expression, and other purposes.

commedia dell'arte   a type of comedy developed in Italy in the sixteenth and seventeenth centuries, characterized by improvisation from standard plot outlines and stock characters, who often wear traditional masks and costumes

commercial   an advertisement on radio, television, or the Internet. Commercials were first developed in the 1920s, for radio.

communication   social interaction through messages; the production and exchange of messages and meanings; the use of specific modes and media to transmit messages

conative   influential on a person's desires and behavior (as a message may be to the addressee)

consumerist   overly concerned with material goods

contact   a physical channel employed in communication; also, the psychological connections that inhere between addresser and addressee

context   the situation (physical, psychological, and/or social) in which a text or spectacle is performed or occurs, or to which it refers

convergence   the erosion of traditional distinctions among media due to concentration of ownership, globalization, and audience fragmentation; the process by which formerly separate technologies such as television and the telephone are brought together by a common technological base (digitization) or a common industrial strategy

culture jammers   a group of social activists, with a popular website and magazine, who are critical of the advertising process itself

culture war   any clash of tastes and ideologies with regard to cultural products

cyberspace   the realm of communication over the Internet. The term was coined by American writer William Gibson in his 1984 science fiction novel *Neuromancer*, in which he described cyberspace as a place of "unthinkable complexity."

decoding   the process of deciphering a text on the basis of its code or codes (systems of meaning) and the medium or media it uses

Digital Galaxy   the new social order ushered in by the Internet. This term is coined in imitation of Marshall McLuhan's neologism of the Gutenberg Galaxy.

digital media   computer-based systems of transmission

e-book   digital book (published on the Internet)

effects models   models of media and pop culture texts attempting to explain any effects (psychological, social, and so on) that these may have on people, societies, and cultures

Electronic Galaxy   the new social order ushered in by electronic media. This term is coined in imitation of Marshall McLuhan's neologism of the Gutenberg Galaxy.

electronic media   devices such as records and radios that allow for the sending and reception of electromagnetic signals

e-mail   electronic mail; an online service that permits people to send messages to each other via the Internet or another computer network

emotive   containing emotional intent (for example, in communicating something)

encoding   use of a code or codes (systems of meaning) to select or create a text using a specific medium

e-toon   a digital comic or cartoon (published on the Internet)

e-zine   a digital magazine (published on the Internet)

feedback   reaction to transmitted messages that informs the sender as to the nature of its reception

feminism   a movement advocating the same rights and opportunities for women as are enjoyed by men. Feminist beliefs have existed throughout history but feminism did not become widespread until the mid-1800s, when women were barred by law from voting in elections or serving on juries and when most institutions of higher education and most professional careers were also closed to women. Many historians regard the feminist movement as a turning point in the history of modern societies.

feminist theory   a theory devoted to showing how media–pop culture texts and social power structures coalesce to define gender categories; a framework for studying images and portrayals of women in the media

fetish   a fascination with a specific object that is believed to have magical or spiritual powers or to cause sexual arousal

fiction   text the content of which is produced by the imagination and is not necessarily based on fact

flappers   stylish and fun-loving young women of the 1920s who showed disdain for the traditional social conventions associated with women

Frankfurt School   a school of critical inquiry founded at the University of Frankfurt in 1922. It was the world's first Marxist institute of social research. Its aim was to understand the way in which human groups create meaning collectively under the impact of modern technology, capitalist social systems, and culture industries. The School was highly pessimistic about the possibility of genuine individuality under modern capitalism and condemned most forms of popular or mass culture as a type of incessant propaganda that indoctrinated the masses and disguised genuine social inequalities. The School's main contention was that typical pop culture fare was vulgar, functioning primarily to pacify ordinary people.

game console   a computer console for game-playing, usually through connection with a television set and operated with a game-controlling device, such as a joystick or game pad

gangsta rap   a style of rap music in which the lyrics deal with themes involving gangs, gangsters, and/or criminal lifestyles

genre   a group of classification for works of literature, art, and the like, and by extension for media (film, television, and so on). A genre is recognizable as distinct because of the subject matter it deals with, the themes it embodies, the style it adopts, and so forth.

global village   a world that has become dependent upon electronic media for information and is thus united, electronically. The term was coined by Marshall McLuhan.

globalization   the process by which formerly separate, discrete, or local cultural phenomena are brought into contact with one another and with new groups of people in an interactive fashion

goth   a form of punk music and lifestyle, especially prominent among youths, characterized by the wearing of dark clothes, the use of dark cosmetics, and other macabre forms of symbolism

Gutenberg Galaxy   the radical new social order ushered in by the invention of the printing press. The term was coined by Marshall McLuhan.

hegemony   the far-reaching power of the dominant class in a capitalist society. The term is most closely associated with the Italian Marxist Antonio Gramsci.

hermeneutics   the art of interpreting texts

hippies   members of a youth movement of the 1960s and 1970s that started in the United States and spread to many other countries

hypertextuality   a system for linking different texts and images within a computer document or over a network

icon   a celebrity who gains culture-wide status

image   a representation of a personality, product, or service used to enhance the aesthetic, social, or economic value of the good represented

Internet the matrix of networks that connects computers around the world

interpretation the process of figuring out what something (such as a word or a text) means

intertextuality allusion within a text to another text

irony the use of words to express something different from and often opposite to their literal meaning

jingle a catchy tune used in commercials

logo a distinctive signature, trademark, colophon, motto, or nameplate of a company or a brand

magazine a paper-based publication consisting of a collection of articles or stories, or both, published at regular intervals

marketing the business of positioning goods and services to the right audience

Marxism a socioeconomic theory developed by Karl Marx and Friedrich Engels. It constitutes the blueprint ideology behind Communism, holding that all people are entitled to enjoy the fruits of their labor but are prevented from doing so in capitalist systems, which divide society into two classes—non-owning workers and nonworking owners.

mass media media such as radio, television, newspapers, periodicals, and the like that reach a large audience

media convergence the transferal of all media into digital formats and, thus, their integration into a single transmission system

medium the physical means or process used to encode a certain type of message and deliver it through a channel

message communication transmitted by words, signals, or other means from one person, station, or group to another with a specific function or meaning

multimedia combining the use of several media, such as movies, music, print, and so forth

mythology a set of latent universally and historically relevant themes or symbols in a media product or pop culture spectacle

narrative something told or written, such as an account, story, tale, or even a scientific theory

narrator the teller of the narrative

narrowcasting   broadcasting designed to reach specific types of audiences

net lingo   forms of language used in all kinds of contemporary electronic communication contexts and media (including chat rooms, text messages, and the like)

newspaper   a paper-based publication, usually issued on a daily or weekly basis, the main function of which is to report the news

noise   an interfering element (physical or psychological) in the communication channel that distorts or partially effaces a message

novel   a fictional prose narrative of considerable length, typically having a plot that unfolds through the actions, speech, and thoughts of the characters

open text   a text that invites a complex interpretation of its meaning

opposition   the process by which ideas and forms are differentiated in binary pairs (for example, *good* vs. *evil* and *night* vs. *day*)

orality   the use of spoken language to transmit knowledge

parody   a work imitating the characteristic style of someone or of another work in a satirical or humorous way

pastiche   a media product or pop culture spectacle that is created in imitation of another similar one, or that is constructed with a blend of borrowed styles

plot   a plan or sequence of events in a narrative

poetic   lyrically and metaphorically communicative

pop art   an artistic movement depicting objects or scenes from everyday life and employing techniques of commercial art and design

pop culture   the culture that has obliterated the distinction between high and low forms, allowing people themselves to evaluate artistic products and expressions

pop language   language that is picked up by the population at large from media spectacles. The term was introduced by linguist Leslie Savan.

pop music   music intended to be appreciated by ordinary people, usually for entertainment and pleasure

pop star   an individual in the media (for example, in music, cinema, or the like) who has become an icon in his or her field

positioning   the placing or marketing of a product for the right audience

post-feminism   an approach to pop culture and media that still holds on to basic feminist criticism but that expands it considerably, especially with respect to the previous restrictive feminist view of women's sexuality

postmodernism   the belief that all knowledge is relative and human-made, and that there is no purpose to life beyond the immediate and the present

print media   media based on paper (or similar) technology

propaganda   the systematic dissemination of doctrines and views that reflect specific interests and ideologies (political, social, and on the like)

pulp fiction   magazines and novels produced on cheap paper, dealing with very popular and titillating themes, such as crime, horror, and sex

radio   a technological system for sending audio signals through the air without wire, via electromagnetic waves

receiver   the person or group at whom a message is aimed

reception theory   a theory that attempts to explain how audiences interpret texts and spectacles

redundancy   repetition of parts of a message to counteract noise in a channel

representation   the process of giving a form to an idea, ritual, or desire

semiotics   science that studies signs and their uses in representation

sender   the transmitter of a message

setting   the place where a narrative unfolds

slogan   a catchword or phrase used to advertise a product

subtext   the concealed system of meanings within a text

tabloid   a small-format newspaper that is roughly half the size of a standard newspaper, usually containing sensationalistic coverage of crime, scandal, gossip, violence, and news about celebrities

technology   a system of objects made by humans

television   a system for sending audio and visual signals through the air via electromagnetic waves

text   a message meant to be interpreted

transmission   the sending and reception of messages

vaudeville   the principal form of popular entertainment in North America before the advent of cinema in the late nineteenth century and early twentieth century. Vaudeville consisted of various acts, which ranged enormously, from juggling, animal acts, comedy skits, recitations, songs, and magic shows to burlesque performances by actresses.

World Wide Web   an information server on the Internet composed of interconnected sites and files, accessible with a browser program

writing   the process of representing speech with characters; the process of laying out ideas or narratives in textual form

youth culture   the various forms of music, clothing, and other styles adopted by young people

REFERENCES

Anderson, W. T. (1992). *Reality Isn't What It Used to Be*. San Francisco: Harper Collins.

Bakhtin, M. (1981). *The Dialogic Imagination: Four Essays*. Austin: University of Texas Press.

———. (1986). *Speech Genres and Other Late Essays*. Austin: University of Texas Press.

———. (1990). *Art and Answerability*. Austin: University of Texas Press.

———. (1993). *Rabelais and His World*. Bloomington: Indiana University Press.

Baron, Naomi S. (2000). *Alphabet to Email: How Written English Evolved and Where It's Heading*. London: Routledge.

Barthes, R. (1957). *Mythologies*. Paris: Seuil.

———. (1975). *The Pleasure of the Text*. New York: Hill and Wang.

Bataille, G. (1962). *Erotism, Death and Sensuality*. New York: City Light Books.

Baudrillard, J. (1983). *Simulations*. New York: Semiotexte.

Bauman, Z. (1992). *Intimations of Postmodernity*. London: Routledge.

Berger, A. A. (2005). *Shop 'Til You Drop*. Lanham, Md.: Rowman & Littlefield.

Blecha, P. (2004). *Taboo Tunes: A History of Banned & Censored Songs*. San Francisco: Backbeat.

Buszek, M. E. (2006). *Pin-Up Grrrls: Feminism, Sexuality, Popular Culture*. Durham, N.C.: Duke University Press.

Carter, A. (1991). *Wise Children*. New York: Chatto and Windus.

Cohen, S. (1972). *Folk Devils and Moral Panics: The Creation of Mods and Rockers*. London: MacGibbon and Kee.

Cook, V. (2004). *Why Can't Anybody Spell?* New York: Touchstone.

Cronenberg, D. (1992). *Cronenberg on Cronenberg*. London: Faber and Faber.

Crystal, D. (2006). *Language and the Internet*. 2nd edition. Cambridge: Cambridge University Press.

Dyer, G. (1982). *Advertising as Communication*. London: Routledge.

Ehrenreich, B. (1991). *The Worst Years of Our Lives*. New York: Pantheon.

297

Ekman, P. (1985). *Telling Lies: Clues to Deceit in the Marketplace, Politics and Marriage.* New York: Norton.

Ewen, S. (1988). *All Consuming Images.* New York: Basic.

Fingeroth, D. (2004). *Superman on the Couch: What Superheroes Really Tell Us about Ourselves and Our Society.* New York: Continuum.

Fishwick, M. W. (1999). *Popular Culture: Cavespace to Cyberspace.* Binghamton, N.Y.: The Haworth Press.

———. (2002). *Popular Culture in a New Age.* Binghamton, N.Y.: The Haworth Press.

Frank, T. (1997). *The Conquest of Cool.* Chicago: University of Chicago Press.

Frankel, A. (2004). *Word Craft: The Art of Turning Little Words into Big Business.* New York: Three Rivers Press.

Gavreau Judge, M. (2000). *If It Ain't Got that Swing: The Rebirth of Grown-Up Culture.* New York: Spence.

Godard, J.-L. (1992). *Projections.* Edited by J. Boorman and W. Donohue. London: Faber and Faber.

Goodwin, A. (1992). *Dancing in the Distraction Factory: Music Television and Popular Culture.* Minneapolis: University of Minnesota Press.

Henderson, J. L. (1964). Ancient Myths and Modern Man. In. C. G. Jung (ed.), *Man and His Symbols,* pp. 95–156. New York: Dell.

Irwin, W., Conrad, M. T., and Skoble, A. J. (eds.). (2001). *The Simpsons and Philosophy* Chicago: Open Court.

James, C. (1983). *Glued To The Box.* London: Jonathan Cape.

Johnson, S. (2005). *Everything Bad Is Good for You: How Today's Popular Culture Is Actually Making Us Smarter.* New York: Riverside Books.

Kiesling, S. F. (2004). You've Come a Long Way, Dude: A History. *American Speech* 69: 321–27.

Kilpatrick, N. (2004). *The Goth Bible.* New York: St. Martin's.

Klein, N. (2000). *No Logo: Taking Aim at the Brand Bullies.* Toronto: Alfred A. Knopf.

Klein, R. (1993). *Cigarettes Are Sublime.* Durham, N.C.: Duke University Press.

Kundera, M. (1991). *Immortality.* New York: Harper Perennial.

Lasn, K. 2000. *Culture Jam: The Uncooling of America.* New York: Morrow.

Lazarsfeld, P., et al. (1948). *The People's Choice.* New York: Columbia University Press.

Leland, J. (2004). *Hip: The History.* New York: Harper Collins.

Leroy, M. (1997). *Some Girls Do: Why Women Do and Don't Make the First Move.* London: Harper Collins.

Levine, E. (2007). *Wallowing in Sex: The New Sexual Culture of 1970s American Television.* Durham, N.C.: Duke University Press.

Lough, J. (2002). The Analysis of Popular Culture. In C. Newbold, O. Boyd-Barrett, and H. Van Den Bulck (eds.), *The Media Book.* London: Arnold.

Lyotard, J.-F. (1984). *The Postmodern Condition: A Report on Knowledge.* Minneapolis: The University of Minnesota Press.

Marcus, G. (1976). *Mystery Train.* New York: Dutton.

Marcuse, H. (1964). *One-Dimensional Man*. New York: Beacon Press.

McLelland, B. (2006). *Slayers and Their Vampires: A Cultural History of Killing the Dead*. Ann Arbor: University of Michigan Press.

McLuhan, M. (1964). *Understanding Media*. London: Routledge & Kegan Paul.

Montgomery, K. C. (2007). *Generation Digital: Politics, Commerce, and Childhood in the Age of the Internet*. Cambridge, Mass.: MIT Press.

Otto, B. K. (2007). *Fools Are Everywhere: The Court Jester around the World*. Chicago: University of Chicago Press.

Paglia, C. (1992). *Sex, Art, and American Culture*. New York: Random House.

Panati, C. (1984). *Browser's Book of Beginnings*. Boston: Houghton Mifflin.

Peril, L. (2006). *Bluestockings, Sex Kittens, and Coeds, Then and Now*. New York: W. W. Norton.

Phoca, S., and Wright, R. (1999). *Introducing Postfeminism*. Cambridge, Mass.: Icon Books.

Pinsky, Mark I. (2004). *The Gospel According to Disney: Faith, Trust, and Pixie Dust*. Louisville, Ky.: Westminster John Knox Press.

Pough, G. D. (2004). *Check It While I Wreck It: Black Womanhood, Hip Hop Culture and The Public Sphere*. Boston: Northeastern University Press.

Reynolds, R. (1992). *Superheroes: A Modern Mythology*. Jackson: University of Mississippi Press.

Robinson, L. S. (2004). *Wonderwomen: Feminisms and Superheroes*. London: Routledge.

Savan, L. (2005). *Slam Dunks and No-Brainers: Language in Your Life, the Media, Business, Politics, and, Like, Whatever*. New York: Alfred A. Knopf.

Scott, L. M. (2005). *Fresh Lipstick: Redressing Fashion and Feminism*. New York: Palgrave.

Shaffer, P. (1993). *Amadeus*. London: Penguin.

Smith, C. (2007). *One for the Girls! The Pleasures and Practices of Reading Women's Porn*. Chicago: University of Chicago Press.

South, J. B., and Held, J. M. (eds.). (2006). *Questions Are Forever: James Bond and Philosophy*. Chicago and Lasalle: Open Court.

Starr, M. E. (1984). "The Marlboro Man: Cigarette Smoking and Masculinity in America." *Journal of Popular Culture* 12: 45–56.

Taylor, T. L. (2006). *Play between Worlds: Exploring Online Game Culture*. Cambridge, Mass.: MIT Press.

Vidal, G. (1974). *Homage to Daniel Shays: Collected Essays 1952–1972*. New York: Random House.

Wachal, R. S. (2002). Taboo or Not Taboo: That Is the Question. *American Speech* 77: 195–206.

Welles, O. (1956). Cited in *The New York Herald Tribune* (12 Oct. 1956).

Wood, R. (1979). *American Nightmare: Essays on the Horror Film*. Toronto: The Festival of Festivals.

FURTHER READING

The following sources provide complementary and/or supplementary information and perspectives to those found in this book.

BOOKS

Abercrombie, N. (1996). *Television and Society*. Cambridge: Polity Press.

Abrams, N., Bell, I., and Udris, J. (2001). *Studying Film*. London: Arnold.

Baran, S. J. (2004). *Introduction to Mass Communication, Media Literacy, and Culture*. New York: McGraw Hill.

Barthes, R. (1957.) *Mythologies*. Paris: Seuil.

Berger, A. A. (1996). *Manufacturing Desire: Media, Popular Culture, and Everyday Life*. New Brunswick, N.J.: Transaction Publishers.

———. (2000). *Ads, Fads, and Consumer Culture: Advertising's Impact on American Character and Society*. Lanham, Md.: Rowman & Littlefield.

———. (2000). *Media and Communication Research Methods*. London: Sage.

———. (2005). *Making Sense of Media: Key Texts in Media and Cultural Studies*. Oxford: Blackwell.

———. (2006). *50 Ways to Understand Communication*. Lanham, Md.: Rowman & Littlefield.

———. (2007). *Media & Society: A Critical Perspective*. Lanham, Md.: Rowman & Littlefield.

Bernard, S. (2000). *Studying Radio*. London: Arnold.

Biagi, S. (2001). *Media/Impact: An Introduction to Mass Media*. Belmont, Calif.: Wadsworth/Thomson Learning.

Boon, M. (2002). *The Road of Excess: A History of Writers on Drugs*. Cambridge: Harvard University Press.

Briggs, A., and Cobley, P. (eds.) (1998). *The Media: An Introduction*. Essex, Mass.: Addison Wesley Longman.

Campbell, R., Martin, C. R., and Fabos, B. (2005). *Media & Culture: An Introduction to Mass Communication*. Boston: Bedford/St. Martin's.

Crothers, L. (2006). *Globalization and American Popular Culture*. Lanham, Md.: Rowman & Littlefield.

Darby, D., and Shelby, W. (2005). *Hip Hop & Philosophy: Rhyme 2 Reason*. Chicago and Lasalle: Open Court.

Davis, S. (2001). *Old Gods Almost Dead: The 40-Year Odyssey of the Rolling Stones*. New York: Broadway.

Dovey, J. (2000). *Freakshow: First Person Media and Factual Television*. London: Pluto.

Duncan, B. (1988). *Mass Media and Popular Culture*. Toronto: Harcourt, Brace, Jovanovich.

Ehrenreich, B. (2006). *Dancing in the Streets: A History of Collective Joy*. New York: Henry Holt.

Eisenstein, E. L. (1979). *The Printing Press as an Agent of Change: Communications and Cultural Transformations in Early-Modern Europe*. Cambridge: Cambridge University Press.

———. (1992). *Visible Fictions: Cinema, Television, Video*. London: Routledge.

Ellis, M. (2000). *Slanguage: A Cool, Fresh, Phat, and Shagadelic Guide to All Kinds of Slang*. New York: Hyperion.

Fiske, J. (1987). *Television Culture*. London: Methuen.

Forman, M. and Neal, M. A. (2004). *That's the Joint: The Hip-Hop Studies Reader*. Routledge: New York and London.

Frith, S. (1983). *Sound Effects: Youth, Leisure and the Politics of Rock*. London: Constable.

Gedalof, A. J., Boulter, J., Faflak, J., and McFarlane, C. (eds.) (2005). *Cultural Subjects: A Popular Culture Reader*. Toronto: Nelson.

George, N. (1998). *Hip-Hop America*. New York: Viking.

Goodlad, L. M. E., and Bibby, M. (eds.) (2007). *Goth: Undead Subculture*. Durham, N.C.: Duke University Press.

Gough-Yates, A. (2003). *Understanding Women's Magazines*. London: Routledge.

Greenwald, T. (1992). *Rock & Roll*. New York: Friedman.

Grossberg, L. (1992). *We Gotta Get Out of This Place: Popular Conservatism and Postmodern Culture*. London: Routledge.

Hall, S. (ed.) (1977). *Cultural Representations and Signifying Practice*. London: Open University Press, 1977.

Hebdige, D. (1979). *Subculture: The Meaning of Style*. London: Routledge.

Heins, M. (2001). *Not in Front of the Children: Indecency, Censorship and the Innocence of Youth*. New York: Hill and Wang.

Herman, A., and Swiss, T. (eds.) (2000). *The World Wide Web and Contemporary Cultural Theory*. London: Routledge.

Hermes, J. (2005). *Re-reading Popular Culture*. London: Blackwell.

Heyer, P. (2005). *The Medium and the Magician: Orson Welles, the Radio Years, 1934–1952.* Lanham, Md.: Rowman & Littlefield.

Hinds, H. E., Motz, M. F., and Nelson, A. M. S. (eds.) (2006). *Popular Culture Theory and Methodology.* Madison: University of Wisconsin Press.

Holquist, M. (1990). *Dialogism: Bakhtin and His World.* London: Routledge.

Inness, S. (1999). *Tough Girls: Women Warriors and Wonder Women in Popular Culture.* Philadelphia: University of Pennsylvania Press.

Innis, H. A. (1972). *Empire and Communication.* Toronto: University of Toronto Press.

Jackson, J. A. (1998). *American Bandstand: Dick Clark and the Making of a Rock ' n Roll Empire.* Oxford: Oxford University Press.

Keren, M. (2006). *Blogosphere: The New Political Arena.* Lanham, Md.: Rowman & Littlefield.

Keyes, C. L. (2002). *Rap Music and Street Consciousness.* Urbana: University of Illinois Press.

Klaehu, J. (ed.) (2007). *Inside the World of Comic Books.* Montreal: Black Rose.

Leiss, W., Kline, S., Jhally, S., and Botterill, J. (2005). *Social Communication in Advertising: Consumption in the Mediated Marketplace.* London: Routledge.

Light, A. (ed.) (1999). *The Vibe History of Hip-Hop.* New York: Three Rivers Press.

Lopiano-Misdom, J. and De Luca, J. (1997). *Street Trends: How Today's Alternative Youth Cultures Are Creating Tomorrow's Mainstream Markets.* New York: Harper Business.

MacDonald, I. (1995). *Revolution in the Head: The Beatles' Records and the Sixties.* London: Pimlico.

Marcus, G. (1991). *Dead Elvis: A Chronicle of a Cultural Obsession.* New York: Anchor Books.

McKinney, D. (2004). *Magic Circles: The Beatles in Dream and History.* Cambridge, Mass.: Harvard University Press.

McLuhan, M. (1951). *The Mechanical Bride: Folklore of Industrial Man.* New York: Vanguard.

———. (1962). *The Gutenberg Galaxy.* Toronto: University of Toronto Press.

———. (1964). *Understanding Media.* London: Routledge and Kegan Paul.

McQuail, D. (2000). *Mass Communication Theory: An Introduction.* London: Sage.

Meehan, E. R. (2005). *Why TV Is Not Our Fault: Television Programming, Viewers, and Who's Really in Control.* Lanham, Md.: Rowman & Littlefield.

Miller, J. (1999). *Flowers in the Dustbin: The Rise of Rock and Roll, 1947–1977.* New York: Simon and Schuster.

Milner, Murray (2004). *Freaks, Geeks, and Cool Kids: American Teenagers, Schools, and the Culture of Consumption.* London: Routledge.

Muggleton, David (2002). *Inside Subculture: The Postmodern Meaning of Style.* New York: Oxford University Press.

Neer, R. (2001). *FM: The Rise and Fall of Rock Radio.* New York: Villard.

Newcomb, H. (2000). *Television: The Critical View.* New York: Oxford University Press.

Noll, M. (2006). *The Evolution of Media.* Lanham, Md.: Rowman & Littlefield.

O'Brien, S., and Szeman, I. (2004). *Popular Culture: A User's Guide*. Toronto: Nelson.

Owram, D. (1996). *Born at the Right Time: A History of the Baby Boom Generation*. Toronto: University of Toronto Press.

Padel, R. (2000). *I'm a Man: Sex, Gods and Rock 'N' Roll*. London: Faber and Faber.

Palmer, R. (1995). *Rock & Roll: An Unruly History*. New York: Harmony Books.

Peiss, K. (1998). *Hope in a Jar: The Making of America's Beauty Culture*. New York: Metropolitan Books.

Perkins, W. E. (1996). *Droppin' Science: Critical Essays on Rap Music and Hip Hop Culture*. Temple University Press: Philadelphia.

Pollock, B. (1993). *Hipper than Our Kids: A Rock & Roll Journal of the Baby Boom Generation*. New York: Schirmer.

Potter, R. A. (1995). *Spectacular Vernaculars: Hip-Hop and the Politics of Postmodernism*. Albany: State University of New York Press.

Queenan, J. (2000). *Balsamic Dreams: A Short but Self-Important History of the Baby Boomer Generation*. New York: Henry Holt.

Reynolds, S. (1999). *Generation Ecstasy: Into the World of Techno and Rave Culture*. London: Routledge.

Reynolds, S., and Press, J. (1995). *The Sex Revolts: Gender, Rebellion, and Rock 'n Roll*. Cambridge: Harvard University Press.

Rodman, G. B. (1996). *Elvis after Elvis: The Posthumous Career of a Living Legend*. London: Routledge.

Siegel, C. (2005). *Goth's Dark Empire*. Bloomington: Indiana University Press.

Slevin, J. (2000). *The Internet and Society*. London: Polity.

Staiger, J. (2005). *Media Reception Studies*. New York: New York University Press.

Storey, J. (2003). *Inventing Popular Culture*. London: Blackwell.

Strausbaugh, J. (2001). *Rock Till You Drop*. London: Verso.

Szatmary, D. (1996). *A Time to Rock: A Social History of Rock 'n Roll*. New York: Schirmer Books.

Twitchell, J. B. (2000). *Twenty Ads That Shook the World*. New York: Crown.

Van Dijk, J. (1999). *The Network Society*. London: Sage.

Van Zoonen, L. (1994). *Feminist Media Studies*. London: Sage.

Vice, S. (1997). *Introducing Bakhtin*. Manchester: Manchester University Press.

Whiteley, S. (1992). *The Space between the Notes: Rock and the Counterculture*. London: Routledge.

Whiteley, S. (ed.). (1997). *Sexing the Groove: Popular Music and Gender*. London: Routledge.

Wicke, P. (1987). *Rock Music: Culture, Aesthetics and Sociology*. Cambridge: Cambridge University Press.

Willis, P. E. (1978). *Profane Culture*. London: Routledge and Kegan Paul.

Wise, R. (2000). *Multimedia: A Critical Introduction*. London: Routledge.

Wright, B. W. (2001). *Comic Book Nation: The Transformation of Youth Culture in America*. Baltimore: Johns Hopkins University Press.

ONLINE RESOURCES

Academy of Motion Picture Arts and Sciences: www.oscars.org

Ad Council: www.adcouncil.org

Ad Forum: www.adforum.com

Adbusters: www.adbusters.org

Advertising age: www.adage.com/datacenter.cms

Advertising history: www.scriptorium.lib.duke.edu/hartman

All music guide: www.allmusic.com

Center for Democracy and Technology: www.cdt.org

Classic television: www.classic-tv.com

Critical communication theory: www.theory.org.uk

Hollywood movies: www.hollywood.com

Images (*Journal of Media Criticism*): www.imagesjourral.com

International Federation of Journalists: www.ifj.org

Internet Movie Database: www.imdb.com

Internet radio: www.radio-locator.com

Internet Society: www.isoc.org/internet

Journal of Popular Culture: www.blackwellpublishing.com

Magazine Publishers of America: www.magazine.org

Marshall McLuhan studies: www.mcluhan.utoronto.ca

Media history: www.mediahistory.umn.edu

Media literacy: www.mediaed.org; www.acmecoalition.org

Movieweb: www.movieweb.com

Net lingo: www.NetLingo.com

Net lore: www.urbanlegends.about.com

Pop culture sites: www.popcultures.com; www.urbandictionary.com

Popular Culture Association: www.h-net.org/~pcaaca

Product placement: www.productplacement.co.nz

Radio history: www.radiohistory.org

Recording Industry Association of America: www.riaa.com

Rock and Roll Hall of Fame: www.rockhall.com

Sundance Film Festival: www.sundance.org

Ultimate TV: www.ultimatetv.com

Web-based *Journal of Mass Communication Research*: www.scripps.ohiou.edu/wjmcr
   /index.htm

Web radio: www.radio-directory.com

INDEX

ABOUT THE AUTHOR

Marcel Danesi is professor of anthropology, semiotics, and communication theory at the University of Toronto. His books include *My Son Is an Alien: A Cultural Portrait of Today's Youth* and *Cool: The Signs and Meanings of Adolescence*. He is also the editor-in-chief of *Semiotica*.